Early Potters and Potteries of Delaware

Historical and Commercial Perspectives

1760-1890

James R. Koterski

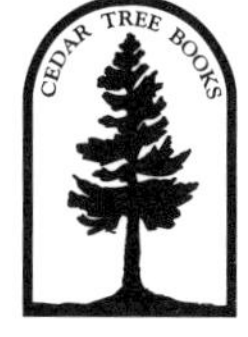

Wilmington, Delaware

Early Potters and Potteries of Delaware

First Edition

Published by: Cedar Tree Books, Ltd.

Any inquiries should be directed to:
Cedar Tree Books
9 Germay Drive
Wilmington, Delaware 19804
(302) 658-3994
books@ctpress.com
www.cedartreebooks.com

ISBN 1-892142-27-9

Title: Early Potters and Potteries of Delaware
Author: James R. Koterski
Book Design and Layout: Bob Schwartz

Library of Congress Cataloging-in-Publication Data

Koterski, James R.
Early potters and potteries of Delaware : historical and commercial perspectives, 1760-1890 / James R. Koterski.-- 1st ed.
p. cm.
Includes bibliographical references and index.
ISBN 1-892142-27-9 (alk. paper)
1. Pottery industry--Delaware--History. 2. Pottery--Delaware--History. 3. Potters--Delaware--History. I. Title.

HD9611.7.D3K68 2005
338.4'766639751'09034--dc22

2005008390

Printed and bound in the United States of America on 60# archival, acid-free paper meeting the requirements of the American Standard for Permanence of paper for printed Library Materials.

TABLE OF CONTENTS

TABLE OF CONTENTS (CONTINUED)

ACKNOWLEDGEMENTS

After retiring a few years ago, the thought came one day, who was William Hare? At that point, I owned about a dozen pieces of his stoneware. Setting out to locate published information about him and his pottery, it soon became apparent that little had been written about this nineteenth century Delaware potter. So starting with the *Wilmington Directory* and census records, and then moving on to land indentures and old newsprint, his story started to unfold. Meanwhile I stumbled across references to other Delaware potters and potteries. When that happened, I jotted down the information or made a photocopy. It wasn't long before I was purchasing notebooks to store this collection and adding numerous electronic files to "My Documents." At one point, I told myself to limit the project to the nineteenth century but then I came across a ledger of Mathew Crips and also recognized that John Andrews, John Jones and Charles Green all operated their establishments during the previous century. Eventually, the collected information became extensive enough to fill the pages of a book. My hope is that others will see a historical and cultural significance to this work and enjoy learning about the lives and interrelationships of these "pot throwers" while gaining some understanding of the commercial aspects of their trade.

Though it may seem trite, old clichés have their place, and truly, "I could not have done this alone!" My sincere gratitude goes out to many individuals and the staffs of several libraries, historical societies and museums.

E.D. Bryan, MD, of Dover, Delaware, spent an enormous number of hours in the early 1990s researching some of the potters who worked in Delaware. He was hoping to uncover examples of their earthenware, stoneware and related ephemera for a state exhibit that focused on this industry. Dave kindheartedly and openly shared all of his files and notes for which I am eternally grateful.

When approached, Constance J. Cooper of the Historical Society of Delaware offered to review the draft of the manuscript without hesitation. Connie's knowledge of Delaware history and her excellent writing skills have left a clear imprint throughout the text. For her help, I am wholeheartedly thankful.

My daughter Sandra, a professional working an extremely busy schedule, found time to review the entire manuscript in its draft form. Her numerous comments and corrections have been incorporated throughout the text. I am particularly indebted to her.

Several libraries hold collections that were very critical resources to this work. They include Hagley Museum and Library, Historical Society of Delaware, Friends Historical Library of Swarthmore College, Delaware State Archives, Winterthur Museum and Library, University of Delaware Morris Library, Cecil County Historical Society, Chester County Historical Society, Delaware County Historical Society, Wilmington Public Library and Milford Historical Society. The staff members of these institutions were always responsive to requests, open to discussion and helpful in locating materials. To all, I thank you very much. But before leaving this subject, I must add my special gratitude and recognition to the staffs at the Hagley Museum and Library and the Historical Society of Delaware.

The late Thomas Beckman of the Historical Society of Delaware developed a special interest in Delaware potters and was in the process of collecting related information for an eventual publication. His notes became part of the society's collections and were particularly useful in resolving some quandaries that this author faced. I will always remember Tom's important contributions to this subject.

The books by M. Lleyn Branin, Arthur E. James and Susan H. Myers are excellent studies of the early pottery industry of central and southern New Jersey, Chester County, Pennsylvania, and Philadelphia, respectively. Each includes a long list of potters they identified, a number of whom have now been connected with the First State. I am grateful for their earlier work and the opportunity to expand our knowledge of these transient craftsmen through their writings.

Through a number of private communications, Carole Wahler provided research leads which helped to understand the life of Charles F. Decker during his stay in Delaware. She also was a key searcher of late nineteenth and early twentieth century census records. I thank her for being there to lend a hand.

Some years ago Keith Phillips studied the ledger of Mathew Crips. He kindly shared his thoughts and interpretations along with his search of Sussex County records. Also his knowledge of early redware was very helpful in examining the pottery fragments that were collected during the archaeological excavations at the site of the Greens' pottery at Smyrna. I truly appreciate his involvement.

Special thanks are due Colonel Kenneth Brown, Professor Jay Custer, David Kenton, Andy Scari, Mr. and Mrs. Craig Stephenson and Deanna Denning Wolfe for allowing access to documents and examples of pottery from private or public collections. Special appreciation is also expressed to Andy Scari for sharing his broad knowledge of nineteenth century ceramics during our frequent discussions and our visit to view the collection of the Historical Society of Delaware.

My two sons-in-law, Sean Fahey and Donald Rose, provided computer support, especially the handling of several photographs and documents. I thank them for enhancing the book's presentation.

Martha Dixon volunteered to proofread the entire text and I am grateful for her interest in this work and her contributions to the accuracy of it.

Finally I wish to acknowledge and thank my wife, Sue. She not only proofread the entire text, but offered her full support throughout this endeavor and steadfastly encouraged me to publish this work.

DEDICATION

TO THE EARLY POTTERS OF DELAWARE

They dug their clay and carted it home
Then milled to mud and turned a pot
Next sat and watched by the kiln alone
Finally sold their wares for not a lot

Chapter I

Setting the Potter's Wheel in Motion

"Time's wheel runs back or stops: potter and clay endure"

Robert Browning
(1812-1889)

One

Pottery makers of eighteenth and nineteenth century America provided both utilitarian and decorative wares that were a mainstay in the everyday lives of the general population. Though they largely served local markets, some potters shipped their handmade products long distances by wagons and sailing vessels. Some excellent books have documented regional studies of this industry which have profiled potters and dated their operations. These treatments also picture examples of their wares and provide insights into the lives and personalities of these craftsmen. Two examples are Arthur E. James' book entitled *The Potters and Potteries of Chester County, Pennsylvania*, and *The Early Makers of Handcrafted Earthenware and Stoneware in Central and Southern New Jersey*, by M. Lelyn Branin. But little has been written about the "pot throwers" of the First State. Given this situation and an avid interest in the stoneware of a Wilmington potter by the name of William Hare, the task of researching eighteenth and nineteenth century Delaware potters and commercial pottery making was undertaken. At the present time, a group representing the Delaware State Museums at Dover is preparing a book about William Hare, the Wilmington potter. With publication anticipated in late 2005 or early 2006, it will focus on the descriptions of over 200 pieces of his surviving pottery and the archaeological excavations at his French Street site.

Introduction

Delaware had its own contingent of early potters. Most of them were centered in New Castle County and Wilmington. Others operated kilns in Kent County. But to date, no commercial pottery of the period has been identified in Sussex County. Census records in 1850 and 1860 for that county are void of individuals with "potter" as their designated occupation. Furthermore, Keith Phillips, a resident of Laurel, Delaware, found no references to potters or potteries in his search of early Sussex County deeds.

The discussion that follows traverses the 130 years from 1760 to 1890 and includes potteries at eleven locations. The dates of operation of each factory are best estimates, recognizing that in some cases there may have been intervening years during which a pottery was idle. Many of the sites had multiple land owners. Some practiced the craft while others leased their property to master potters or business proprietors who employed those skilled in the art. At times partnerships were involved. It should also be pointed out that this work excludes the making of bricks and drain tiles unless those who produced them also crafted the typical household wares of a potter like pitchers, pots, plates and jugs.

Over 80 individuals who were associated with Delaware's pottery industry during this 130 year period have been identified. This contingent includes owners, operators, partners and those potters who labored as hired hands. In many cases, names have been linked to a specific pottery and period of time. In addition, early craftsmen had the reputation for changing locations over the course of their lives. Potters were no exception and several who worked in Delaware also applied their talents other places. In fact, about 30 percent of those who played a role in the potting industry of the First State crossed the borders of Pennsylvania, New Jersey, Maryland, Virginia or Tennessee at some point during their active careers. And more than 10 percent were born in Europe, most in the more progressive states of Germany. Largely from Baden and Bavaria, these artisans fled their homeland when political reforms failed. Many came to America starting around 1850.

One of the most prominent and prolific Delaware potters was William Hare. In business for over 45 years on French Street in Wilmington, he marked many pieces of his stoneware with his name and the location of his pottery. Decorated examples are especially prized by today's collectors. Had other Delaware potters done likewise, we could, as with Hare, use surviving forms to better understand the breadth and extent of their work.

Numerous sources were searched to collect this information. These included the population and manufacturing censuses, land deeds, tax records, old newspapers, city directories, account books, wills and estate inventories. Records from Friends Monthly Meet-

Delaware Potteries
1760-1890

Location	Owners/ Operators	Period
Wilmington		
King/French Streets	1	1760-1798
Orange & Third Streets	6	1763-1838
Water & Orange Streets	7*	1783-1880
French Street	7	1827-1885
Madison & Seventh Streets	5	1850-1853
Eleventh Street	1	1880-1890
Hockessin		
Above Yorklyn Road	1	1860-1866
Smyrna		
Main Street	2	1778-1817
Main Street	2	1817-1838
Smyrna Landing	4	1867-1870
Milford		
Pear Street	1	1843-188?

** Excludes heirs of John Jones' family who leased his pottery to others for 55 years following his death.*

ings also provided some important information since Wilmington enjoyed a contingent of early potters who were Quakers. Yet this author would not be surprised to learn of potters and potteries that are unknown at the time of this writing and would be most interested in any that come to light. In sketching the personal and business lives of those who practiced the art in Delaware, speculation and conjecture unquestionably are woven into the accounts. However, rationales are presented to support liberties taken in an attempt to "fit together fragments of the pot." But knowing the extent to which some information was found in obscure places, it would not be surprising to yet discover bits that would enhance a story told here.

The number of potteries that simultaneously produced wares in Delaware during the nineteenth century was fewer than in neighboring rural Chester County, Pennsylvania. At least six kiln sites were operating there in 1820 while three are known to have been active in the all of Delaware in the same year. Yet Delaware's population of nearly 75,000 was well above Chester County's 44,000. The preponderance of clay in neighboring Pennsylvania compared to downstate Delaware may partly explain this difference, although it is also quite possible that some Delaware potteries remain buried in history. Arthur James refers to a number of Chester County operators as "Bluebird potters," using this term to describe farmers or tradesmen who engaged in this craft on a part-time basis. With the large number of farmers that were active in Delaware, it is quite conceivable that one or more of them fired a kiln from time to time. This may also help explain the lack of documented potteries in Sussex County.

Undoubtedly, the life of a potter was demanding and the proprietor of a pottery faced frequent tribulations. These included procuring large amounts of heavy materials, locating and employing skilled artisans, dealing with a kiln full of poorly fired product, building a solid customer base and finding a competitive advantage in light of imported and other locally and regionally produced wares. And eventually the market was invaded by not-in-kind replacements of tin and glass and impacted by changing technologies. These cut into the potter's revenues. A view of economic history also provides some key insights into the success and failure of these potteries and will be discussed in Chapter IX. Yet for all of this, as late as 1870, a Milford potter extracted an average of 12 cents for each piece of earthenware he sold.

Early Pottery

Among the types of handmade pottery of the eighteenth and nineteenth centuries, earthenware, or what is more commonly referred to today as redware, was produced from the type of clay found along creek banks and in brickyards. These clays were high in iron oxides which imparted reddish colors to the finished pieces. The temperature used to fire a variety of forms, including plates, bowls, cups, jars, jugs and pots, was in the range of 1,100°C, lower than for stoneware or porcelain. The resulting pottery was quite fragile and porous so it would seep liquid. A glaze, in many cases one that contained lead, was applied before firing to overcome this deficiency. A lead glaze for earthenware was formulated from red or white lead, sand and a colorant. The lead oxide and other ingredients were ground into a fine powder and then combined with water to make a liquid which was applied by dipping or pouring and swirling. The lead glazes fired clear, but to add color, oxides of manganese (dark brown to black), copper (green) and iron (yellow) were incorporated. Multiple colors were occasionally used to enhance the aesthetics of the pottery. An 1822 advertisement placed by a Market Street hardware store in the *Delaware Gazette* offered oxides of lead for sale. Though used in a variety of applications, the subscribers specifically offered them "For potter's use."

AMERICAN
WHITE LEAD,
Warranted well ground & unadulterated.
Also,
RED LEAD AND
LEAD ORE.
For Potter's use, all of the best quality; together with a general assortment of PAINTS, and OILS, for sale at the
HARDWARE STORE,
No. 50, Market-street, Wilmington, (Del.)
N. B. A quantity of COACH LACE, of the newest patterns, just received from the Manufacturer, and for sale as above.
Thomas S Newlin,
Samuel Woolston.
July 23—tf

Delaware Gazette, August 13, 1822

Other low-fired ceramics included yellow ware and Rockingham. Both became quite common well into the nineteenth century, although in order to compete with Queensware imported from England, some potters began to produce pottery from yellow clay in the early 1800s. An alkaline glaze, which fired clear, was another characteristic of yellow ware. In the second half of the nineteenth century, yellow ware was typically molded rather than formed by hand on a potter's wheel. Rockingham was a decorated type of yellow ware in which a glaze containing manganese was applied to give the pottery a glossy and spattered appearance.

Stoneware was another type of ceramic product of some potteries. The clay used for it vitrified when held at kiln temperatures in the range of 1200°C to 1300°C, rendering the wares non-porous. Even though stoneware would hold a liquid after firing, a salt glaze was usually applied by throwing or shoveling sodium chloride into the kiln once the peak temperature had been reached. The sodium reacted with silicate in the clay leaving a glassy appearance on the surface of the fired stoneware.

Porcelain was the most difficult to produce, requiring even higher temperatures of around 1400°C. Less available and more specialized clay compositions were needed. Few potters tackled its manufacture. Of those that did, many abandoned their kilns after little success.

Some potters signed, impressed or stenciled their mark on a portion of their output. Redware was seldom identified with the potter's name and, though it was more common for stoneware to be marked, the makers of the majority of it remain unknown. As mentioned previously, the only Delaware potter who is known to have signed or marked some of his work was William Hare of Wilmington.

Several techniques were used to decorate earthenware and stoneware. Besides the colored glazes already mentioned, cobalt oxide fired blue, and is the color most typically found on stoneware. Commonly used techniques to apply colors included sponging, dripping or hand brushing. Besides adding colorations, sharp tools were used to incise or cut into the green ware before firing. And in the second half of the nineteenth century, some manufacturers stenciled on decorations before firing, though no such enhancement has been observed on a Delaware piece.

Wood was used as the heat source, although later in the nineteenth century, some potters fired their kilns with coal. Local supplies of wood were plentiful; it could take four or five cords for one kiln burn which lasted several days. Wilmington potters were paying four to six dollars per cord during the third quarter of the nineteenth century making this fuel for their kilns a significant contributor to their manufacturing costs.

A book entitled *American Stonewares, The Art & Craft of Utilitarian Potters* by Georgeanna H. Greer is an excellent source should one want to locate more information about early pottery making. It includes a discussion of kiln construction, clay preparation and the use of the potter's wheel among other subjects.

That All-Important Clay

Clay was the potters' most important raw material. Many dug and carted their own supply. These early craftsmen saw the advantage of locating their pot house and kiln near a reliable source. New Castle County and the surrounding areas of Pennsylvania and Maryland hold a variety of deposits ranging from common "brick" clays, somewhat adaptable for manufacturing earthenware, to white clays, a key ingredient in porcelain. These latter high-end clays are rich in kaolin. In the middle of the nineteenth century, potters valued earthenware clay at two to three dollars per ton or, as some reported, per wagon load. There was an additional premium attached to clays capable of producing stoneware or porcelain.

The availability of local clays was recognized well before Delaware's eighteenth century potters were even born. The names of two New Castle County creeks, the Red Clay and the White Clay, attest to the presence of this potter's necessity. Some would say these labels describe the colors of their waters after a heavy rain storm. When and by whom they were tagged is uncertain but land records that go back over 300 years—1679 in the case of the Red Clay and 1688 in the case of the White Clay—refer to them by these names in describing property lines. Both deeds are in the files of the Historical Society of Delaware.

Clay consists largely of silica, alumina and water in varying amounts. Its properties differ depending on the relative proportions of each along with the kinds and amounts of other materials present. Plasticity, strength, shrinkage, color and fusibility were important physical properties to the potter and he often blended his clays to produce a usable "mud." Clays can be described in terms of the type of ceramic they produce. Earthenware clay is only slightly richer in alumina than common earth. Stoneware clay and kaolin show increasing purity with higher amounts of alumina and water replacing impurities like iron and other oxides, and organic material. Clays are found in a variety of colors including yellow, gray, blue and red. Their colors are imparted by these impurities.

Earthenware clays are high in iron oxide and usually burn from yellow to orange to reddish brown in color. The color of most stoneware that has been salt-glazed varies from cream to light brown and gray. Color variations are produced by the type of clay and the conditions inside the kiln. Most of the more prized and decorated stoneware of the Mid-Atlantic region is gray in color. Potters were known to mix common clays with those best for stoneware, presumably to stretch their inventory of the less available stoneware variety. Sand or flint was also used to temper the clay to reduce any cracking in the final product. One sees color differences in the stoneware made by the Wilmington potter, William Hare. His less common and more carefully crafted wares are more typically gray in color while his preserve jars, which he must have fired by the tens of thousands, are found in varying shades of creams, browns and grays. Hare probably sourced his clay from a number of deposits and also "blended down" the clay with some lower quality ones in some cases. In fact, there is a likeness to the color of redware in some of his stone preserve jars. Though salt-glazed, the salt failed to reach parts of the necks and shoulders of some jars due to the stackers he used to separate them in the kiln. The color of the unglazed surface bears a noticeable resemblance to redware. In stretching his supply of the better clay, more would have been saved for his higher quality pieces and blending would have helped control the material costs of his common jars.

That Delaware held veins of stoneware clay is suggested by a statement made by Phil Schaltenbrand in his recent book on Pennsylvania pottery. Though no source of the information was given, he wrote that Daniel Shenfelder, a Reading potter, used carloads of clay shipped from Delaware for the manufacture of stoneware. His pottery began operation in the 1860s. Besides Delaware, surrounding counties in Pennsylvania and Maryland provided these clays richer in alumina. Stoneware clay was probably also imported from the Amboy region of New Jersey, an area well known to early potters for the quality of its clay. The port of Wilmington could receive loads by ship and the birth of the railroads in the second quarter of the nineteenth century opened up another means of transport.

Various clays were found within a day or so by wagon from most of Delaware's potteries, though access to the purer clays diminished as one headed south. *Geological Survey of the State of Delaware* authored by James C. Booth provides deeper insight into the clay deposits within the state. Published in 1841, the research for this work was conducted during 1837-38. In his survey, Booth observed clays in a variety of colors—red, yellow, blue and white—and wrote that "There are deposites of clay in many parts of the state affording a sufficiently fine material for the manufacture of earthen ware, stone-ware, and even fine pottery or English ware." However, he did not mention potters by name nor did he dwell on specific commercial deposits other than "the white clay below the town of New Castle" along the banks of the Delaware River. Usually found below the high-water mark, this clay was often dug from inside coffer dams once the water had been removed. Booth noted that the clay had been exported to various parts of the United States to manufacture glass-pots or crucibles for melting glass. He added that it belonged to a class of infusible clays called plastic or pipe-clay and had been excavated for some 40 years as a raw material for crucibles. No mention was made if this product was manufactured locally.

One of the purposes of Booth's survey was to identify ways to find commercial uses for Delaware's geological resources. An item he included in his report spoke to the preparation of clay for the manufacture of earthenware. The geologist wrote, "If clay be stirred up in water, the gravel, sand and coarser matter will subside, and if the muddy liquid be poured off, the finest parts will finally settle down and may be obtained by pouring off the clear water and partially drying the remainder. Carrying out the same operation on a large scale, we obtain a fine-clay adapted to earthen ware."

Attempting to tie specific clay deposits to a Delaware potter in most cases is virtually impossible, though a few references to a potter's source were found. One would expect a prolific eighteenth century potter like Mathew Crips to have used clays from across New Castle County and even from inside what are today, the city limits of Wilmington. Indeed his ledger references digging the material at Stedham's brickyard. Other early brickyards were also known. According to Anna T. Lincoln's book on the history of Wilmington, Thomas Coxe was operating a Wilmington factory as early as 1750 on land bordered by Lombard, Poplar, Seventh and Ninth streets. But entries in his ledger confirm that Crips also purchased this important material from Philadelphia. Thomas Stroud supplied 24 car loads from that city in 1782. A few years later, Mathew scrolled a note to himself saying "I want clay at Hanrey Kinsley his brickyard in Philadelphia has bottoms clay." Per the *Philadelphia Directory,* Henry Kinsley manufactured brick on Cherry Street between Ninth and Tenth streets.

To be discussed in Chapter VI, Abner Marshall was instrumental in initiating the kaolin industry in the Hockessin area of Delaware in the early 1850s. And earlier, deposits from nearby Chester County were used by well-known Philadelphia porcelain makers. William Ellis Tucker was the founder of a Philadelphia pottery in 1826 and Winterthur Museum's collection of ceramics includes porcelain manufactured at this factory. But, apparently unrecognized to date, Delaware's geology also played a role in the manufacture of Tucker's fine ceramics. The Historical Society of Delaware holds minutes of the Delaware Academy of Natural Sciences, and as early as 1827, Eli Hilles was appointed to investigate feldspar found on a farm owned by the Dixon family. (Feldspar is a mineral component of kaolin clay.) According to the minutes of July 1, 1830, "Dixon's farm ... affords some of the finest feldspar in the world a large quantity of which has been shipped to England for the manufacture of porcelain. Tucker's porcelain factory near Philadelphia derives its supply from the same place." Another reference to the mineral followed in the minutes of July 7, 1831, in which its export and use by Tucker were reiterated. And it was added that the mining is now in several quarries. In Chapter VI, we will see where two German immigrants attempted to establish a porcelain factory in Wilmington using Delaware clay.

A prominent advertisement in the June 19, 1867, issue of the *Wilmington Daily Commercial* further points out the commercial recognition given to kaolin. "KAOLIN! KAOLIN!!" The notice announced the public sale of 32 acres of land that contained a recently discovered mine. The deposit was located eight and one-half miles from Wilmington on the Lancaster turnpike along the Delaware & Chester County Railroad. This site is probably the one that eventually became the Kaolin Works of Hamilton and Graham in Hockessin.

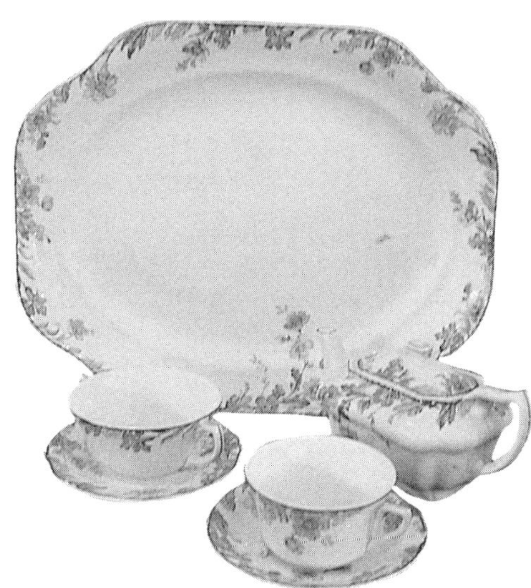

This porcelain dinner service was molded from clay refined in Hockessin, Delaware. *Courtesy of Mr. & Mrs. Craig Stephenson.*

Golding and Sons was another prominent miner of clays in the Hockessin area; the last general manager of the mining and mineral processing facilities was William Cook. In 1929, he and his wife gave their daughter, Lillian, and her new husband, LeRoy Stephenson, a porcelain dinner service as a wedding present. The set of china had been crafted at

Golding's pottery in Steubenville, Ohio, from clay refined in Hockessin. After firing, the molds for this set were destroyed. Numerous pieces of the ivory and floral decorated dinner service have survived, and are currently owned by descendents of the Stephensons.

Archaeological Excavations

Of the eleven pottery sites that will be discussed, archaeological investigations have been conducted at only three: the first pottery of the Green family in Smyrna, the manufactory on French Street in Wilmington and the remains of the late nineteenth century operation in Smyrna Landing. All were limited in their investigations. Development over the years has likely precluded excavations at many other locations.

Though an official report was never issued, the Charles Green pottery on Main Street in Smyrna underwent limited salvage operations in two stages during 1991 and 1992. Initially, the Delaware Bureau of Archaeology and Historic Preservation, and the Kent County Archaeological Society attempted to locate sub-surface features and collect examples of pottery produced at the site. Subsequent salvage operations were continued by the University of Delaware's Center for Archaeological Research. Excavation of a number of test and waster pits produced numerous earthenware fragments and kiln furniture that are believed to be associated with the Green pottery. However, no intact or nearly intact vessels were unearthed. The recovered fragments might be classified as typical Philadelphia redware, suggesting their similarities to pottery of the Delaware Valley. Photographs of some recovered shards have been included on the dust cover and in Chapter VII of this book.

In 1990, Louis Berger & Associates issued a report entitled *Archaeological and Historical Investigation of Block 1184, Wilmington, Delaware*. Submitted to the Delaware Department of Transportation under the Christina Gateway Project, this research program focused on a block bordered by Spring Alley and French, Second and Walnut streets. The William Hare pottery was located within these boundaries and ceramic wares uncovered in an area designated in the study as Lot 4 were attributed to his pottery. The recovered items consisted mainly of stoneware and redware kiln furniture, clay shapes that were placed between unfired wares during loading of a kiln. These prevented individual pieces of pottery from fusing together during firing. In addition, some salt-glazed stoneware, red-bodied earthenware fragments and partial vessels were uncovered.

A word of caution regarding attribution should be added here. As will be discussed later, William Hare was not the only potter to manufacture ceramics on French Street. The locations of Test Units 1 & 2 on Lot 4 coincide with property that other potters worked beginning by 1831 and probably a few years earlier. According to the report, the recovered artifacts were prepared for permanent storage at the Delaware State Museums in Dover.

The Berger report also references an earlier limited excavation of a waster pit associated with the William Hare pottery. No formal report was apparently written but notes from the three-day project in October of 1985 are on file at the Wilmington Department of Planning. The lead archeologist was Conrad Goodwin. Numerous artifacts were recovered, mostly from surface reconnaissance. These included shards from jugs, mugs, cups, jars and chamber pots along with kiln furniture. The collection was washed but not catalogued, and is in storage with the Delaware State Museums in Dover.

Several years ago, E.D. Bryan, MD, of Dover identified the location of a pottery at Smyrna Landing. In 1991, he and a group of friends made a one-day visit to the site and collected numerous stoneware fragments. The team turned over their find to the Delaware State Archeologist and the shards are also in storage at Dover. After washing and inspecting the stoneware fragments, no evidence of a potter's mark or decoration was found on any of them. No further excavations have been carried out.

Indentured Apprenticeships

Early artisans commonly learned a trade by serving an apprenticeship under a master craftsman for several years. Usually minors, these apprentices spent a specified period of time, typically three to six years, learning to produce the wares of their chosen craft. An end point in many apprenticeships was the twenty-first birthday for men and the eighteenth birthday for women. In 1826, Delaware enacted a law to regulate apprenticeships and the first registrations occurred the following year. This act provided a formalized opportunity for any young man or woman to be trained in a trade, although it was especially applicable to orphans and the children of paupers. The typical indenture regarding a potter read in part as follows:

> ... the said master shall use the utmost of his endeavours to teach or cause to be taught or instructed the said ap-

> prentice in the trade or mystery of pottery and shall well support and clothe him and procure and provide for him good and sufficient meat, drink, lodging and washing suitable for him during the said apprenticeship, and the said master shall give the said minor reasonable education in reading, writing and arithmetic to the single rule of three inclusive (excluding vulgar and decimal fractions) and shall at the regular expiration of said apprenticeship, furnish the said apprentice with two good suits of clothes, suitable to his condition ...

The document executed by the master and apprentice to record the agreement was referred to as an indenture. From 1827 to 1850, a total of 7,853 apprenticeships were recorded statewide, forty percent of which were for farming. Only five of these apprenticeships were for learning the trade of pottery.

Four of the five indentures were executed in New Castle County and these four apprentices served in Wilmington. Some related data put a perspective on the relative level of need for and popularity of apprenticeships for potters. During this 23 year period (1827-1850) in New Castle County, the apprentice count for blacksmiths totaled 63 and for cabinetmakers 55. Similar to potters, five young men agreed to become silversmiths and six pledged to learn the barbering trade. In researching this book, many hours were spent scanning old Delaware newspapers and only one of the many advertisements for apprentices sought a potter. Most common, subscribers were seeking boys to learn blacksmithing, printing, tanning, cabinetmaking, and papermaking. Normally, only two potteries were operating in Wilmington simultaneously and the total employee count was less than a dozen. And several of the potters had sons whom they trained in their own craft without executing any formal agreement. These facts serve to rationalize then the low number of young men who were indentured in the "mystery of pottery."

The lone advertisement for a potter's apprentice was placed in the July 10, 1846, issue of the *Blue Hen's Chicken*. The subscriber was William Hare, the master under whom William Rogers had indentured in 1844. Hare sought a "good industrious BOY, about 16 years of age, to learn the pottery business." Either Hare never found an acceptable candidate or, if he did, he chose not to execute a formal record of the apprenticeship.

Potter Apprenticeships

County	Master	Apprentice	Date
New Castle	Andrew Maxfield*	William Hair	4/27/1832
New Castle	Andrew Maxwell	William Henry Logan	2/08/1833
New Castle	William Hare	William Rogers	4/06/1844
New Castle	Nathan Dolbey	Henry S. Lambdin	4/26/1847
Kent	John H. Denning	Alfred Stevens	7/21/1846

** It will be argued in Chapter V that Andrew Maxfield was actually Andrew Maxwell, who also apprenticed William Henry Logan.*

Census of Manufactures: Before 1850

While the population census was initiated in the United States in 1790, the Census of Manufactures did not make its debut until 1810. Then, a total of 194 potteries were reported to have produced $260,000 of "Potters wares," or an average of about $1,300 worth of products at each. Clearly, the data were incomplete and inconsistent since no Delaware factory was included, and 80 percent of the entire country's factories were claimed to have been located in Pennsylvania. In comparison, only 22 glass manufacturers were acknowledged, but their product value exceeded a million dollars.

It was not until 1840 that any potteries were included in the Delaware census yet, even then, the operators of the two state's factories were not named. Only the following summary was published in that census:

No. of potteries	2
Value of manufactured articles	$4300
No. of men employed	9
Capital invested	$1100

So some detective work is required to identify the two operations and their proprietors.

That census also did not differentiate these two potteries by county. But as luck would have it, a separate compendium was published which provides an extremely useful piece of information. It identified New Castle County as the location of both. Just prior to 1840, three potteries were in operation in New Castle County and, in fact, all were in Wilmington. One was on Water Street at Orange Street, another was a few blocks up Orange Street at Third Street, and the third was located on French Street between Second and Third streets. So which of these two were active in 1840?

Leading up to 1840, William Hallowell was the proprietor of the pottery at Orange and Third streets but, as we will see in Chapter III, he had closed his business by about 1838. By the next year Hallowell had retired to Philadelphia, where he was listed as a "Gent" in that city's directory and was residing with his daughter. And no evidence has been found to suggest that another potter followed Hallowell at this location. That leaves the French Street and Water Street sites as those compiled in the 1840 Census of Manufactures. And it will be argued that William Hare and Nathan Dalbey were the respective proprietors.

The French Street property was undoubtedly turning out clay products in 1840 under the proprietorship of William Hare. An entry dated 1840 in the ledger of the Wilmington Fire Insurance Company housed in the Winterthur Library: Joseph Downs Collection of Manuscripts and Printed Ephemera clearly shows William Hare as a policy subscriber. Hare was covered "on his stock of potters materials and wares manufactured and unmanufactured with his tools and fixtures including horse dearborn." The description went on to note that the pottery establishment belonged to Smith and Hilles and was located in Wilmington on the easterly side of French Street between Second and Third streets. A property indenture (Q 4 175 1832) confirms their ownership at the time. Also of interest, the "dearborn" referred to here was Hare's wagon which, as will be discussed in Chapter V, overturned on two occasions in later years while William was driving on the streets of Wilmington.

The pottery at the corner of Water and Orange streets was established by John Jones in the eighteenth century and a number of proprietors turned out wares at that location in the years that followed. Newspaper notices in 1848 reported the financial failure of Nathan Dalbey at that corner. But by 1840, Dalbey, sometimes spelled Dalby or Dolby, was already in business there. And he was in Delaware well before 1840. Lelyn Branin, in his book on New Jersey potters, mentions a Barton "Dolby" who was born in Delaware and died in 1852 at the age of 24. Barton was the son of Nathan and would have been born around 1828, already placing Nathan in Delaware then. Though not included in the 1830 population census, Nathan shows up as a head of household in Wilmington ten years later. So, Nathan Dalbey was the other proprietor whose operation was included in the manufacturing census for 1840.

Besides the Census of Manufactures, there was an attempt by the federal government in 1832 to gather detailed data on manufacturing industries across the country. The House of Representatives passed a resolution on January 19, 1832, "to collect facts and information on the production of wool, cotton, flour, iron ... and such other articles that are manufactured to a considerable extent." A survey format of 40 questions was used. The feedback from the industrial community of Delaware, captured in what has been referred to as the McLane Report, was more complete than that of most states. However, no reply was received from a potter. In fact, Josuha Gilpin, the organizer of the state's compliance, only called on one potter, Branch Green. This operator sold his factory in the year of the survey which probably explains Green's lack of response. Three other potteries were in business at that time but their level of activity may not have met the survey's or Gilpin's criteria.

Census of Manufactures: 1850-1880

The federal censuses of 1850 and subsequent decades provide more detailed information regarding the operation of individual Delaware potteries than in 1840. These reports consist of the following: the amounts and values of raw materials consumed, typically clay and wood; the amount of capital invested in the business; the number of employees and total wages paid; and the value and types of products crafted. The table on the following page shows the number of potteries in operation as reported each ten years during the period 1850-1880 along with the combined product values, names of the operators and locations.

Rather than iterating the data here, the manufacturing statistics for individual potteries will be presented in the chapter in which each potter and his business are discussed. It should also be noted that the data reported for 1870 do not include George Ziegler of Wilmington. Either that was an oversight of the census, or his operation was not very active that year since other evidence supports that he was working on Water Street at the time. On the other hand,

Census of Manufactures
1850-1880

Year	Potteries	Product Value	Operators	Location
1850	3	$8,400	William Hare	Wilmington
			Richard Lowe	Wilmington
			John H. Denning	Milford
1860	4	$13,387	William Hare	Wilmington
			George Ziegler & Albert Neumayer	Wilmington
			Abner Marshall	Hockessin
			John H. Denning	Milford
1870	3	$9,800	William Hare	Wilmington
			Reese Bell	Smyrna
			John H. Denning	Milford
1880	3	$8,500	William Hare	Wilmington
			Albert Neumayer	Wilmington
			John H. Denning	Milford

that Ziegler was not counted in the 1880 census is not surprising. He was at the end of his business career then and probably did not operate the entire year.

The location and operation of the eleven individual potteries, each beginning with its earliest known owner or operator and proceeding until its demise, are covered in several subsequent chapters. A chapter then follows which provides more detailed information on other potters who were born and/or worked in Delaware. In addition, a chapter is included which attempts to connect economic history with the viability of some potteries, and presents a discussion of marketing approaches and the competitive influences these potters faced. Finally, an alphabetical checklist of potters and those associated with the state's ceramic factories is included for quick reference to their names.

Chapter II

Mathew Crips in the Eighteenth Century

Two

The earliest identified potter who turned clay into ceramic wares in Delaware was **Mathew Crips**, and, to date, more has been written about him than any other potter from the First State. But the longest treatment of Crips is only about a page and a half long and several histories of Delaware limit mention of him, at most, to a few paragraphs. But previously unpublished information, especially that found in some land indentures and a business ledger, help to tell a more complete story. The ledger is in the archives of the Hagley Museum and Library in Wilmington. So the discussion of this eighteenth century potter will attempt to blend information that is already published with that newly researched.

The spelling of Mathew Crips' name takes different forms. In some documents, his first name may be spelled with a double "t," and in others his surname is found with a double "p." But in a 1787 note to an esteemed friend in which he agreed to purchase red lead, the potter appears to have signed his name "Mathew Crips" so this spelling will be used throughout these writings.

Esteemed Friend Wilmington. November 10 1787.
William Hanson
If thou'd be agreeable to me I would Oblige me to send me the Half a Ton of Red Lead with the Bill thereof which I agree for last Week when I was at Philadelphia I also 1 C. of Magnus or a Keg more or less & it will Oblige thy Friend Mathew Crips

Mathew Crips' ledger shows his signature in a signed note to a friend in Philadelphia dated 1787. *Accession Number 1756. Courtesy of Hagley Museum and Library.*

Mathew Crips was born circa 1740 and died in February of 1805; he was buried in Wilmington's Old Swedes Cemetery. The potter's birthplace is unknown, though a small shred of evidence points to Wilmington. His brother, Andrew, also lived in the city throughout his adult life, suggesting that northern Delaware may have been the family's lifelong home. Mathew married Elizabeth Stidham (Stedham); she was about five years his junior. Elizabeth was a fourth-generation descendent of Tymen Stidham, a Swedish immigrant, and the granddaughter of Timothy Stidham. The Stidham family was very prominent in early Wilmington so one might imagine the life as a potter's wife would not be very attractive to a woman of her social status. In any event, Mathew and Elizabeth had three sons: Cornelius, Simon and Timothy, and a daughter, Pricilla. This conclusion was reached using information in Mathew's will (NCC Q-1-65) and a Stidham family genealogy which can be found at the Historical Society of Delaware. Simon died sometime in 1787 while Cornelius succumbed to yellow fever on October 24, 1798. His other children apparently survived him and Mathew named Timothy one of his executors and Pricilla an executrix of his estate. Regarding Timothy, Mathew noted in his will that he was at sea. Whether he returned and assisted in handling his father's estate is uncertain. Elizabeth Montgomery, in her book entitled *Reminiscences of Wilmington*, makes a statement that "Mr. Crips' only daughter was heir to the estate, which she never enjoyed, neither did her heirs." What she meant by that is unclear.

It has been written by Thomas Scharf in his *History of Delaware*, that Mathew started his pottery about 1760 on land he purchased east of King Street between Seventh and Eighth streets. No doubt that this was Crips' eventual location. A newspaper advertisement in 1795 noted that earthenware could be purchased by applying to Mathew Crips in King Street. But there is some doubt whether the potter began his factory there. While Crips purchased property (T 1 51) in Wilmington as early as 1759, its location was on the east side of French Street and appears to have been between Fourth and Fifth streets, about three blocks from the one mentioned by Scharf. Other recorded land acquisitions took place during the next few years (U 1 645 1761 and U 1 644 1762), though neither was near the location Scharf ascribed to the pottery. It was not until 1767 that the potter bought part of the land (Y 1 163) bounded by King, French, Seventh and Eighth streets. In that indenture, the property was described as being south of Kent Street, which, in 1835, was renamed

Eighth Street. And in 1771, Crips expanded his real estate holdings in this block (B 2 500). If the site between Seventh and Eighth streets was his original location, Mathew probably began by leasing the site. Then, once established, he acquired it. Or, he may have begun nearby, say down French Street, and then moved to King Street below Eighth Street after he bought that parcel in 1767. So, though he was in business for over 38 years, Crips' early location has some uncertainty attached to it.

Similarly unclear is where Mathew learned his potting skills. He was already identified as a potter when he acquired his earliest piece of property in 1759. Philadelphia would have been a likely place to apprentice, but if in Wilmington, it would have been under the tutelage of a yet unidentified Delaware potter.

The earliest sale of pottery found in Crips' ledger was dated April 7, 1761, and consisted of a large lot of earthenware to Joseph Shaw for £15.4.11. Many of the ledger's transactions do not show an itemized list of the pottery sold, but rather use the phrase, "parsel of erthenware." Some 37 years later, the last cash sale appears to be on December 15, 1798, at which time the potter recorded a transaction for eight milk pans, three dozen pint bowls and one dozen quart bowls. For these he charged £1.5.10. But this sale did not totally deplete his inventory since he continued to offer his earthenware to workmen in exchange for their services in building his new mansion. That this craftsman was prolific in turning out his wares is indeed an understatement. One only has to scan his ledger to see the size of some of the orders he filled and note a newspaper advertisement from 1795 in which Crips stressed the large quantity of product he could deliver in wagons, crates or vessels.

Like many earthenware potters, Mathew Crips produced a wide variety of pottery forms. Most of them were highly utilitarian and found practical applications throughout the home. But use in the kitchen and setting the

A Large Quantity of Earthenware

Upon hand, and for ſale, upon as low terms as the times will permit of, where ſtorekeepers and watermen may be ſerved and well packed, either in waggons, crates or veſſels, by applying to Matthew Crips, in King Street, near the Academy, in Wilmington, who ſtill carries on the potting buſineſs as uſual.

Delaware Gazette, May 30, 1795

table predominated. Records of his sales to merchants provide long itemized lists of specific pieces. They show that Crips offered "potts" of various sizes, some of which were for milk, "picklen," butter or flowers. The chamber pot was also a common item; the customer could either choose one that was single-glazed or pay a premium for a double-glazed one. The latter, glazed both inside and out, was more aesthetically pleasing and offered added assurance of a leak-free vessel in a service that might justify the added expense. Table wares included mugs, cups and saucers, plates, bowls and porringers. Mathew also produced jugs, milk and pudding pans, jars and pitchers. Besides his own ceramics, the ledger contains a few transactions involving Queensware. Probably imported and resold by the potter, Queensware referred to white-glazed earthenware that the English were producing to resemble porcelain.

According to his ledger, Crips also sold tiles and bricks that were fired in his kiln, although entries referring to these products are sparse. It does not appear that he mass produced common house brick but rather a specialized form which in one case he called "hard brick." It was not unusual for potters to make fire bricks, some of which were used for their own kilns, and this was probably the case with Crips.

One line in a long list of items sold to John Moore reads "2 Doz Black Chamber potts." Some early potters applied a black glaze to earthenware. Manganese dioxide was used to color that finish. Its use supports the notion that the Wilmington potter on King Street manufactured some higher priced, more decorative wares. Indeed, Mathew charged £1.4 for these 24 pots, a shilling each. His typical pot could be bought for about six pence, half the price. In 1795, there are two entries for black chamber pots.

Many pieces of Crips' earthenware in 1767 sold for less than a shilling each. A shilling (s.) equals 12 pence (d.). And by 1784, prices were not very different. For one thing, Crips' ledger shows he sold more large orders with items priced by the dozen in 1784 so some of the prices used in the following analysis for an individual piece are based on those bulk prices. This would tend to slightly lower a 1784 single-item price relative to 1767. But regardless, Crips' selling prices changed little over nearly a twenty year period as illustrated in the table on the following page.

Admittedly, some items, for example, large jugs and pitchers, commanded higher prices than the items shown, but the numbers of these sold were much lower. The selection of these years was arbitrary though the intent was to reflect a fairly wide span of time.

Comparative Selling Prices of Crips' Pottery

Item	Selling Price (d.) 1767	1784
Porringer	2	2
Plate	3	6
Single-glazed chamber pot	6	6
Double-glazed chamber pot	8	9
Butter pot	8	6
Small pot	3	-
Pint bowl	-	3
Quart bowl	4	5
Pudding pan	4	3
Half gallon jug	8	9

So how active was Crips' pottery? Taking liberties, some estimate of his annual production can be made based on information from his ledger. Revenues from his earthenware sales were summed for each of these same two years, 1767 and 1784. Then the average price for each of these two years was estimated. Using seven and eight pence for 1767 and 1784, respectively, the tabulated data below show the results of converting these revenues and selling prices to the number of pieces produced each year:

Year	Estimated Revenues (£)	Average Selling Price (d.)	Estimated Pieces Fired
1767	370	7	12,700
1784	700	8	21,000

Finally, if Mathew loaded his kiln with 250 to 500 pieces for a burn, he would have fired it 25 to 50 times in 1767 and nearly twice that often in 1784 just to produce saleable pottery. And kiln burns were not always completely successful so some products had to be discarded. Also these estimates of annual productions are possibly quite low since, throughout this ledger, there are references to at least eight others which may have recorded additional earthenware sales. Anyway, recalling that Crips was in business for at least 38 years, and assuming the lower production rate of 1767 across the entire period of his operation, nearly 500,000 saleable pieces of pottery were likely manufactured by Mathew during his lifetime. Clearly, the eighteenth century pottery of Mathew Crips must have been a showplace of activity on a daily basis. Wagons would have been hauling in clay and wood while others would have been loading with wares before heading to local customers and various shipping points. Typical days might have seen green ware waiting to be loaded while a kiln of earthenware was under fire. It is also quite likely Crips operated more than one kiln, so the stoking of a fire under one may have been in progress while another was cooling down.

Mathew Crips used a number of routes to market his clay products. While he sold directly to the general public, the potter moved large quantities through an extensive network of resellers. Transactions ranged from a single item to those that exceeded 50 dozen pieces. Some customers visited his pottery to complete transactions. Others sent a servant to make their purchase or leave an order that was later delivered by wagon. Prominent Delawareans were customers of Crips. In 1787, John Dickinson, the Delaware statesman and governor, purchased "2 potts" from Mathew's pottery. Two years later, Crips sold milk pans to the lawyer Gunning Bedford who referred to himself as Gunning Bedford, Jr. He was a member of the Delaware legislature, a delegate to the Continental Congress and attorney-general of the state. The millers William Shipley and Vincent Gilpin were also listed as purchasing earthenware from Crips.

Crips' ledger recorded a sale of earthenware to the Delaware governor, John Dickinson, in 1787. *Accession Number 1756. Courtesy of Hagley Museum and Library.*

The earthenware from Crips' pottery reached far beyond Wilmington. Ledger entries identify numerous customers in Pennsylvania, New Jersey, New York, Maryland and North Carolina as well as in other parts of Delaware. Many large transactions were with merchants and storekeepers who undoubtedly resold his wares. They included:

- David Nilson (Nelson), a merchant as noted by the abbreviation "merch" scripted next to his name in one entry. He purchased large quantities of pottery from Crips as early as 1770 and as late as 1798. It's unclear where Nilson was in business but tax records suggest Christiana Hundred (Wilmington). The city was a seaport and one would suspect Nilson was shipping Mathew's products along the east coast and possibly beyond.
- Tobias Rudolph, a merchant at Head of Elk, Maryland, which today is known as Elkton. Some ledger entries were to Tobias but others suggest that Rudolph had business partners from time to time. For example, several sales to Rudolph Murray & Son were recorded by Crips.
- Alexander McBeath, a merchant with the notation "New York." Presumably he was located in New York City since otherwise Crips would have likely first written the name of the city or town and then followed the entry with "New York" to identify the state.
- Robert Wilkin, a storekeeper in Kennett Square, Pennsylvania.
- William Hemphill, a merchant and wharf owner in Wilmington, Delaware. Some of Crips' sales to Hemphill include a reference to a ship's captain. Though difficult to decipher, the seaman's name appears to be John Powell who delivered Crips' earthenware as far away as Wilmington, North Carolina.

Another repeat customer, though not a merchant, was Henry Hollingsworth, at Elks Neck, Maryland. Following the War for Independence and the lifting of the blockade by the British navy, Hollingsworth built a large shipping business at the northern end of the Chesapeake Bay. So he may have been distributing Mathew's earthenware wherever his ships sailed. During the war, Hollingsworth was George Washington's commissary for the Eastern Shore of Maryland.

This early Wilmington potter also had business transactions on three occasions with a colleague in Philadelphia by the name of John Justice. According to Susan H. Myers in her book entitled *Handcraft to*

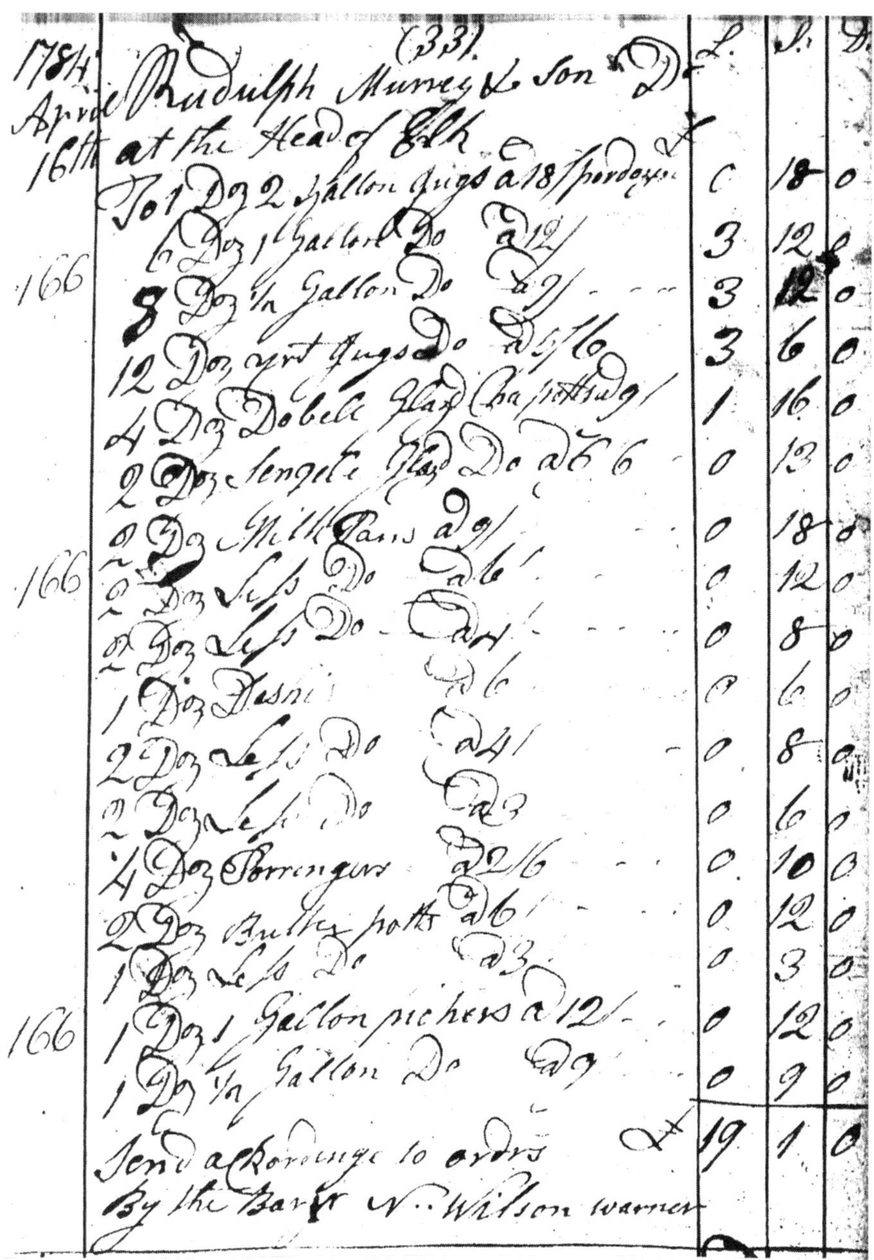

(33)

1784		£	s	d
April 16th	Rudulph Murrey & Son Dr at the Head of Elk			
	To 1 Doz 2 Gallon Jugs a 18/ per dozen	0	18	0
	6 Doz 1 Gallon Do a 12/	3	12	0
166	8 Doz 1/2 Gallon Do a 9/	3	12	0
	12 Doz quart Jugs Do a 5/6	3	6	0
	4 Doz Dobele Flap Chamber pots a 9/	1	16	0
	2 Doz Sengele Flap Do a 6/6	0	13	0
	2 Doz Milk Pans a 9/	0	18	0
166	2 Doz Less Do a 6/	0	12	0
	2 Doz Less Do a 4/	0	8	0
	1 Doz Basins a 6/	0	6	0
	2 Doz Less Do a 4/	0	8	0
	2 Doz Less Do a 3/	0	6	0
	4 Doz Porringers a 2/6	0	10	0
	2 Doz Butter potts a 6/	0	12	0
	1 Doz Less Do a 3/	0	3	0
166	1 Doz 1 Gallon pichers a 12/	0	12	0
	1 Doz 1/2 Gallon Do a 9/	0	9	0
	£	19	1	0
	Send acordinge to orders By the Barge N. Wilson warner			

Mathew Crips sold a large, itemized lot of earthenware to Rudolph Murray & Son, a Maryland merchant, in 1784. *Accession Number 1756. Courtesy of Hagley Museum and Library.*

Industry: Philadelphia Ceramics in the First Half of the Nineteenth Century, John Justice was a Philadelphia-based potter on North Second Street. She dated his tenure there from 1791 to 1799. However, the reference to John Justice in Crips' ledger suggests that he was potting some ten years earlier. One wonders if their relationship even preceded business transactions and if Justice might have apprenticed with Crips. In any event, Crips and Justice, potter, exchanged "tea potts" and "lead" in November of 1780. The lead was either red lead, an oxide used in the glazing of earthenware, or lead metal which Crips burned to form the oxide. It was especially common in colonial times for merchants, craftsmen and farmers to trade their wares or services for the products or services needed. But what was unusual about this one was the monetary value of £675 placed on the transaction. And even more astonishing, they completed two similar business dealings later that month. John paid Mathew £1044 in cash for another large lot of tea pots. And Mathew sought more lead from John. In another cash transaction, he paid £1125 for the metal. So during one month, the value of transactions between these two potters totaled £2844. But times were not normal in 1780 and these monies must have reflected the high rate of inflation in the colonies that was brought on by the Revolutionary War. In fact, in the same year, Mathew traded pottery valued at £1125 for a horse owned by Thomas Maguire. Before the war and after the value of currency stabilized following the end of the conflict, £25 or £50 was a more typical price to pay for this work animal. Besides the ledger entries recording exchanges of pottery for raw materials and a horse, others documented the trading of earthenware for various items including flour, eggs, rum, fish and feathers. Some of these were consumed by the Crips' family while others Mathew resold. In 1776, for example, Crips dealt Samuel Jervis, "cordwinder," pottery for "value in shoes."

Like most Wilmington potters, Crips probably obtained much of his clay locally in parts of New Castle County, Delaware, and lower Chester County, Pennsylvania. Also, one cannot rule out neighboring Cecil County, Maryland. With all of his earthenware that was delivered there, the back-hauling of clay would have been a logical enterprise. But his ledger does offer some specifics and one finds him even going to Philadelphia for this raw material. The Stidham family owned a brick yard in Wilmington and an entry logged payment to Mathias Jinnet for digging 46 loads of potter's clay at that location. And in the early 1780s, Crips bought this potter's necessity from Thomas Stroud and Henry Kinsley (Kenssley) in Philadelphia. Eight years later, his ledger shows that "John Robnet shallopman" transported 24 loads of clay and some lead from Philadelphia to Wilmington for the potter. Crips paid four shillings to have the vessel loaded. Glazing materials also were supplied from this city up the Delaware River. The ledger shows that red lead was procured in a half ton quantity from William Sansom, and in the same transaction, Mathew acquired "1 C. of Magnus," an oxide of manganese. To fire his kiln, Mathew burned several types of wood, especially the hard woods, oak and hickory. Much of his wood was obtained in exchange for his earthenware. To produce such large quantities of earthenware, Crips must have employed a number of journeymen, apprentices and laborers. But for the most part, the names of these workers are buried in history. Of his three sons, Cornelius was apparently the only one who took up his father's craft, though he did not spend his entire life at the Wilmington pottery. Since he inherited some land from his maternal grandfather, New Castle County land indentures provide some details of his earlier life. Named as grantor in two 1791 deeds (L 2 424 and X 2 155), **Cornelius Crips** is identified as a farmer residing in Lancaster County, Pennsylvania. But by 1796, another indenture (P 2 524) signals his return to Delaware, identifying residency in Wilmington and his occupation as a potter. Land transactions (R 2 284 and S 2 426) during the next two years likewise name him as a potter in Wilmington. And both before and after the time he spent in Pennsylvania, one can find references to Cornelius, potter, in his father's ledger.

Mathew noted in his ledger in 1783 that he hired, Jacob, son of the widow Webb, for 30 shillings per month. In colonial times the value of currency fluctuated over a wide range, but a conversion factor generally applied in non-inflationary periods is seven shillings and six pence to the dollar. On that basis, Webb's monthly wages approximated $4.00. Though Jacob learned the art of turning clay from Crips, he did not spend his entire potting career in Wilmington. In his book on Chester County, Arthur James noted the name **Jacob Webb** as working at the Westtown, Pennsylvania, pottery of Aaron James in 1796. By then, Crips was nearing the end of his potting career and it may have been for that reason that Webb left Wilmington for Pennsylvania.

Two other probable employees of Crips are found in the 1959 writings of John N. Pearce in his master's thesis submitted to the University of Delaware. Pearce identified **John Brown** as an apprentice of Crips and **John Andrews** as a potter who was possibly employed by the pottery owner.

A Wilmington Friends Meeting certificate named John Brown ("a Ladd") as an apprentice to Mathew Crips in 1762. In that year, Frances, John's mother, applied for a certificate to move him from Haddonfield, New Jersey, to the Wilmington Monthly Meeting. After a short time in Delaware, John was granted a certificate on September 9, 1768, to the Gunpowder Monthly Meeting in Baltimore. There he established his own pottery where, according to that city's directory, he was still in business in Old Towne on Fridge Street in 1796. Pearce's thesis provides an in-depth look at Baltimore potters for the period of 1763-1850 and it includes a lengthy treatment of Brown's potting life after leaving Wilmington in the 1760s. Using Pearce's words, "he and his family, and apprentices, monopolized the production of pottery in Baltimore for thirty years."

In his writings, Pearce suggests that another individual, John Andrews, possibly worked with clay at Crips' pottery. As a grantee in a 1767 land deed, Andrews was identified as a Wilmington potter. The deed was witnessed by Crips. But, interestingly, Crips noted in his ledger that he sold clay to a "John Andrew" on two occasions in 1769, suggesting John had his own kiln. That Andrews did in fact operate his own pottery business will be discussed in Chapter III.

Moses Bryan(t) is identified as a potter in a 1782 deed, and undoubtedly he practiced his craft in eighteenth century Delaware. It is possible he was employed by Crips. More will be said about Bryan in Chapter VIII.

Brief references in Crips' ledger to some other individuals—Patrick Mullen, labourer; Andrew Nelson, labourer; and John Hade, brick moulder—suggest they may have worked at Mathew's pottery. Typically, these entries were noted "to cash"... "by work done."

The tax assessments of 1782 demonstrated Crips' relative wealth. Few, probably less than ten percent of the population, were assessed at a higher rate than the potter. In fact, Mathew was quite wealthy by the time of the American Revolution. According to Anna T. Lincoln's writings, travelers passing through Wilmington singled out his home, gardens and fruit trees on Market Street above Eighth Street. During the British occupation of Wilmington in 1777, officers occupied various houses, including that of Crips. For that year, Crips' ledger is void of any entries. Following the war, Mathew filed for £150 in damages to his property inflicted by the invading British army. Crips, along with two operators of the eighteenth century pottery on Orange Street—John Andrews and Isaac Starr—was a member of the Delaware Militia's North Division of the Borough of Wilmington during the war.

Though his home on Market Street must have been one of the most prominent, Mathew erected a new mansion on the site of his King Street pottery at the end of his manufacturing days. In her book, Elizabeth Montgomery wrote that this occurred somewhere around 1797. Matthew's ledger contains many references to this construction activity. The brunt of the project occurred in 1798 and it continued into 1799. Finishing touches were added in 1800. One of the key contractors was a bricklayer by the name of John Webster. In one 1798 notation alone, Crips paid Webster nearly £100 for razing existing structures, building an oven, laying 67,418 bricks and turning 15 arches over windows, among other tasks. Entries in 1799 record the purchase of plaster and nails. In 1800 he paid a carpenter in tea pots and cups from his remaining inventory. After his death, this three-story brick home was leased by a number of occupants and for a time became known as the Old Boarding School. Here, Eli Hilles, with different partners, operated a school for young women. One of the most successful educators of the time, Eli was elected the first president of the Board of Education of Wilmington. As will be discussed in Chapter IV, this is the same Eli Hilles, who along with David Smyth, purchased the French Street pottery from one potter, Branch Green, and later sold it to another, William Hare.

Chapter III

Wilmington Potteries on Orange Street

Three

Two potteries, located within three blocks of each other, were established in Wilmington along Orange Street during the eighteenth century. The first one appears to have been started in the 1760s at the corner of Orange and Third streets while the second, begun in the early 1780s, was at Water Street, just above the Christina River. Under various operators, both were active for many years. In fact, the property at Orange and Water streets served as a pottery for nearly 100 years. Today, the site is covered over by roadways and possibly some of the embankment and tracks that carry Amtrak® and other trains up and down the busy northeast corridor.

The Corner of Orange and Third Streets

From an ownership perspective, the property on the northwest corner of Orange and Third streets had its ups and downs. As we will see, the potter who apparently built the works died at age 42. Two subsequent owners, a miller and a skinner, ran into financial difficulties and lost the property through court actions and sheriff's auctions. Between their ownership, a hatter held the deed for a few years. In all three cases, these businessmen were quite successful and substantial land holders when they acquired the property so it is reasonable to presume their intent was to manage the pottery or lease it to those skilled in the craft. But in the end, the final owner of this lot that contained a "Pot House" and "Pot Works" was a trained pot thrower.

During the discussion of Mathew Crips, it was suggested that while **John Andrews** may have worked for him, he likely fired his own kiln at some point during his clay working days. According to records at the Friends Historical Library of Swarthmore College,

Property Ownership
Northwest Corner of Orange and Third Streets

Owner	Period	Occupation	Use
David Ferris	Pre-1778	Yeoman	Pottery
Sarah Andrews (1)	1778 -1780	Widow	Unknown
Isaac Star (2)	1780 -1800	Miller/Potter	Pottery
Elisha Starr	1800 -1804	Hatter	Unknown
William Robinson	1804 -1823	Skinner	Pottery
William J. Hallowell & Heirs (3)	1823 -1865	Potter	Pottery

(1) Inherited property from her father, David Ferris; her sister Mary Lightfoot and husband, William, were co-inheritors. Sarah was the wife of John Andrews, potter.
(2) Isaac Starr was apparently involved in the pottery's operation from the very late 1780s into the 1790s.
(3) Hallowell closed his business in about 1838. No evidence was found to suggest he or his heirs leased the property as a pottery after that date.

John married Sarah Ferris on August 25, 1763. A son, Samuel, became a well-known Wilmington printer. Sarah's father, David Ferris, was a large landowner in northern New Castle County. In 1780, two years after John's death, widow Sarah Ferris, along with William and Mary Lightfoot, sold a piece of property on the northwest corner of Orange and Third streets in Wilmington. The land indenture (W 2 257) noted that this property contained a "Pot House" and "Pot Works." John was probably the first to operate a pottery at this location, although one cannot discount a previous operator. In any event, as we will see later, he was not the last.

That John Andrews was a Wilmington potter is confirmed by a 1767 property deed on file at the Historical Society of Delaware in which his occupation was noted. Fellow potter Mathew Crips was a witness to its execution.

According to other Friends' records, John, son of William and Miriam, was born on June 2, 1736, and died on November 11, 1778. Some six years earlier, he had been disowned by the Wilmington Friends for taking strong drink to excess. The Friends' archives also document a brief stay in Philadelphia. In February of 1759, John was granted a certificate to the Philadelphia Monthly Meeting. He returned to Wilmington in February of the following year. During his short stay in the City of Brotherly Love, one can speculate that Andrews was employed as a potter and then, on returning to Wilmington, worked for Mathew Crips. After marrying Sarah, John established a pottery on land owned by her family. Interestingly, the unrelated property he purchased in 1767 was granted to Andrews by Nicholas Sellers, a brick maker. Some Wilmington brickyards were located on land that was rich in clay. While John may have produced bricks there, his purpose for acquiring the site could have been to provide a source of clay for his pottery. Probably like his colleague Crips, Andrews produced household earthenware from red clay high in iron content.

In 1780, Sarah and the Lightfoots conveyed the Orange Street property to **Isaac Starr (Star)**, a Wilmington miller. Isaac was then in his fifties and well established in business when he acquired the pottery. In a 1791 indenture recording another land purchase of his, Isaac was again referred to as a miller. But the next year, in granting approximately four acres of land to John Lea, Isaac Starr, potter, signed over that property. It's doubtful whether Isaac ever became adept at using a potter's wheel himself. One would suspect that he either managed or leased out the pottery during his ownership, though the identities of potters who may have worked there during the Starr years remain unknown. One piece of evidence that Isaac had his hands in the business comes from an account book of Samuel Bush which is part of the collection of the Historical Society of Delaware. Bush operated a sloop from the wharf at the foot of French Street that transported freight and passengers to and from Philadelphia. At this location on the Wilmington riverfront, he also bought and sold numerous articles of commerce. An entry in his ledger dated October 17, 1789, recorded a transaction with Isaac "Star" of four loads of clay. Whether Starr was buying, selling or shipping the clay is unclear but the entry does connect him with a primary material of a pottery as early as 1789.

The genealogy files at the Historical Society of Delaware provide some pertinent information regarding the Starr family. Isaac Starr, born January 7, 1728, was one of nine children of Isaac and Margaret Lightfoot Starr. The father, a native of Ireland, settled in Pennsylvania around 1710. Isaac, the son, was twice married. His first wife, Elizabeth Ashbridge, died in November of 1776 before Isaac acquired the pottery. By then he had remarried since his wife, Rachel, was named in the deed recording its purchase. Her maiden name was Green and she was the widow of John Pritchett. The Starr and Pritchett families had another relationship. Isaac, one of the sons of Isaac and Elizabeth, was involved in a business partnership with a Jesse Pritchett in Philadelphia in the 1790s. These partners were agents for the Insurance Company of North America. Interestingly, like Mathew Crips and John Andrews, Isaac, the miller and potter, was a member of the Delaware Militia's North Division of the Borough of Wilmington during the Revolutionary War.

Though following the related land indentures is somewhat confusing, the Starr family owned the Orange Street pottery from 1780 until it was sold to **William Robinson**, apparently in 1804 (C 3 368). In the interim, however, a judgment had been placed against Isaac and his recently deceased son, Isaac, Jr., in 1800 to satisfy the son's debt to Lewis Stone. When the property was auctioned, **Elisha Starr**, the younger brother of Isaac, Jr., stepped forward and acquired it in September of 1800 (U 2 411). During the period of about 26 years (1778-1804), the level of activity at which the pottery operated is unknown, though it must have at least functioned during some of the 1780s and '90s under Isaac Starr's ownership.

In 1808, with ownership now in the hands of William Robinson, **Jonathan Beeson** began manufacturing and offering a good assortment of earthenware at this pottery on Orange Street. In his advertisement, he not only sought the business of the general public but also offered special terms to those who would purchase his products for resale.

His published notice further identified Beeson's location as a few doors below High Street, now Fourth Street. Early on, not all of Wilmington's streets starting at the Christina River were named based on numbers. Prior to 1835, in order, they were Water, Front, Second, Third and

Earthen-ware Manufactory

THE subscriber respectfully informs his friends and the Public that he has commenced the Potting business in Orange Street, a few doors below High Street, (near the New Market) where he offers for sale, on reasonable terms, a good assortment of Earthen-ware. As he is determined that nothing shall be waning on his part to give general satisfaction to his customers, he hopes to merit a share of public favour.

Country store-keepers, and others who purchase to Sell again, will be supplied on advantageous terms.

Jonathan Beeson, Jun.

The Museum Of Delaware and General Advertiser, August 6, 1808

High. But a Wilmington City Ordinance renamed several, including High Street, effective December 31, 1835. This description of street names is important since it clearly distinguishes the location of John Jones' pottery at Water and Orange streets from this one announced by Beeson on Orange Street between Third and High streets.

According to records at the Friends Historical Library, a Jonathan Beeson was born to Thomas and Rebecca Kellum Beeson on July 18, 1762; he died on December 12, 1813. Additional records there show that Jonathan married Elizabeth Shipley, daughter of Samuel, on December 18, 1793. They had a son, Thomas S., and a daughter, Jane. Elizabeth died on February 10, 1823, at the age of 48. Her obituary appeared in the *Delaware Gazette* on February 18.

The Delaware censuses of 1800 and 1810 include Jonathan Beeson as a head of household and, in each case, one of the designated age categories counting males is consistent for an individual born in 1762. According to New Castle County land indentures, Jonathan bought and sold several parcels in Wilmington and in rural Brandywine Hundred between 1788 and the year of his death. Some were multiple acreages and, when his occupation was identified, it was that of a grazer or farmer. It's unlikely then that Beeson ever trained as a potter prior to the opening of the Wilmington pottery in 1808. He was 46 years old at the time. In fact, Beeson was counted in Brandywine Hundred in the 1810 census and, in his book on Delaware history, Thomas Scharf wrote that Jonathan Beeson voted in a district election in that locale in 1812. This information suggests that he may have devoted more time to his agricultural interests than to producing earthenware. So why did Beeson open a pottery? Mathew Crips had died a few years earlier and quite possibly Beeson believed there was a business opportunity in filling this void. Furthermore, Thomas Jefferson had just imposed an embargo on imports from across the Atlantic. In fact, Beeson used the phrase, "Potting business," in his advertisement. To carry on this venture, he would have had to hire some experienced potters and, while none has been clearly identified, William J. Hallowell is a probable candidate. But Beeson's interest in this pottery business was fairly short-lived since he died only five years after its inception.

There is an anomaly in the connection made in the previous paragraphs with Jonathan Beeson, the farmer of Brandywine Hundred and Jonathan Beeson, pottery proprietor. The newspaper advertisement placed by Beeson identified the subscriber as Jonathan Beeson, Jun. Errors in printed matter were not uncommon in the 1800s so it is conceivable that the "Jun." attached to the subscriber's name was an error. Clearly, Beeson, the farmer, was not the son of a Jonathan. But an extensive search of various records to locate a Jonathan Beeson who was given his father's first name came up empty.

William J. Hallowell was a successor to Jonathan Beeson on Orange Street at Third Street. According to the surname file at the Historical Society of Delaware, he was born on January 30, 1784, probably in nearby Pennsylvania. As a minor, a Friends' certificate accompanied his move from the Concord to the Wilmington Monthly Meeting on May 14, 1800. In October, 1807, William J. "Hollowell" (Potter), wife Mary and a child George P. were listed as members of Wilmington Friends. This timing suggests that he possibly apprenticed under John Jones, a Wilmington Quaker, and may have worked for Jonathan Beeson when this member of a Quaker family took over the pottery at Orange and Third streets.

Hallowell was not named in the 1810 Delaware census, but these early data are not always complete. Next, he appears on the 1813 New Castle County tax assessment rolls. A year later, William is listed in the 1814 *Wilmington Directory* as a potter on Orange Street between Third and High streets. Hallowell probably took over leasing the pottery's operation following Jonathan Beeson's death. In the 1816-17 tax lists for New Castle County, William Robinson was assessed for a house and lot in tenant of Wm Hallowell. No location was given but recall that Robinson was then the owner of the pottery site. Hallowell eventually purchased this property at the northwest corner of Orange and Third streets through a sheriff's sale (Z 3 446). The court ordered the action to satisfy the debts of William Robinson, his earlier landlord, following the tanner's death on March 3, 1823. He was 59 years old. On April 26, 1823, the potter acquired five adjoining lots with frontages on Orange and Third streets of 111 feet and 100 feet, respectively. For these Hallowell paid $1,505.00. Some years later, Hallowell shows up in New Castle County tax records. In 1837 and again the following year, he was assessed for several pieces of property, one of which was identified as a "Pot House" on Orange Street. According to the same records, his stable was located around the corner on Third Street.

Hallowell appears in both the 1820 and 1830 censuses for Wilmington. In the first case, five individuals are counted under him. The male and female in the category of 26 to 44 years old presumably were the potter and his wife, Mary. The two females under ten were daughters Sarah and Rebecca. Some major family events occurred around the time this census was taken. Mary Pierce, a third daughter was born on January 3, 1819, but is not included in the census. On the other hand, William's wife is listed, although she died four days later, possibly from complications related to the birth of Mary Pierce. A male, 16 to 25, was also counted. More than likely, he was a young potter working for William since this census records two individuals engaged in manufacturing in the household. By 1830, only William (40 to 50 years old) and two females (15 to 20) are listed.

Hallowell does not appear in the 1840 census for Delaware. But through information provided by E.D. Bryan, MD, of Dover, William can be the traced to Pennsylvania following the closing of his pottery in about 1838. In that year, he was still assessed for real estate valued at $2,700. Taxed at a rate of six percent plus a head tax, he was billed for $210. The properties included a pot house on Orange Street and a lot and stable on Third Street. A year later, he is listed in the *Philadelphia Directory* as a "Gent" residing at 45 South Fifth Street. There he was living with his daughter, Sarah, and son-in-law, Lee Buffington, MD. The Buffingtons and Wm. J. Hallowell appear in the 1850 census in the South Mulberry section of Philadelphia. William is listed as a 68-year-old gentleman. Hallowell presumably died before the next decennial census since he is not included with the Buffington family in 1860.

After Hallowell left Wilmington, he and then his family retained the property on Orange and Third streets for a number of years. It was not until 1865, in an indenture (A 8 480) dated March 17, that his heirs sold a large portion of it to Peter Springer for $4,500.00. Between Hallowell's retirement to Philadelphia and the property's sale, it must have been leased to one or more businesses, possibly the leather trade, since no evidence was found to support any continuation of pottery making there. His earlier landlord, William Robinson, was identified as a "skinner" in several land transactions and, in the 1845 *Wilmington Directory*, a leather store was advertised at the corner of Third and Orange streets. In the ad, the store's new proprietor pointed out that he was the successor to Jos. Robinson and Samuel Williamson. Presumably Joseph was a member of the leather processing Robinson family.

So based on the information uncovered, Hallowell, after learning his craft in Wilmington, worked as a journeyman and proprietor from about 1806 until 1823. Part of this time he leased the factory from William Robinson before acquiring it in 1823. No newspaper announcement of Hallowell's pottery was found so, unlike most of his colleagues, this potter did not use this medium to advertise his wares. Most likely William limited his operation to the manufacture of earthenware. That he produced this type of ceramic is substantiated through an entry in an account book of Joseph Bringhurst. Owner of a Wilmington drug store, Bringhurst purchased a nondescript lot of earthenware from W. Hallowell on November 14, 1820. Besides confirming the type of pottery Hallowell produced, it further lends creditability to the argument that William was operating the pottery prior to purchasing the real estate in 1823.

14 Two White Chambers at 20 Cents ... 40
Earthenware of W. Hallowell ... 50
Sundries ... 25

Joseph Bringhurst, a Wilmington druggist, purchased earthenware from William Hallowell in 1820. *No.73x250.1a. Courtesy, The Winterthur Library: Joseph Downs Collection of Manuscripts and Printed Ephemera.*

Like many nineteenth century city residents, William Hallowell was active in a fire company. In his case, service spanned at least 15 years with the Reliance Fire Company. A newspaper notice in 1814 named him as a hose conductor and another in 1829 announced Hallowell was elected a staff man. This fire company was located on Third Street between Market and Shipley streets, less than two blocks from Hallowell's business. John Jones, owner of the pottery on Water Street, was a member of the same fire fighting unit.

Water Street at Orange Street

John Jones is another Wilmington potter who began his career in the eighteenth century. In an indenture made April 7, 1783 (S 2 66), John Jones, potter, purchased 33 perches of land in the city from the Millers of Chester County, Pennsylvania, for £171.8.7. The property was bordered by Front Street to the northeast, Water Street on the southwest, Orange Street to the southeast and Thorn Street on the northwest. Water Street was about 100 feet below Front Street and very close to the Christina River. The indenture makes no mention of a pottery on the site so it's somewhat safe to conclude Jones was the first to turn and fire various clay forms there.

Where on his property did John construct his pot house and kiln? The first issue of the Wilmington Directory, dated 1814, does little to clarify the location since it listed John Jones, potter, on Orange Street between Front Street and the Christina Creek. The next year, Joshua Stroud, in an advertisement in the November 7, issue of the *Delaware Gazette and Peninsula Times*, informed the public of his plaster mill on the corner of Front and Orange Streets, opposite Jones' Pot House. But information in a later land deed (U 4 36) in 1834 used the back walls of the pot house and kiln house to define property lines in a sale of the northeast corner of Jones' tract. Reading the description in this indenture, it becomes clear that a strip of land, roughly 20 feet wide above and along Water Street, holds a pot house and kiln house. It placed the pot house at the corner of Water and Orange streets and the kiln house to the west toward Thorn Street. Sometime later, a stable was added at the corner of Water and Thorn streets to fully utilize the property facing Water Street. From dimensions in the deed and assuming the exterior walls were built on the property lines, the pot house was a rectangular building 17 feet 8 inches by 34 feet 10 inches. Meanwhile the kiln house and the eventual stable covered an area 23 feet 8 inches by 42 feet 6 inches where the kiln house was nearly twice the size of the stable. And a city atlas and map in the 1860s and '70s placed the pottery at the intersection of Water and Orange streets. While Jones may have started his venture at Front Street and later moved his pottery down Orange to Water Street, it is more likely that the corner of Water and Orange streets was its location from the beginning.

According to Benjamin Ferris' book on Delaware history, John Jones was born in 1758 and much can be leaned about him through Friends' records held in their library at Swarthmore College. In October of 1776, the Philadelphia Monthly Meeting produced a certificate from the Gwynedd Monthly Meeting identifying Jesse Jones as the father of John Jones who had recently been placed as an apprentice with "John Thomson." While the craft was not mentioned, John Thompson operated a pottery on Fourth Street in Philadelphia. Susan Myers placed him at that location by 1785, but now it appears he was there ten years earlier. After Jones' training, he probably stayed on in Philadelphia as a journeyman potter for a few years. Presumably he arrived in Wilmington by 1783 since, in the deed granting him the property at Water and Orange streets, he was identified as a resident of Wilmington. At that point, he was about 25 years old. But for some unexplained reason, John Jones, his wife Sarah and four minor children did not transfer to the Wilmington Monthly Meeting until 1791. It is possible that the Jones family maintained two residences until then.

Sarah was a member of the Green family of Smyrna, Delaware. According to the probate records of Rachael Jordan of Duck Creek Hundred dated September 3, 1814, she was a cousin of Charles Green. This would have been Charles Green, Jr., the Kent County potter. As will be discussed in Chapter VII, it is believed that Charles learned his craft and worked in Philadelphia in the 1770s. John Jones was there during part of that period so Charles and he may have crossed paths while working at the same pottery. Maybe John met Sarah through Charles.

The Wilmington potter from Orange Street lived to be 67 years old. The January 14, 1825, issue of the *American Watchman & Delaware Advertiser*, published in Wilmington, noted that John Jones, "an old and respectable inhabitant of this borough, died yesterday morning." He was buried in the Wilmington Friends' Meeting Yard. No reference to the exact birth date of Sarah, his wife, was found but she died soon after her husband on April 5, 1826. She was in her 65th year and was also buried at Wilmington Friends. A John Jones, consistent with a birth date of 1758, is found in the 1800, 1810 and 1820 censuses of Wilmington. The 1820 census also counted the number of individuals within a household who were engaged in manufacturing. In Jones' case, the number was three, and presumably all worked at his Water Street pottery. One would have been John, himself, while the other two, by the census, were 16 to 25 and 26 to 44 years old. The younger of the two may have been an apprentice, Andrew Maxwell. The other individual could have been Abraham Ritchie. More will be said about them later. We will also see that a potter by the name of John Bannard most likely worked for Jones during this time frame. He was about 54 years old in 1820, and married. John was probably the John Banners recorded as a Wilmington head of a family in the 1820 census. His age and that of his wife, Jane, match a man and women counted in the Banners' household.

In the earlier profiling of Isaac Starr, Samuel Bush was mentioned as a Wilmington businessman involved in general trade at a wharf on the Christina River. Bush's account book includes three transactions with John Jones for materials critical to a pottery's operation. All occurred in 1792:

April 23	3 cask of lead
May 12	15 bushels of sand
December 10	12 loads of clay

Sand was a component in the preparation of earthenware glazes and was also added to clays to prevent the finished pottery from cracking during heating. Lead was a basic ingredient used to formulate a clear glaze. Potters typically purchased red lead, an oxide, for this purpose. But some early operators made their own oxide by burning metallic lead. The ledger does not specify the form of lead but it was more likely the metal itself, since red lead was a common term in the eighteenth century and probably would have been used to distinguish the material purchased.

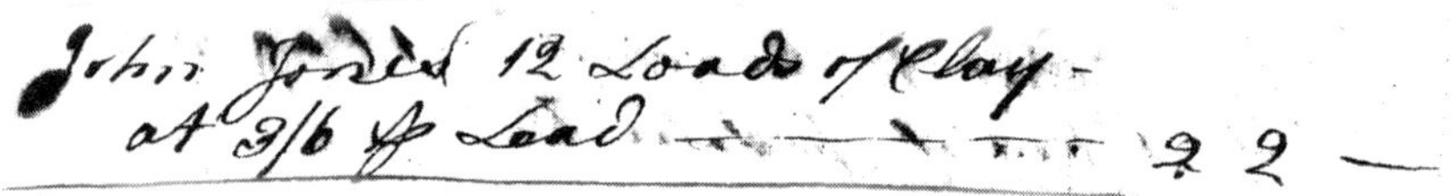
John Jones 12 Loads of Clay -
at 3/6 pr Load ——— 2 2 —

Samuel Bush sold clay to the potter, John Jones, in 1792. Account Book of Samuel Bush. *Courtesy of the Historical Society of Delaware.*

The Historical Society of Delaware holds a receipt book of Elizabeth and Rachael Montgomery in which they recorded signatures of those to whom they paid money. An entry dated August 14, 1804, was scripted by a John Jones, though the reason for Rachael's payment was not given. Quite likely this is the signature of the potter.

Rec'd 8th mo. 14. 1804 of
Rachel Montgomery, One
Pound 3/6 in full —
£1. 3. 6 John Jones

The signature of John Jones was recorded by Rachael Montgomery in 1804. Receipt Book of Elizabeth and Rachael Montgomery. *Courtesy of the Historical Society of Delaware*

No doubt John Jones was still manufacturing clay wares at or close to the time of his death. His estate inventory included the following entries related to his business:

Lot of earthenware in house No 1	$25.00
Lot of earthenware in ware house No 2	50.00
Lot of earthenware in ware house	125.00
Lot of earthenware in kiln house	50.00
Lot of green ware and "pott of glasing"	90.75
Pine wood estimated at 10 cords	35.00
1 load blue clay	5.00

No examples of pottery attributed to Jones' factory are known to exist today. But from his final inventory, it is clear that he produced the utilitarian forms of glazed redware typical of the period. If, as suggested earlier, John and Charles Green were from the same Philadelphia training ground, the photographs of fragments from Green's pottery may also reflect the production and style of Jones. Sometimes newspaper advertisements provide clues to a potter's product line, but none was found for Jones. However, a card in the genealogy catalog in the Reference Room at the Wilmington Library indicates that the December 4, 1797, issue of the *Delaware & Eastern Shore Advertiser* contained a note regarding the pottery operation of John Jones. But disappointment prevails since a copy of that newspaper has not been located in any library.

In his will executed in 1824 (NCC-S-1-59), Jones bequeathed all his real and personal property to Sarah. Israel D. Jones, a son, and Reuben Webb, a son-in-law, were named executors of his estate. In their accounting of receipts and disbursements, four names are recognizable as associated with pottery making in Delaware and some mention has already been made of them:

- The estate collected $23 from John Bannard. While no reason for the payment was given, it could have been for rent. A potter, Bannard must have worked for Jones.
- The estate owed William "Hollowell" $1.245. No reason for the payment was noted. William was operating his own pottery up Orange Street at the time.
- A. Maxwell paid $16.66 to the estate for rent. An Andrew Maxwell was a Wilmington potter who later took

on apprentices in 1832 and 1833. Maxwell may have apprenticed and worked for Jones.

- The estate paid A. Ritchie or Abraham Ritchie from $7 to $20 on four occasions. Though no reasons were logged, it could have been to manage pottery operations after Jones' death. Beginning in the late 1820s, Abraham Ritchie is known to have managed another pottery, one in Smyrna, Delaware, following the death of its owner, Daniel Green.

John Jones' pottery enterprise must have been reasonably successful. Not only did this business span over 40 years but he purchased several other properties in northern Delaware during his lifetime. The extent of his ventures into real estate can be gleaned from an advertisement his executors placed several months after his death. In it, they announced the sale of properties in both the Wilmington and Smyrna areas of Delaware. Some were undeveloped lots while others contained residential buildings that undoubtedly he had rented out. Two parcels of land, which apparently held no structures, may have been related to his pottery. One, a lot of 3.25 acres, had been purchased in 1803 at auction for $520 (A 3 386). It was situated in Clement's Creek Marsh and was one that his executors advertised. Three years earlier, John had acquired a somewhat smaller piece of land (X 2 328) along Marsh Road for $232.50. Though speculation, these parcels may have been sources of clay for his pottery. The properties in Smyrna could have come to Sarah from holdings of the Green family. Besides the prop-

Valuable Real Estate for Sale,

Late the property of JOHN JONES, dec.

TO wit: in Smyrna, Del., on the 21st of the present month, at Lockwood's Tavern—No. 1, a lot of land in Main St, opposite Lockwood's Tavern; 21 ft 6 inches front, and 63 ft. deep, with a new frame house, one story, 19 ft. square, with a kitchen adjoining.

No. 2, a lot of land adjoining No. 1—22 ft. 6 inches front and 68 ft. deep.

No. 3, a lot of land adjoining No. 2—17 ft. front and 68 ft. deep.

No. 4, a lot of land 20 ft. front, and 526 ft. deep, with a good two story brick house, 16 ft. 6 inches in front, on the road leading to the landing.

At Wilmington, Del., on the 26th of the present month,

No. 1, a lot of land 213 ft. on Front street, extending back to 2d street 247 ft.—bounded on Justus street; part of which is under lease to Evan Thomas & Co., containing in the whole about 1¼ acres.

No. 2—3 acres and 23 perches in Clement Creek marsh, adjoining lands of Joseph Haily and others, near the Black Horse Tavern, being divided into two lots: it will be sold to suit purchasers.

No. 3, a house and lot in Market St. occupied by Joseph Pogue as a dry goods store.

Conditions will be made known on the day of sale, by

ISRAEL D. JONES,
REUBEN WEBB,

11th mo., 1, 1825. 95—6t *Ex'rs.*

American Watchman and Delaware Advertiser, November 18, 1825.

erty that Jones amassed, some personal items in the inventory of his estate reflect the level of his wealth—two mahogany dining tables, two arm chairs and six Windsor chairs.

The entrepreneurship of Jones extended beyond the manufacture of earthenware. In the March 3, 1809, issue of the *Museum of Delaware and General Advertiser*, John Jones announced the dissolution of a partnership between Jones and Johnson, brewers. With such a common name as John Jones, can one be sure the subscriber of this notice was the potter from Water Street? Later newspaper notices add a high degree of certainty that he had his hands in the brewing business. Another of Jones' obituaries, this one, in *The Wilmingtonian & Delaware Register* on January 13, 1825, the date of the potter's death, reported that "John Jones, Brewer, of this borough, died this morning in the 67th year of his age." Earlier in 1819, John Jones & Son announced that they had commenced brewing beer for the season. The son referred to in this advertisement was most assuredly Israel D. Jones. In early 1825, Israel advertised the availability of "Draught Beer, Porter and Ale" at No. 34 Second Street. Apparently this was the brewer's retail outlet. Subsequent to John's death, Israel announced that a property at the corner of Tatnall and High streets was available for lease. He went on to say in this "NOTICE To *Manufacturers*" that it was formerly occupied as a brewery but could now be used for a variety of manufacturing operations.

Jones' business property holdings went beyond pottery making and brewing. In the assessments in New Castle County for 1816-17, Jones was taxed for "1 lot on rent to S. Baldwin." In a notice in the *American Watchman* on February 6, 1819, Samuel Baldwin was named as the recent occupant of an iron foundry. Located in Wilmington, it included two air-

NOTICE TO
Manufacturers

To let for a term of years, that large and commodious building in the Borough of Wilmington, formerly occupied as a Brewery, situated on the corner of Tatnall and High Streets, 120 feet long and 30 feet deep, with a dwelling attached, and a never failing spring of excellent water in the cellar, to pump by horse power. This building is well calculated for a Manufactory, particularly weaving or distilling, it being in a central part of the Borough, with a good brick stable on the premises. The subscriber thinks it unnecessary to say any thing further, as any person wishing to rent would first view the premises.

Israel D. Jones

Delaware and American Watchman, February, 16, 1828

furnaces. The newspaper item headed with the byline, "For Rent," went on to identify John Jones as the person in Wilmington to whom to apply for terms. The property was only vacant for a few months since in the *Delaware Gazette & Peninsula Advertiser* on July 31, Evan Thomas announced that "he has taken the Delaware Air Furnace, lately occupied by Samuel Baldwin, where he will receive orders for any description of iron castings." Two references to a "furnace lot" also appear in Jones' final estate accounting. He owed approximately ten and a half dollars for the fabrication of 34 posts and fence for this facility.

John Jones' involvement in the Wilmington community went beyond his business interests. The Reliance Fire Company was the second to be organized in Wilmington and Jones served it in various capacities over the years. According to an announcement in the March 10, 1799, issue of the *Delaware Gazette*, Jones was then its clerk. In an advertisement titled "Fire Buckets," John sought their return following loss at the last fire. The buckets were marked with the inscription—RELIANCE FIRE CO. No. 27. In 1814, he also served as one of its engineers according to the author, Thomas Scharf. This fire company, started in 1796, held the distinction that Caesar A. Rodney, grandson of Delaware's representative to the Continental Congress and a U. S. Senator in his own right, was one of its organizers. The duties of an engineer were not only to take care of the engine but also to clear the way and secure the nearest source of water. Jones was the first in a line of potters to play a role in the city's fire protection. No doubt they felt a sense of duty since their kilns provided ignition sources in their neighborhoods. In fact, Jones lost the roof of his pot house in a fire in 1798. In another capacity, the *Wilmington Directory* published in 1814 lists John Jones, potter, as an inspector for the Humane Society of Wilmington. The Society served as the rescue service of the era since its "objects were the recovery from apparent drowning, suffocation from burning charcoal or other noxious vapors, drink-

Fire-Buckets

Lost, at a late fire with an inscription on the front—RELIANCE FIRE CO. No. 27—Supposed to be taken in mistake. Whoever has it, will oblige the Company, by sending it to the subscriber, or informing him thereof.

JOHN JONES

Delaware Gazette, March 10, 1799

ing cold water, strokes of the sun, damps of wells, lightning or other similar casualties." Apparently Jones held a paid position since his estate logged a $2 receipt from the Humane Society.

Following John Jones' death in 1825, a number of proprietors worked the pottery on Water Street. But throughout the entire period, his descendents continued ownership and leased the property until the potter's wheel turned for the last time in 1880. Then heirs sold the property to Sarah Murphy (Q 11 208), whose husband, James, was in the coal business. An announcement in the *Delaware Gazette* on April 1 of that year provided insight into Murphy's plans. Per the notice, the pottery of Jacob Ziegler on the northwest corner of Orange and Water streets was purchased with the intent to tear it down and, in its place, erect a stable and office. (Actually, it was George, not Jacob Ziegler, who was operating the pottery at the time.) A portion of Jones' property below Water Street was also part of the transaction and Murphy planned to convert it to a coal yard. Whether James followed through with his plan is uncertain since the outlines of the original pot house, kiln house and stable are still shown in a 1901 atlas of the city published by Baist. In any event, the purchase by the Murphys sounded the end to nearly 100 years of pottery making on land along Water Street between Orange and Thorn streets. During the long rein of this manufactory, potters turned and fired tons and tons of clay into various forms of earthenware, though no known example with attribution to the pottery has survived. In addition, no documentary evidence has been found that stoneware was ever produced on this site by any of its operators.

On Tuesday last, a fire broke out in the pot-house of Mr. John Jones, of this town; which thro' the prompt attention of the engines, and activity of the citizens, was happily extinguished. We do not hear that any material loss was sustained besides the destruction of the roof.

Delaware Gazette, December 27, 1798

So who operated the pottery on Water Street after 1825? As mentioned earlier it is quite possible that the Jones family engaged Abraham Ritchie to temporarily manage the Water Street pottery after John's death. And Samuel Preston Moore may also have been a short term proprietor. However, neither has been included in the chronological listing of operators since at this point their involvement is conjecture. More will be said about these two individuals in Chapter VIII.

The Pottery on Water Street

Operator	**Time Period***
John Jones	1783-1825
Nathan Dalbey	182?-1848
Richard Lowe & John Stüber	1848-1850
Richard Lowe	1850-1854
Lawrence Messick	1854-1855
John Stüber	1855-1859
George Ziegler & Albert Neumayer	1860-1864
George Ziegler	1865-1880

*John Jones and his descendants retained ownership of the pottery during this entire period.

This table shows the chronological order of the proprietors of the pottery located at Orange and Water streets. The dates are best estimates based on available information, some of which is limited.

The proprietor who can next be linked to this pottery is **Nathan Dalbey**, sometimes spelled Dalby or Dolby. When he assumed its operation is unclear, although it could have been as early as the late 1820s. Several pieces of information place him in Wilmington then, and into and through the next decade. Nathan had a son, Barton, who was also a potter. He is mentioned in M. Lelyn Branin's book on New Jersey potters and more will be said about him in Chapter VIII. Suffice it to say here that Branin cites Barton as born in Wilmington, Delaware, and age 24 when he died in 1852. That information places the Dalbey family in Wilmington in about 1828. Available Wilmington tax records show Nathan Dolby was assessed a personal tax in 1833. And according to the 1840 Delaware population census, Nathan was 30-39 years old with three young males listed in his household. One categorized as 10 to 14 years old was undoubtedly Barton. Additional evidence that Dalbey was in Delaware in the early 1840s is supported by a ledger of Wilmington foundry operators Betts and Stotsenburg. On September 6, 1841, an entry, "To furnace" for Nathan Dolby in the amount of $6.18, was recorded. Nathan settled the account "By cash" in May of 1843. This ledger is in the collection of the Hagley

Museum and Library. As for his occupation, Nathan Dalbey was listed in the 1845 *Wilmington Directory* as a potter dwelling on Thorn Street below Water Street. That would place his residence just around the corner from the Jones' pottery.

As further evidence of his craft, Dalbey executed an apprentice indenture on April 26, 1847, in which he agreed to teach **Henry S. Lambdin** the "Trade or Mystery of Pottery." Henry never completed his apprenticeship under Dalbey since Nathan announced the failure of his business in a newspaper notice in May of the next year. Soon thereafter, Nathan must have left Wilmington. Though not indexed in the 1850 census of either Delaware or New Jersey, Nathan Dalbey of Burlington County, New Jersey, was appointed administrator of his son's estate on April 29, 1852. Nothing more is known of him.

> *Failure* – We regret to learn that Mr. Nathan Dalby, potter, of this city, has failed. We hope he may be able to commence again.
>
> *Blue Hen's Chicken, May 24, 1848*

But while it is clear that Dalbey manufactured pottery in Wilmington, what information is there that connects him with the operation at Water and Orange streets? In April of 1848, **Richard Lowe** and **John Stüber (Stiiber)** advertised that they have taken over the old establishment of Mr. Nathan Dalbey at the corner of Water and Orange streets where they were "prepared to manufacture all kinds of EARTHENWARE." More than likely, these two potters met while working for Dalbey. When his business folded, they stepped in. As we

EARTHENWARE MANUFACTORY

The subscribers respectfully inform their friends and the public generally that they have taken the old established stand, recently occupied by Mr. Nathan Dalbey, corner of Water and Orange streets, where they are prepared to manufacture all kinds of **EARTHENWARE**, in a superior manner and on the most accommodating terms.
They hope by strict attention to business, and a determination to please their customers to merit and receive a liberal share of public patronage.

LOWE & STIIBER

Blue Hen's Chicken, April 17, 1848

will see, Lowe came to Wilmington before 1845, though Stüber arrived closer to the date of their announced partnership.

Richard Lowe appears in the 1845 *Wilmington Directory* and also in the 1850 Delaware census. At that point, he was 40 years old and married with four children, the oldest of whom was 14. Both Richard and his wife, Mary, were born in New Jersey, he in about 1810 and she in 1816. They relocated to Wilmington from Monmouth County, New Jersey. According to Lelyn Branin, Richard "Low" operated a pottery in Middletown Point in the late 1830s. There, as on Orange Street, he manufactured all kinds of earthenware. One historian wrote that Lowe worked at this New Jersey location until 1850. However, Branin discounts that report based on a newspaper advertisement in which another potter announced in 1842 that he then occupied Richard Low's stand. The *Wilmington Directory* attests to the correctness of Branin's conclusion since Lowe had already arrived in Wilmington and was living on Poplar Street between Front and Second streets by 1845. Though Lowe did not own this Wilmington property, he was granted a lot at the corner of Poplar and Front streets in 1846 for $900 (T 5 5). The family resided there until he sold it in June of 1851 (F 6 453) for $100 more than he paid. Richard then apparently moved his family onto the site of the pottery.

According to probate records, Richard Lowe died in 1854. An inventory of his goods totaled $784.87. In addition, $652.93 were listed as "Cash from" numerous individuals who probably owed Lowe for previous purchases. Inventoried raw materials from his pottery included clay, wood and red lead. Product entries were sparse with only five references. The combined estimated value of unfired and finished earthenware was set at $192 by the appraiser. That amount is quite low compared to the $3,500 of earthenware Lowe reported producing in 1850. Several pieces of equipment used in the pottery were also listed in the inventory. His wife, Mary, identified a number of disbursements in the total amount of $460.71. Of those named, one might expect that some potters would have been due wages if the pottery was operating at the time of Lowe's death. But no names of known potters were recognized in the listing. This and the small inventory of products suggest that the pottery was inactive for a period of time prior to his death, possibly because of Richard's illness. There were, however, two references to William Hare, a potter who was working on French Street at the time. Hare's signature is one of two at the end of the inventory. Who better to appraise pottery and materials and equipment used in its making than a master potter like Hare? William was also named to receive $44.83 for stoneware Lowe had apparently purchased from him. This suggests that Lowe was reselling Hare's stoneware since $45 worth would have consisted of more than a hundred pieces, far more than a typical household would need. Even if they were highly decorated or unusual forms, it would take a substantial number to total that amount of money. Today from time to time, one sees unsigned stoneware preserve jars in local antique shops that are identical in shape and color to those produced and marked by Hare. William might have funneled some of his unmarked jars to a potter like Richard Lowe for resale.

Selected Items from Richard Lowe's Estate Inventory

Materials	
25 cords fire wood	$150
10 cart loads clay	20
500* red lead	40
Equipment	
2 wheel barrows	3
2 wagons	75
2 horses & gears	180
1 glazing mill	5
Wares	
un-burnt ware	40
180 feet tile	18
manufactured ware	125
drain pipe	7

*Units associated with the quantity of red lead cannot be discerned.

Little is known about the pottery forms that Lowe produced. We read in his advertisement with Stüber that they were "prepared to produce all kinds of earthenware," but no details were provided. A similar product description, "Earthen Ware of all Kinds", was reported by Lowe in the 1850 Census of Manufactures. As we will see later, by the time of this census, the Lowe-Stüber partnership had been dissolved. Other details of the census show how equal in size Lowe's operation was to that of the French Street potter, William Hare. Both operators employed four men and paid an average of $80 in monthly wages. Lowe produced ceramics he valued at $3,500, only $100 less than Hare's product value. Richard's clay and wood consumptions were somewhat less but one might expect that since Hare also produced stoneware.

Lowe's estate inventory does not help much either. Tile and drain pipe were the only specific items mentioned. Otherwise the listing included single lots of un-burnt and manufactured wares which were surely references to assortments of typical forms of redware. And it is clear that Richard glazed some products. Both a glazing mill and red lead were inventoried in his estate.

Apparently Mary Lowe continued to reside in Wilmington until her death, though the date is unknown. Both she and Richard were buried in the Wilmington and Brandywine Cemetery, Lot 63, Section Z. Two of their sons, **William A. Lowe** and **Frederick Lowe**, also became potters and more will be said about them in Chapter VIII.

John Stüber (spelled with an umlaut in his native language) was born in Baden, Germany, about 1802. Baden was homeland to several immigrant potters. Germany was also the birthplace of his wife, Clara, and six children, the youngest being eight years old per the 1850 population census. That suggests the family arrived in America after 1842, but quite possibly after 1845, since John is not listed in that year's *Wilmington Directory*. In 1853, the same publication shows John residing at the corner of Washington and Sixth streets. In fact, Stüber had purchased that property in August of 1850 (F 6 22). Ten years later, the census lists John as a potter with real estate and personal property valued at $1,500 and $500, respectively. By 1870, Stüber was a retired grocer with $2,500 in real estate. Based on the filing of letters of administration (NCC D-2-527) on November 19, 1877, regarding his estate, John must have died earlier that year.

But the Lowe and Stüber relationship didn't last long. In July of 1850, they announced dissolution of their partnership. Richard purchased John's interest and as already mentioned, continued in business until his death in 1854.

So why did John Stüber dissolve his partnership with Richard Lowe in early 1850? Though conjecture, it is quite possible he left the Orange Street pottery to join the firm of Reiss and Hutman; they were erecting a porcelain manufactory in Wilmington at the time. In fact, in the 1850 census, John's 15-year-old son, **Herman**

DISSOLUTION of PARTNERSHIP

THE Partnership heretofore existing between Richard Lowe John Stiiber, under the firm of LOWE & STIIBER, is this day dissolved by mutual consent. All persons indebted to said firm, either by note or book account, will please present them for settlement to either of the subscribers.

RICHARD LOWE,
JOHN STIIBER

HAVING purchased Mr. John Stiiber's interest, I would most respectfully inform my friends and the public, that I will carry on the EARTHENWARE MANUFACTORY at the old stand, corner of Orange & Water Streets in all its various branches.Thanking for past patronage, I respectfully solicit a continuance of the same.

RICHARD LOWE

Blue Hen's Chicken, February 8, 1850

Stüber, was listed with an occupation, "porcelain," suggesting that he worked for the two German immigrants in their attempt to bring the production of fine china to the city. More will be said about the porcelain venture in Chapter VI, but it is important to note here that the enterprise failed in early 1851 and the timing coincides with a career event in the life of Stüber. In its January 10, 1851, issue, the *Blue Hen's Chicken* reported that Mr. John Stüber has commenced the grocery business at the corner of Sixth and Washington streets. This location was also his residence. But we will see that soon after Richard Lowe's death, John Stüber returned to pottery making on Water Street.

Following Richard Lowe, the next individual with an interest in the pottery at Orange and Water streets appears to have been **Lawrence Messick**. Perusing the *Wilmington Directory* in the 1850s does not connect him to a pottery. Instead he was referred to as a trader and grocer. Those occupations are further confirmed in the May 7, 1859, issue of the *Delaware Inquirer* in which he is described as being engaged in the grocery and provision business near Front and Jefferson streets. But an advertisement in the *Delaware State Journal* in 1855 also links Messick with the old pottery established by John Jones and the same notice announces the reentry of John Stüber. In it, Stüber said he had purchased Messick's interest in the pottery business and vowed to carry on at the old, established stand, corner of Water and Orange streets. Whether Messick was the pottery's proprietor or a financial supporter in partnership with Stüber or someone else before 1855 is not clear. Newspapers of this time period are full of announcements creating and dissolving partnerships but none was found naming a Messick partner. Lawrence's heritage, according to the 1870 census, was like that of others associated with the Water Street pottery, including Stüber. He was born in Baden, Germany. Apparently after Richard Lowe's untimely death in 1854, Messick and Stüber teamed up to continue the production of earthenware on Water Street.

POTTERY

THE undersigned, having purchased the interest of Lawrence Messick in the **POTTERY BUSINESS**, would respectfully inform his friends and the public generally, that he still continues to carry on the above business in all its branches at the old established stand, **CORNER OF WATER AND ORANGE STREETS**, and hopes by strict attention to business to merit and receive a share of public patronage.

JOHN STIIBER

Delaware State Journal, September 21, 1855

Then within a year, Stüber bought out Messick's interest. Their acquaintance may have even begun some years earlier due to their similar roots.

John Stüber's return to the potting business continued until about 1859-60. Though the 1860 population census records him as a potter, one no longer finds him listed in the *Wilmington Directory* after that year with that occupation. In the October 7, 1859, issue of the *Delaware Gazette*, Stüber was named as having purchased a New Castle County retailer's license for $2.50. The business wasn't specified so the license could have been for the pottery. However, it is more likely the license was for his grocery business since a pottery was considered a manufacturing rather that a retailing enterprise. The *Wilmington Directory* for 1862-63 shows John was once again a grocer.

The pottery at Orange and Water streets was next occupied by **George Ziegler** and **Englebert (Albert) Neumayer**. Both were named in the 1860 Census of Manufactures as operating a factory that fashioned earthenware of various kinds. Employing three men, they produced wares valued at nearly $1,800, about one-third that of their Wilmington competitor, William Hare. The two German potters reported only $300 in capital, suggesting that the pottery they had taken over under lease required little in new investment. (Hare claimed capital of $6,000.) In the same year, the potters were cited in a newspaper note as manufacturers of superior wares that were sold throughout Delaware. Federal tax records beginning in 1862 assessed them for manufacturing pottery ware at Orange and Water streets. These assessments continued until January of 1865 when Ziegler is named as the only one assessed. In an advertisement in 1862, these partners informed the public that they were not only continuing to manufacture earthenware but also offered Rockingham ware. They went on to say that their flower pots, vases, and other forms excelled in beauty of finish and strength. Their reference to finish and the mention of Rockingham indicate

---

Ziegler & Neumeyer, potters, corner of Water and Orange Streets, manufacture superior ware, and we are pleased to hear that our merchants and others in the lower portion of the State are giving them a liberal share of their patronage. They manufacture good and cheap articles and must have a demand for them.

Delaware Republican, June 7, 1860

that these potters were applying glazes to the external surface of at least some of their products. And their Rockingham was most probably formed in molds rather than by hand using a potter's wheel. As with most other Delaware potters, no wares attributed to them are known today.

Listings in the *Wilmington Directory* are consistent with the tax data of the early 1860s. Both are denoted as co-operators of this pottery in the 1862-63 printing. But publication was interrupted for a few years and on its return in 1865-66, only Ziegler's name is ever associated with a business interest in the pottery. The fact that Ziegler's operation was not included in the Census of Manufactures in 1870 must have been an oversight. Not only was his pottery listed in that year's *Wilmington Directory*, but a reference to it is found in the *Delaware Gazette* on September 22 of the following year. In publishing the weekly paydays honored by various Wilmington manufacturers, the newspaper reported that George Ziegler, potter, paid his five employees on each Saturday suggesting that these craftsmen worked a six day week. The *Wilmington Atlas* published in 1876 attached the name "Ziegler's Pottery" to the buildings along Water Street between Orange and Thorn streets, though George never owned the property or the structures on it. He continued to produce ceramic products at this location until 1880.

POTTERY

THE subscribers would respectfully inform the public that they continue to manufacture Earthen and Rockingham Ware of all kinds at the corner of Water and Orange streets. Everything in their line kept on hand at the lowest figures. Orders for any article filled at the shortest notice. Flower pots, vases, &c., tastefully gotten up atmoderate prices. Their work for beauty of finish and strength cannot be excelled. Those in want will please give them a call.

ZEIGLER & NEUMAYER

Delaware Republican, June 7, 1860

The name George Ziegler first appeared in the *Wilmington Directory* in 1857 and then in the city's census of 1860. Both he and his wife, Justina, were born in the same part of Germany as John Stüber. But it seems that Ziegler arrived in Delaware several years before his name appeared in those publications. At the time of the 1860 census, the Zieglers had five children, four of whom had been born in Delaware. Pennsylvania was the birthplace of the firstborn.

The oldest of the four born in Delaware was nine years old in 1860, suggesting that the family was in Wilmington by about 1851. Where and for how long they resided in Pennsylvania is unknown. For many of their years in Wilmington, the family lived at 616 Tatnall Street. This two-story brick dwelling was purchased on March 25, 1858 (A 7 342).

Surely George learned his craft in Germany but may have worked at a Philadelphia pottery for a short time after arriving in America. But once in Wilmington, his initial place of employment is an open question. At first thought, one might conclude he worked on Water Street because of the birthplace he held in common with John Stüber. But William Hare on French Street cannot be discounted. Years later, near the end of his career, George did work for Hare. But there is another possibility. For some reason, George's occupation in the 1860 census was given as "china maker." Did this reference reflect his early training and previous employment? If so, was George associated with the attempted production of porcelain on the west side of Wilmington described in Chapter VI? The timing was right, and in his book, Edwin A. Barber wrote that early experiments of the eventual American Porcelain Company were conducted in Philadelphia and Wilmington. On his arrival in America, George's short stay in Philadelphia may have been associated with that venture followed by a move to Wilmington to participate in its next phase. Whatever his early leanings, earthenware was his forte once he became established in Wilmington.

Based on deeds and supported by an 1876 atlas, the Orange Street pottery apparently changed little in size and layout during the nearly hundred years of its operation. The 1876 map shows the pottery in three sections, two adjacent brick structures to the west along Water Street, and a frame building, likely used as a stable, at the corner of Water and Thorn streets. The distance along Water Street was approximately seventy-seven feet. Recall during the discussion of the John Jones era, it was pointed out that an 1834 land indenture provided the relative locations of the "Pot House" and "Kiln House." They appear to coincide with this 1876 map, even to the offset of six feet at the back walls of the two buildings.

The James F. Wood & Company, located at the corner of Front and Orange streets, fabricated products in tin, brass and iron in the 1870s. There the company was a neighbor to George Ziegler's pottery manufactory. As additional proof that Ziegler was so engaged comes from a daybook of Wood & Company which is

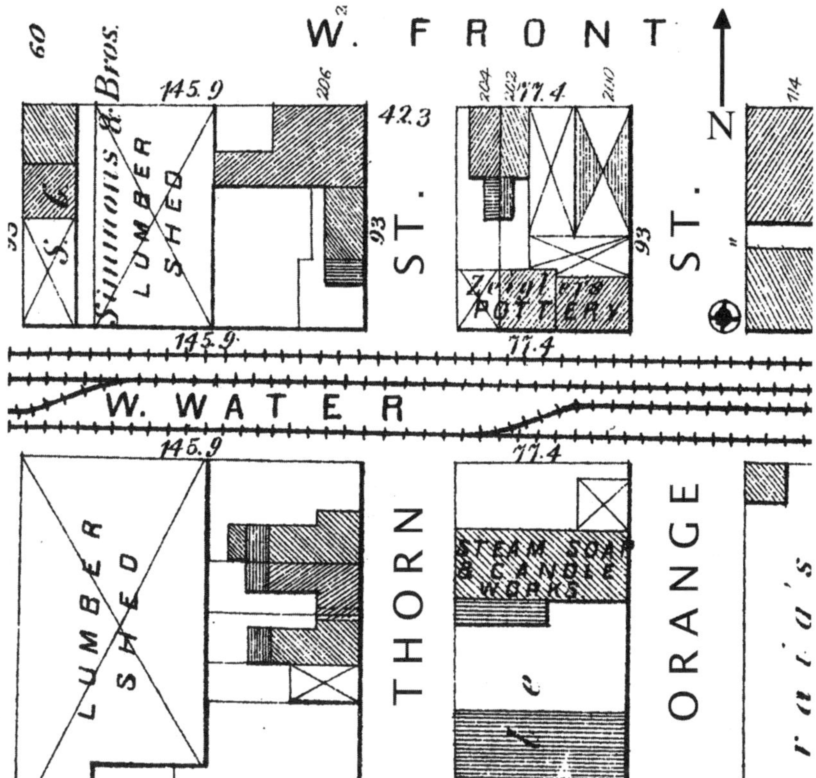

An outline of the pottery on Water Street leased by George Ziegler was published in 1876. The dimensions coincide with those in an earlier land deed (U 4 36 1834). The kiln house was located between the pot house and stable. *City Atlas of Wilmington, 1876*

archived in the Winterthur Library: Joseph Downs Collection of Manuscripts and Printed Ephemera. It contains three transactions between the company and Ziegler between 1870 and 1875. The one in 1875 records Ziegler's purchase of three pieces of pipe with "Potter" following his name.

An advertisement in a Wilmington newspaper in 1876 provides some insight to the types of pottery Ziegler was producing at that point in his life. His use of the words yard, hanging, gardener and green house demonstrates recognition that the market for the earthenware forms used inside the home was shrinking. The change in his product line was not unlike the reaction of other manufacturers of low-fired redware in the latter stages of the nineteenth century. The move of households toward the use of finer ceramics for table settings and glass for food storage reduced the demand for this simple pottery.

During the 1800s, newspapers routinely reported fires that occurred in Wilmington and, from time to time, the city experienced a rash of "incendiaries." Ziegler was a victim of a deliberately set fire, though it did not happen within the pottery itself. One night, his wagon loaded with hay was setting outside of his pottery at Water and Orange streets when a man applied a match to the contents. The event was witnessed by a passerby but the culprit escaped. The fire department kept the flames from spreading, though the wagon was "considerably damaged." The account was published in The *Delaware Gazette* on April 4, 1875. Ziegler may have been planning to load his wagon for a delivery, since potters commonly packed their wares in hay for safe transport.

EARTHENWARE MANUFACTORY

COR. OF ORANGE & WATER STREETS
WILMINGTON, DEL.

I keep constantly on hand a full assortment of CROCKERY WARE, made in the best manner, and sold at prices to suit the times.
Also Yard Vases, Hanging Vases, Gardeners' and Green House Pots. All articles in my line made to order at short notice.

GEORGE ZIEGLER

The Daily Gazette, November 4, 1876

Once George Ziegler closed his pottery, he was employed by William Hare until that potter's death in 1885. This segment of George's career can be followed using the *Wilmington Directory* into the mid-1880s. Furthermore, George is named in the final settlement of Hare's estate as due $15.68 for labor at the warehouse. According to the *Every Evening* published on January 1, 1887, Ziegler had died suddenly a day earlier at the age of 65. At the time, he was walking on Fifth Street near Market Street when he was stricken with a hemorrhage. George was buried from Sacred Heart Church, the city's Roman Catholic German parish, and laid to rest in Old Cathedral Cemetery in Wilmington. Justina continued to live in Wilmington until her death on April 6, 1893.

Two sons, **William F. Ziegler** and **Ferdinand Zeigler**, worked as potters for their father during the 1870s. After the pottery closed, William, while continuing to board on Tatnall Street at the family residence, briefly took his potting skills to Chester, Pennsylvania.

There he probably worked for the Trapnells on Hayes Street at the corner of Front Street. Like his father, the Trapnells manufactured earthenware. Years earlier, members of this family had potted in Maryland and Smyrna. But William Ziegler returned in the late '80s to once again work with clay in Wilmington, this time for Neumayer, his father's former partner. Ferdinand, on the other hand, changed occupations and became a carriage trimmer. The first-born son, Valentine, met a tragic death at age 12 when he drowned in the Christina River in 1862.

There is a reason that little has been said at this point about Englebert Neumayer other than to have identified him as Ziegler's early partner. Englebert eventually established his own pottery on the east side of Wilmington and the story of that venture will be told in Chapter VI.

Several of those associated with the pottery on Water Street were immigrants from parts of Germany that were both politically progressive and Catholic in the practice of religion. As Wilmington grew, new parishes were established and churches built. Not unlike today, donations were sought from the laity for this purpose. On January 22, 1858, the *Delaware Gazette* published a list of contributors for a new church, Saint Mary's, at Sixth and Pine streets. Donations were pledged by members of the "Orange Street contingent": Lawrence Messick ($100), George Ziegler ($30), John Stüber ($20) and Englebert Neumayer ($12).

Chapter IV

French Street in Wilmington Before 1840

FOUR

In 1831, **Branch Green** announced his relocation from Philadelphia to Wilmington and the opening of his pottery on French Street under the name of Branch Green & Co. He advertised that he had been manufacturing stoneware in Philadelphia for over twenty years and was taking **William Streatch (Stretch)** into copartnership in his Delaware venture. Though he mentioned several types of clay products, the headline touted stoneware. Green was probably the first potter to manufacture this type of ceramic in Wilmington and in Delaware. He apparently saw a niche opportunity since it is likely that all contemporary and earlier potters had only produced lower temperature earthenware. Of significance and worthy of brief mention at this point is that Green's pottery on French Street eventually became the business center of one of Delaware's longest surviving potters, William Hare. Today, that potter is especially known for his stoneware.

Not only did Green advertise his stoneware, but an account book of Joseph Bringhurst, a Wilmington drug store proprietor, documents the purchase of "6 stone milk pans" and "1 jar 5 gal" from Branch Green in June of 1832 for $1.00

STONE-WARE
BRANCH GREEN

Who carried on the Manufacturing of *Stone-ware* in Philadelphia for more than twenty years, informs his friends and former customers, that he has removed to Wilmington, Del. and that he has taken into co-partnership WILLIAM STREATCH under the firm of BRANCH GREEN & Co. — They have commenced the manufacturing of *Stone-ware, Earthen-ware, Fire brick, Cylinders* and *Clay Furnaces*; corner of Second and French Streets, opposite the Custom House; where they intend keeping all the above articles for sale, WHOLESALE & RETAIL, on the most favorable terms.

BRANCH GREEN & Co.

Delaware Journal, May 16, 1831

and $0.75, respectively. These sales occurred about four months before Green sold his Wilmington factory. While signed examples of Branch Green's stoneware—a jug made in Philadelphia and another he probably fired before his arrival there—are known, no pieces from his days in Wilmington have yet been attributed to him.

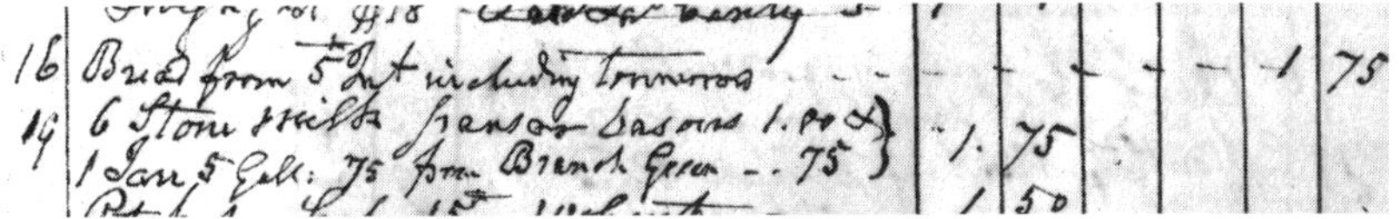

Joseph Bringhurst purchased stone milk pans and a jar from Branch Green in 1832. No. 73x250.2. *Courtesy, The Winterthur Library: Joseph Downs Collection of Manuscripts and Printed Ephemera.*

Branch had a life as a potter before Philadelphia. According to a book by Broderick and Bouck, Green was the first documented potter in Troy, New York, as early as 1799. Next he moved to New Jersey, and by 1805 opened a pottery with others at the South River Bridge. Then it was on to Philadelphia in 1809 where, per the *Philadelphia Directory,* he operated a pottery on Second Street above Germantown Road. In about 1827, he sold this pottery to Henry Remmey, one of the deft potters of the famous family by that name.

In April of 1831, just a few weeks before Green ran his newspaper advertisement in Delaware, he and David Cooke purchased property on French Street in Wilmington for $600 (4 P 59). At the time, Cooke was identified as a resident of the District of Kensington in the Northern Liberties section of Philadelphia. Unlike Green, Cooke was apparently not a potter; his interest in the operation may have been purely financial or commercial. During the 1820s, a David Cooke is listed as a merchant in the *Philadelphia Directory*. Some 18 months after acquiring the lot in Wilmington, Green and Cooke sold it and its improvements for over three times the original purchase price. But what circumstances might have warranted this high return in so short a period of time? It is quite probable that Green was the first to produce pottery on the site. In the deed granting them the property, it was described as a house and lot; no pottery or kiln house was mentioned. Thus, Branch may have had to build a kiln and make other capital improvements to the property. He had the experience and know-how to do that, and cash was available from the sale of his Philadelphia pottery and from his partner, Cooke.

This suggestion that Branch Green developed the potting facilities on French Street is based on land indentures and prior ownership. In 1814, Jacob Fussell advertised the private sale of a bake house on French Street between Second and Third streets. Interestingly, the notice touted the presence of a stone bake house of rather large size, a drying room and hoisting machinery. The description sounds like the property would have been an excellent candidate for conversion to a pottery. However, Fussell had no takers and he died soon thereafter, leaving to his wife, Esther, the task of selling the property to settle his estate. In 1816, the property was transferred to John Boyd and William Murdock (T 3 5). Nothing in the deed hinted the site had the capability to manufacture pottery at this early date. In August of 1830, David C. Wilson acquired Murdock's interest after it was seized by the New Castle County sheriff. No separate record of this transfer was found but mention of it is made in the indenture granting the property to Green and Cooke. However, when Green and his wife, Mary, and Cooke, and his wife, Mary W., transferred the property to Eli Hilles and David Smyth in 1832 (4 Q 175), the phrase

---

BAKE HOUSE &c. for SALE. — To be sold at Private Sale; a lot on French Street, in Wilmington, Del. between Second and Third Streets, 40 feet front by 118 deep, with a large and convenient Bake House thereon; 21 feet by 36 feet, having two ovens of 11 feet deep with soap stone fronts and iron doors, with a complete set of baking utensils, a large Drying Room, Hoisting Machinery, &c. A further description is thought unnecessary since any person inclining to purchase may view the premises by applying to the subscriber living thereon.

JACOB FUSSELL

* The Aurora & Baltimore Patriot will please to insert the above to the amount of one dollar, and send their accounts to the advertiser, for payment.

American Watchman, May 7, 1814

"stone messuage" (premise) was now part of the indenture. Though it is not totally clear to what the phrase referred, it was new to the property's description since the prior sale. However, by the next transfer to William Hare in 1846, the words, "stone pottery," are found in that deed. After the Fussell sale and before the purchase by Green and Cooke, the use to which the property was put is unclear, though it will be suggested that Branch Green established his pottery on the property of Boyd and Murdock as early as 1827.

Ownership of Property on French Street

Period	Owner(s)	Purchase Price	Use
1800-1816	Jacob Fussell	—	Bake House
1816-1830	John Boyd & William Murdock	$1450	Unknown
1830-1831	John Boyd & David Wilson	—	Pottery?
1831-1832	Branch Green & David Cooke	$600	Pottery
1832-1846	Eli Hilles & David Smyth	$2000	Pottery
1846-1885	William Hare	$2200	Pottery

In the 1831 indenture transferring property ownership to Green, he was identified as already residing in Wilmington. Recall he had sold his pottery in Philadelphia in 1827. So when did he arrive in the Delaware city? Census data for Pennsylvania and Delaware do not provide the answer. However, there is one piece of evidence that supports his arrival soon after the sale of his pottery. It was reported in the *Delaware Advertiser* of December 13, 1827, that Branch Green, along with many others, attended a meeting in Wilmington for the purpose of forming a temperance society. Eli Hilles also attended that meeting. Green continued his association with the Delaware Temperance Society for some time. In its March 17, 1831, issue, the same newspaper named Branch Green as one of several who had subscribed to the society's constitution. The name of a William Stretch, the partner Green mentioned in his stoneware advertisement, was also on the list of subscribers.

The whereabouts of Branch Green are uncertain after he sold his pottery on French Street in 1832 until he again appears in the *Philadelphia Directory* in 1841. At that point, he is no longer referred to as a potter. Instead, Green is listed as a dry goods merchant until 1844. Thereafter, no occupation is associated with his name so presumably he lived out his life in retirement until his death in 1847.

So far, little has been said about William Stretch, Green's co-partner. But in researching him, a better understanding of Branch's life after he left Wilmington and before he returned to Philadelphia may have been uncovered.

Working with several spellings of his surname—Streatch, Streeh, Strech and Stretch—leads to a reasonably clear understanding of William Stretch's movement during his life as a potter. A William Strech, age 40 and labeled a potter, is listed in the 1850 census for the second ward of Kensington in Philadelphia County, Pennsylvania. (Recall that David Cooke, Green's partner in the property purchase, was from Kensington.) According to this same census, William was born in Maryland and John Pearce gave a birth date of May 12, 1808, in his master's thesis. However, the year would have been 1807 based on his apprentice indenture also cited by Pearce. Maryland's census in the early 1800s shows a Samuel Stretch in Baltimore, and in the 1810 record, a male was counted in his household as under ten years of age. An apprentice indenture, which will be discussed in more detail later, confirms that Samuel was William's father. Per the *Baltimore Directory* in 1837-38, Samuel's occupation was noted as a tailor. William's first son was also named Samuel as it was not unusual for the eldest male to be named after the paternal grandfather.

Continuing to look at the information in the 1850 census, two of William Stretch's sons were born in Delaware. At the time of that census, Samuel was a 19-year-old potter and William (Jr.) was a 17-year-old boat maker. The birthplaces of seven other children of William and Mary, his wife, included Maryland, Pennsylvania and the District of Columbia. So, much about Stretch can be tracked through this census and a summary of several life events is shown on the following page.

At first thought, one might assume that this young potter began his apprenticeship under Branch Green before the offer of a partnership. John Pearce, however, found in his work on early Baltimore potters that a William "Sketch" was bound by himself and his father, Samuel, to James Burland on September 4, 1821, for a period of 6

Life Events of William Stretch, Potter

Approximation Year	Age	Life Event
1821	14	Bound to apprenticeship in Baltimore
1828	21	Scheduled to complete apprenticeship
1831	23	Green purchased the French Street property and took Stretch into partnership; son, Samuel, was born in Delaware
1832	24	Green sold the French Street pottery
1833	25	Second son, William (Jr.), was born in Delaware
1835	27	Third son was born in Maryland
1839	31	First daughter was born in the District of Columbia
1841	33	Fifth son was born in Pennsylvania
1850	42	Listed in the Kensington, Pennsylvania census

*Note: William's ages are based on a birth date of 1807 rather than on age 40 in the 1850 census. Based on a birth date of 1808, he would only have been 20 in 1828.

years, 8 months and 8 days. Burland was in partnership with David Parr. Stretch's Baltimore County apprenticeship was scheduled to end in 1828 on William's twenty-first birthday. (Note there is a discrepancy in the dates cited by Pearce. If born in 1808 as noted in the previous paragraph, his twenty-first birthday would have occurred in 1829, not 1828.) But Burland turned to the grocery trade around 1824 and died the next year so William did not finish his training under his original master. At this point, Stretch may have stayed on at the David Parr pottery continuing to train with others or, for some unknown reason, the young teen may have relocated to Philadelphia and connected with Branch Green to finish out his learning experience. In any event, by 1831, and probably sooner, Stretch had relocated to Wilmington and was working with Green on French Street.

As already mentioned, Green and Cooke sold the French Street pottery to Eli Hilles and David Smyth in 1832 but, based on the birthplace of Stretch's second son, William must have stayed on in Wilmington for a few years after the sale. Then he returned to Baltimore where he was listed as a potter in that city's directory in 1835-36 and again in 1837-38. Interestingly, in the later reference, the entry tags him as a stoneware potter, further substantiating his potting specialty that dates back to his partnership with Green in Wilmington. Eventually Stretch returned to Pennsylvania, notably about 1840 or 1841. And it was about then that Branch Green reentered the Philadelphia scene. One finds him in the *Philadelphia Directory* in 1841. Is it a coincidence that they both reappeared in Philadelphia about the same time? Although speculation, one can suggest that Green followed the same eight to nine year itinerary as Stretch between the time he sold his Wilmington pottery and his return to Philadelphia. As we have seen in his early life, moving was not foreign to Green and by the 1830s, any children would have been grown, allowing him even a more mobile lifestyle.

As for Stretch's later life, William is found residing in Bedminster, Bucks County, Pennsylvania, in the 1870 census. In his 60s then, presumably he was retired, though his occupation was recorded as "potter." William was living with his son, William (Jr.), who was listed as farmer.

Eli Hilles and **David Smyth** acquired the French Street pottery in 1832 from Green and Cooke and retained ownership for 14 years. Neither of these new owners was a potter. Hilles was a highly respected educator who co-founded a private school for young women on King Street between Seventh and Eighth streets. By coincidence, this location was the site of the former pottery and mansion of Mathew Crips, the wealthy eighteenth century earthenware potter discussed in Chapter II. Eli eventually moved his school a few blocks up King Street to a new facility. David Smyth was a Market Street merchant who dealt in china and glassware. Presumably Hilles and Smyth purchased the pottery as an investment, either with the idea of leasing it or hiring someone to manage it for them. One might have expected that if they sought a manger, the individual would have been a skilled potter. But regardless of the type of business arrangement that was struck, the next operator had no experience in the pottery business.

The first clues linking **Thomas Hayhurst** to a Wilmington pottery were uncovered in newspaper advertisements. In the *Delaware Gazette* on January 7, 1840, Charles Warner & Company, a Wilmington grocery store, announced that they had been appointed an agent of a Baltimore stoneware manufacturer. In the advertisement, they went on to say that they were now prepared to supply any or-

POTTERY FOR SALE

ALL that extensive Pottery now occupied by Mr. Thomas Hayhurst, situate on French street, near Second street. The lot is 40 feet front on French street, extending back about 118 feet, on which is erected a large stone building with kiln attached, and all necessary buildings suitable for ware houses, mill house, stables, carriage houses, & c., in good repair.

This property has long been established as a pottery, and capable of affording to any person having knowledge of the business, profit enough to pay for the premises in a very few years, and will be sold a bargain on easy terms. Apply immediately to **W. H. NAFF**
No. 1 West 4th street

Delaware State Journal, January 11, 1839

ders in that line "at *Thomas Hayhurst's* old prices." Another newspaper notice sheds even more light on Hayhurst. In an 1839 issue of the *Delaware State Journal,* the sale of a pottery was advertised and Thomas Hayhurst was named as its occupant. The advertisement gave the location as French Street, near Second Street. Undoubtedly, this was the pottery that Branch Green started and William Hare eventually purchased. W.H. Naff was the agent representing Eli Hilles and David Smyth, property owners at the time.

Thomas Hayhurst first appeared in the Delaware census in 1830 at which time he was listed with an age of 40 to 49. A later census identified Pennsylvania as his birthplace. A further search of census data and records at Friends Historical Library of Swarthmore College leads one to conclude that he was born in Bucks County, Pennsylvania, around 1790. In his early years, Quaker monthly meeting records place him in various Pennsylvania locations—Wrightstown, 1809; Muncy, 1809; Kennett, 1816; and Middleton, 1817. The first census in which he was named as a head of household was in 1820. In that year, Thomas Hayhurst was residing in Middleton Township, Bucks County, Pennsylvania. Patricia C. O'Donnell, a Friends' library staff member, suggested Thomas may have been a teacher, since frequent movements such as these were a characteristic of a Quaker of that profession.

Indeed, according to Thomas Scharf's *History of Delaware,* Thomas Hayhurst was a teacher at Wilmington Friends School on West Street near Fourth Street "several years after 1828." A current staff member confirmed from the school's archives that he taught there from 1830 to 1831. During this time at Friends, other activities acknowledge his interest in the intellectual and the religious. According to the minutes of the Delaware Academy of Natural Sciences in the collections of the Historical Society of Delaware, Hayhurst was proposed and elected to membership on

January 2, 1830, and elected a curator in June of the same year. He served the academy in various capacities until at least January of 1837. By 1838, he was not reelected. Some of Hayhurst's other pursuits were not without controversy. His name, along with those of Benjamin Ferris and others, appears as an addressee of a letter from Robert Dale Owen in which this author disagreed with principles William Gibbons had published in a pamphlet entitled *An Exposition of Modern Scepticism*. Benjamin Ferris, an important Wilmington Quaker, was a colleague of Gibbons, a surveyor involved in the design of the Wilmington Friends Meeting House and the author of the book, *A History of the Original Settlements on the Delaware and a History of Wilmington*.

So how did Thomas Hayhurst become associated with the French Street pottery then owned by Eli Hilles and Smyth? Eli was also a member of the Wilmington Friends Monthly Meeting and a respected educator. Besides these similarities, Hayhurst and Hilles crossed paths on other occasions. Hilles was also an addressee of the letter written by Robert Owen, and he was the treasurer of the Delaware Academy of Natural Sciences during most of the 1830s. Soon after acquiring the pottery from Branch Green, Hilles must have looked for someone to handle its operation. Maybe he even had Thomas in mind when he and Smyth bought the pottery in 1832, since 1831 was Hayhurst's last year on staff at Wilmington Friends. This new proprietor would have needed to hire some skilled craftsmen to produce quality wares. Andrew Maxwell may have been employed by Hayhurst. That potter took on an apprentice in 1832 and another in the following year. Those extra hands may have been part of the staffing up that Hayhurst had to do. Recall that one of those apprentices to Maxwell was William "Hair." As suggested earlier, it is quite likely that William Stretch and Branch Green stayed on as potters for Hayhurst for some period of time following the 1832 sale of the pottery. Both were experienced in stoneware making and that is what this proprietor's operation specialized in since the Warner & Company advertisement referred to stoneware at Hayhurst's prices.

But by the late 1830s, the pottery under Hayhurst must have run into financial difficulty. Not only was it up for sale but, in 1839, Thomas Hayhurst assigned all of his goods, chattels, rights and credits to Eli Hilles and Samuel Buzby to satisfy his creditors.

Meanwhile, Hayhurst left Wilmington for Chester County, Pennsylvania, where he is found in the censuses of both 1840 and 1850.

The Academy then proceeded to the Election of Officers for the ensuing year. Thos Hayhurst and Saml Buzby were appointed Tellers, and upon balloting, the following ~~Officers~~ persons were duly elected

Dr William Gibbons — President
E. W. Gilbert — Vice Pres.
Eli Hilles — Treasurer
Darling Lippincott — Rec. Secy
Dr Henry Gibbons — Corresponding Secty
Ziba Ferris
Lea Pusey
Saml Smith
Thos Hayhurst } Curators. —

The slate of officers elected in 1832 to lead the Delaware Academy of Natural Sciences included Eli Hilles and Thomas Hayhurst. *Minutes of the Delaware Academy of Natural Sciences. Courtesy of the Historical Society of Delaware.*

In his "new life," Thomas again changed occupations. In the November 11, 1846, issue of the *Village Record*, Thomas Hayhurst, as secretary of the Pure Spring Water Company, declared an eight percent dividend payable to its stockholders at his office in Kennett Square. This company, with a supply basin located near Linden and Broad streets, provided the borough with its water.

At the time of the 1850 census, Thomas and his wife, Martha, were residing with John and Mary K. Darlington in Kennett Square. John was identified as a farmer and may have been the Hayhursts' son-in-law. Thomas' occupation was given as

ASSIGNEE'S NOTICE. - Whereas Thomas Hayhurst, of the city of Wilmington, county of New Castle and State of Delaware, did on the 22nd day of the 3d month, (March) 1839, execute a deed of assignment of all and singular, his goods, chattels rights and credits, unto Eli Hilles and Samuel Busby of the city, county and state aforesaid, in trust for the benefit of his creditors. And all persons indebted to the said Thomas Hayhurst on Book account or otherwise, are requested to make payment to either of the undersigned, without delay- and those having claims, will present them on or before the first day of the 5th month (May,) in order to avail themselves of the benefit of said assignment.

ELI HILLES,
SAMUEL BUZBY,
Assignees.

Delaware Gazette, March 27, 1840

"none." The Darlington family liquidated its personal property, livestock and farm utensils at a public sale in 1856. They do not show up in the 1860 census. Thomas probably died during the 1850s. Martha apparently then went to live with her son, Dr. Jerimiah Hayhurst, a graduate of the Philadelphia College of Dental Surgery, until her death. According to her obituary in the *Daily Local* published on June 14, 1881, she was 85 years old.

Once Hayhurst's business failed, Eli Hilles and David Smyth had to look elsewhere to find a proprietor for the pottery on French Street. Since their newspaper notice failed to capture interest in its sale, they turned to a potter who was probably already employed there, William Hare. While Hare did not acquire the property until 1846, he was definitely in business on the site in 1840 and probably embarked on his proprietorship the previous year. Earlier, he was assessed a head tax per the New Castle County records in 1837, probably his first full year as a journeyman potter. It is likely he continued in that capacity until some time into 1839, since in January of that year, Thomas Hayhurst was still occupying the facilities according to the advertisement in the *Delaware State Journal*, "POTTERY FOR SALE."

The next phase in the story about "turning pots" on French Street will explore the life and pottery ownership of William Hare. His factory became the longest surviving, continuously operating pottery under a single operator in eighteenth and nineteenth century Delaware.

Proprietors of the French Street Pottery

Branch Green	1827-1832
Thomas Hayhurst	1832-1839
William Hare	1839-1885

Chapter V

William Hare, Over 45 Years on French Street

Five

William Hare left a distinctive mark on Delaware's pottery industry by impressing his own mark on numerous pieces of surviving stoneware. In addition, his factory was the most advertised of all of the state's potteries. Combined with census records, land deeds and an extensive estate inventory, these resources permit more to be written about this man than any other pottery proprietor of the First State.

The Family

According to his obituary in the December 17, 1885, issue of *The Delaware Republican*, William Hare was born in Columbia, a town in western Lancaster County, Pennsylvania, along the Susquehanna River. Birthdates in both 1814 and 1815 have been attached to him and will be sorted through later in this chapter. In the 1880 census, William said that his parents were also natives of Pennsylvania. Attempts to trace his family with any certainty through the Lancaster County Historical Society have been unsuccessful, though the 1820 census lists a number of Hares in Manor Township near Columbia. It will be suggested later that his father's name was John.

E.D. Bryan, MD, found that William married Abigail Shepherd in Philadelphia on October 10, 1842. The marriage took place at the Nazareth Methodist Church and was performed by the Rev. William A. Wiggins. The marriage produced three sons and a daughter. Abigail, born on July 10, 1809, in New Castle County, Delaware, was her husband's senior by about four years. Her father, George, and mother, Hannah, farmed 140 acres in Brandywine Hundred about three miles from Wilmington. Abigail died on March 1, 1882, of dropsy, according to N.B. Morrison, her attending physician.

DEATH

HARE—On March 1, Abigail Shepherd Hare, wife of William Hare, in her 73rd year. Relatives and friends are invited to attend the funeral from the residence of her husband, No. 230 French street on Friday, March 3, at 2 o'clock p.m. Interment in the Wilmington and Brandywine cemetery.

Every Evening, March 2, 1882

The Hares' first son, William S., was given a middle initial probably to distinguish him from his father and quite possibly in honor of Abigail's maiden name. No exact birth date has been found, but William S. was likely born in 1843 or 1844. In the 1850 census, he is listed as 7 years old and when he joined the Union Army on November 12, 1862, his muster-in record shows he was 18 years old. He was assigned to Company C of Delaware's Fifth Infantry Regiment and served until August 10, 1863. These Civil War records can be found at the Historical Society of Delaware. William did not practice his father's craft. After the war, he worked as a bookkeeper for a short time in Wilmington, possibly for his father. Then, according to the *Wilmington Directory* of 1867-68, he went into a soap manufacturing partnership, Miller & Hare, with W. Miller on Fifth Street. The directory lists a butcher, William Miller, at Second and Market streets. He may well have been the W. Miller in partnership with Hare since the by-products of butchering were a basic ingredient for soap making. This partnership was short lived and William S. next is found in the 1870 *Philadelphia Directory* as a salesman. In 1875, Hare was associated with McLear & Kendall on North Broad Street in Philadelphia. This Wilmington-based firm was known to the Hare family and dealt in carriages. Interestingly, William's house, located at 1501 Spring Garden, was next door to his sister, Anna, and her husband, Albin Pyle, who resided at 1503. In 1877, though still listed, no occupation was given, and after that year he was not listed at all. Confusion then sets in when attempting to track him further. One might conclude William S. died before late 1885 since he was not named as an heir in his father's will. Rather his wife, Nellie Rosalie Hare, was designated to share the estate equally with Anna H. Pyle, daughter of the potter. But William S. is not referred to as "deceased" in the will and his father's obituary mentioned that a son survived him. It is quite possible that his marriage to Nellie failed and the surrounding circumstances were disapproved by the family. Searching further, a William S. Hare is listed in the 1880 population census for Olean in western New York State. His age and place of birth of his father, mother and himself match the expected description of a son of William Hare, the potter. The census also reported that he was married to Margarette Bell. They had two children, 8-year-old Margarette and 5-year-old Abigail. The older daughter was born in Pennsylvania and the younger one in New York, suggesting that the family moved from Pennsylvania in about 1873 or '74. Though Hare was still listed in Philadelphia then and for a few years after, listings in early directories were not always timely. As for his earlier marriage to Nellie, no record or any other information regarding her or any children from their marriage has been found.

William and Abigail had two other sons, neither of whom saw their third birthday. John K. was born on July 22, 1845, and died November 11, 1847. George H. was born on March 2, 1855, and died on December 3, 1857.

The Hares named their only daughter Anna. Though the exact date of her birth has not been uncovered, the year appears to be 1849 based on tombstone records. In the census for 1850, she is listed as two years old. Anna married H. Albin L. Pyle on March 3, 1874. They spent much, if not all of their married lives together in Philadelphia. Following her husband's death in 1891, Anna returned to Wilmington and purchased property on Adams Street near Tenth Street where she lived until her death on June 14, 1905. Her obituary was published the next day in the *Every Evening*.

The Hare Family

William Hare (1814-1885)	Married (1842)	Abigail Shepherd (1809-1882)
	Children	
Son	William S. Married Nellie Rosalie	(1844-?)
Son	John K.	(1845-1847)
Son	George	(1855-1857)
Daughter	Anna Married H. Albin L. Pyle	(1849-1905)

H. A. L. Pyle can be found in the *Wilmington Directory* and later in the *Philadelphia Directory*. He first clerked and then tried his hand as a merchant tailor in Wilmington. In the very early 1870s, no occupation accompanied his listing. He was apparently studying law since, within two years, he was listed as an attorney. Albin established a law practice in Philadelphia and, for a time, it was located on Fifth Street. Later he relocated his office to Chestnut Street. He died in Philadelphia on May 20, 1891, per the *Every Evening* of May 25, 1891.

In a private communication, the late Thomas Beckman, registrar at the Historical Society of Delaware, confided that he had traced a grandson, Albin F. Pyle, to New York City. Indeed, census data and *Wilmington Directory* listings support that and fill in parts of his life before and after his stay in Manhattan. Clearly, Albin did not follow his grandfather's trade. About 25 years old in 1900, the young man was living with his widowed mother, Anna, in Wilmington and was employed as a collector and agent. Within a few years, he apparently married Laura Allen. However, the marriage must have been very brief since by 1904, Albin was no longer listed and Laura A. Pyle was now employed and residing at a different address. Albin F. Pyle can next be found in the New York census for 1910 where he was working as a salesman in a dry goods store. This record also shows that he had been married for six years to Gertrude P., a 33-year-old woman from New Jersey. No children were recorded. In the next decennial census, the couple was back in Wilmington where Albin was in the real estate business.

William Hare died in his 72nd year on December 15, 1885; the attending physician, Willard Springer, listed the cause of death as apoplexy (stroke). He had written his will about a year and a half earlier. In it, he bequeathed his real and personal estate in equal shares to Nellie Rosalie Hare, wife of his son, William S., and to Anna H. Pyle, his daughter. George Allmon, Hare's nephew through his marriage to Abigail, served as executor. Allmon was a partner in Frist and Allmon, a Shipley Street firm that manufactured carriages. More details regarding Hare's estate as they relate to his pottery will be covered later.

Death of William Hare

William Hare, an old and well-known citizen, died of general debility last evening at his home, no. 230 French street. For many years he was engaged in the pottery business.

Every Evening, December 16, 1885

William Hare

WILLIAM HARE, WHOSE DEATH WAS ANNOUNCED YESTERDAY, WAS BORN IN COLUMBIA, PA. AND WAS IN THE 72ND YEAR OF HIS AGE. FOR 45 YEARS, HE WAS IN THE POTTERY BUSINESS ON FRENCH STREET BETWEEN SECOND AND THIRD. HE JOINED THE WASHINGTON STEAM FIRE AND HOOK AND LADDER COMPANY ABOUT 25 YEARS AGO AND WAS ONE OF ITS OLDEST MEMBERS. A SON AND A DAUGHTER SURVIVE HIM.
HE WILL BE BURIED FROM THE HOME OF GEORGE S. ALLMON, NO. 511 WEST SEVENTH STREET, ON SUNDAY AFTERNOON.

Every Evening, December 17, 1885

The Hare family burial plot, Lot 19, Section B, is located in the Wilmington and Brandywine Cemetery on Delaware Avenue in Wilmington. A large four-sided monument stands in the center of this lot that holds eight burials. William and Abigail along with three of their children—John, Anna and George—and H. A. L. Pyle are buried there. In addition, the lot is the resting place of Hannah Shepherd and Mary Solomon. Hannah was Abigail's sibling. As the older of the daughters, she advertised the sale of their father's farm following his death in 1836. The relationship of Mary Solomon is unknown; she may have been another sister of Abigail.

In any number of early potteries, family members were often involved and carried on the operation and tradition in later generations. Such was not the case with William Hare. Only one son reached adulthood, and if associated with his father for a short time, it was in an administrative role. He soon left Wilmington. By the time a grandson would have reached "potting age," William had already died and his pottery had been closed.

Earlier the suggestion was offered that William's father might have been named John. That is based on a pattern one sees in the names that William and Abigail selected for their three boys. The first-born was named after his father, although the initial "S" was probably added to differentiate him and could very well have come from Abigail's maiden name, Shepherd. Their second and third sons may have been named after their paternal and maternal grandfathers, respectively. If so, the grandfathers' names would have been John and George. Indeed, George was the name of Abigail's father.

So, it is quite possible that William's father was John Hare. On page 353 of the 1820 census of Manor Township in Lancaster County, a John Hare is listed as head of household, with a male under ten years of age also in the family. William would have been about six years old at the time of that census. This may be the closest we will come to identifying William Hare's roots.

The Young Man

It is not clear why William Hare headed to northern Delaware and Wilmington as a young man. One can speculate, however, that his heritage and early years in Lancaster County, Pennsylvania, had some influence. Wilmington was well-known to Lancaster County farmers as their preferred port for shipping grain. The route to Wilmington had benefits over those to Philadelphia and Baltimore. Also, Hare was most likely Irish or Scotch-Irish, and many of that ethnicity had preceded him in relocating to Wilmington from Lancaster County.

William Hare began his apprenticeship in Wilmington with Andrew Maxwell in 1832, although he did not serve the full apprenticeship under him. Maxwell died in 1835, a year or so before the term of the indenture was to be completed. At that point, Hare probably continued his learning process under another master at the same pottery.

The Delaware Public Archives holds a formal indenture dated July 14, 1832, between Andrew "Maxfield" and William "Hair." The term stated in the document was four years, five months and twelve days thus specifying the agreement would end on December 26, 1836, or, as a stated alternate, the apprentice's 21st birthday. So why are the names "Maxfield" and "Hair" enclosed in quotation marks? The answers do not come simply but in the end, a strong case can be made to support the earlier statement—William Hare began his apprenticeship under Andrew Maxwell.

The Hair indenture is on file at the Archives in two different formats, and a clue to this was found in the notes of the late Thomas Beckman at the Historical Society of Delaware. What must have been the official agreement contained all the wording common to these indentures as a printed form. Then blanks were filled in to add the names, dates and craft or skill to be taught. In the second format, the entire document is handwritten and apparently served as a copy of the original. Stated in the bodies of both indentures, the apprentice, William Hair, was bound to Andrew Maxfield but, the official one was signed, Andrew Maxwell. And, though the copy was signed Andrew Maxfield, the signature was written in the hand of the person who transposed the document. Having already used the name Maxfield in the body of the document, the clerk then signed the same name at the bottom of the indenture. But is there any other evidence that supports the Maxwell theory? First and foremost, the following year Andrew Maxwell agreed to teach the art of potting to another apprentice, and his signature on that document matches the Andrew Maxwell on Hair's original indenture. Second, the only time throughout this extensive research effort that the name Andrew Maxfield was found was in the indenture, yet references to Andrew Maxwell appeared on several other occasions.

Misspellings in old documents are not uncommon. In fact, "the real" William Hare was listed in the 1850 population census as William Haire. This was undoubtedly a mistake since, according to the entry, the man was a potter, had a wife named Abigail, a son named William S., and a daughter named Anna, all of which fits William Hare without question. As for the indentured William, he could not read nor write when he executed the agreement. He marked it with his "X" and his master was obliged not only to teach him the trade or mystery of pottery, but also to give him reasonable education in reading, writing and arithmetic. Also keep in mind that the name Hare was not common in Wilmington at this time; in fact, the 1814 *Wilmington Directory* is without a Hare and in 1845, there was only one, the potter on French Street. So one can envision a situation where a young lad who can't read or write arrived in a city unacquainted with the spelling of his name, so the officials used one that sounded very familiar to them—"hair." One can also argue that it would have been highly coincidental to find both a William Hair and a William Hare in a community with less than a dozen potters and their apprentices.

There is also another discrepancy in the indenture—his birth date. On that occasion it was recorded as October 15, 1815, yet years later, cemetery records show January 13, 1814. This earlier date coincides with his obituary which reported him in his 72nd year. Besides this being "just another recording error," a better rationale may relate to a limitation placed on the duration of apprenticeships. For a man, they did not go beyond one's 21st birthday. If born on the 1814 date, William's agreement would have ended on January 13, 1835, just two and a half years after its signing. So to ensure a training period of a meaningful length, the young man may have provided an inaccurate birth date. At that point in history, most births were not officially recorded or certified.

William Hare must have been a gifted young man, and Andrew Maxwell and any other early instructors taught him well. When William arrived in Wilmington, he was an orphan. His indenture begins: "This Indenture witnesseth I William Hair now of New Castle and State of Delaware having no father mother nor guardian ...." Nor could he read or write. But he quickly learned to throw and fire both earthenware and stoneware pots. Hare developed a beautiful writing script as can be seen from his signature reproduced and included later in this chapter. And through his business prowess and marketing savvy, Hare kept his pottery going without interruption for some 46 years.

In Later Life

We are limited in trying to understand much about William Hare. As far as we know, he left no memoirs and no photographs. Nor have any writings from anyone who knew him personally been found. But let's see what we can do.

Much more will be said about William Hare's pottery business later but in profiling this man, it is important at this point to offer a few words about it now. No other Delaware pottery survived longer under a single operator. William must have been an astute businessman in addition to possessing the manufacturing skills of a potter. And, to be discussed in Chapter IX, his newspaper advertisements clearly show that he understood how to develop a product and target a market niche.

Hare lived through adversity within his family. He and Abigail lost two young sons when both were still toddlers. Their first son may have been disowned or at least distanced from the family. And Abigail succumbed nearly four years before William. The occupation of a potter was extremely demanding and a single pot, jar or plate might only sell for a nickel or dime. Yet Hare continued to operate his pottery and sell his wares on French Street until his own death, quite possibly because he still had a mortgage to satisfy.

At one point in Hare's life, horse-drawn wagons and he did not mix very well. Within a period of a year, William had two accidents while driving in the city of Wilmington. In the first case, one Monday he was thrown from his wagon and badly bruised and injured. His recovery was quite speedy since by Friday, according to the newspaper account, he was doing well.

Wm. Hare, Esq. (Potter) an excellent citizen, was thrown from his wagon near the Bridge, on Monday last, and badly bruised and injured. Dr. Ashley was called to him, who conveyed him home in his carriage. He is now doing well.

Blue Hen's Chicken, July 12, 1850

In the second event, he and two young boys were exiting into King Street when the wagon Hare was driving overturned and the three were caught under the vehicle. Luck must have been on their side since they escaped with little injury. One of the boys might have been his son, William S., who would have been about seven years old at the time. The potter was visiting merchants, one of whom was Mr. Smyth, who had long owned a china store. Maybe he resold Hare's ceramics and William was making a delivery. Otherwise, he would have likely walked there since his pottery was only a few blocks away.

Another adversity, fire, struck Hare. On one occasion, the conditions were especially dry and the wind was out of the south. It was the night of April 15, 1867. Several frame stables containing tons of hay caught fire which spread rapidly. Located at Walnut Street below Second, they were within a block of Hare's business. According to the account in *The Delaware Gazette*, the pottery of Mr. Hare was on fire, but soon extinguished. Were it not for the noble and diligent work of the energetic firemen, the blaze, which illuminated the whole neighborhood, might have destroyed the entire block.

In his obituary, mention was made that William Hare was one of the oldest members of the Washington Steam Fire and Hook and Ladder Company of Wilmington. It was located on French Street in the block north of his pottery. Hare was a member for about 25 years. This fire company relied largely on volunteers.

Upset – On Thursday evening as Mr. Hare, the potter, was driving a horse attached to a dearborne wagon out of the alley leading from the stores of Messrs. Smyth and Peterson into King Street, the horse sprang suddenly aside and over-turned the vehicle. There were two little boys with Mr. Hare and the whole three of them were completely caged the wagon turning bottom upwards. Fortunately the horse stopped at once and they escaped with little injury.

Blue Hen's Chicken, July 4, 1851

In 1856, he was elected R. S.—which may stand for recording secretary—of the newly instituted Columbia No. 26 Lodge of the Independent Order of Odd Fellows and the following year he was elected the same Lodge's Grand Guardian. Holding these positions suggests Hare may very well have been instrumental in establishing Columbia Lodge. During 1859 in Wilmington, the fortieth anniversary of the Odd Fellows was celebrated with a parade; William Hare was the Grand Marshall's Aid for Division 1 formed in Third Street between Market and King streets. Hare also held Odd Fellow offices at the state level. For the year ending July 1862, he was Grand Treasurer of the Grand Lodge of Delaware and earlier served as a director of the Odd Fellow's Library that consisted of over 1,400 manuscripts at a time when the Wilmington Library housed 5,000 volumes. Prior to this involvement with the Odd Fellows, William was active in the New Castle Temperance Society and was elected a delegate from Independent Division No. 9 in 1848. And society was aware of the role he played. In the newspaper account of his first wagon incident, he was dubbed an excellent citizen and some 35 years later in his obituary, the *Every Evening* referred to him as a well-known citizen.

His family, the pottery, the Odd Fellows and the fire company must not have been enough to exhaust his energy. William also raised fine Isabella grapes as a hobby. In September of 1859, the editor of the *Delaware State Journal and Statesman* wrote:

> **FINE GRAPES** - Our friend, Mr. William Hare, favored us on Wednesday with a stem from his grape vine containing ten or twelve full bunches of as fine Isabella grapes as we have seen for some time .They were raised in the private garden attached to his house in French Street, below Third. The yield from this vine this year has been very great, and the bunches are generally full and large. Mr. Hare has upon former occasions sent sample bunches from this vine to our Horticultural exhibitions, where they have been generally admired. No wonder, Mr. Hare takes as much pains to manufacture at his extensive Pottery in French Street, the very best kind of Air-Tight Fruit Preserving jars. He knows the value of good fruit and intends so far as his Jars are concerned that it shall be well preserved.

Delaware State Journal and Statesman, September 30, 1859

Hare's French Street Properties

William Hare first appears in the New Castle County tax assessment records in 1837, the year after he probably finished his apprenticeship. These records identified an individual's various taxable holdings including land, houses, livestock and slaves. But in the young potter's case, it is not surprising that he held none of these. His only assessment was a poll tax. The following year his name again appears with this simple tax attached to him. There is then a break in the surviving records until 1841. That year, Hare's tax assessment consisted of two components, $400 for a head tax referred to as "capitation" and $75 for stock, probably taxing the horse that turned his clay mill and pulled his "dearborne" wagon. These records can be viewed at the Delaware State Archives.

The potter from Pennsylvania bought his first piece of real estate, the family residence at 230 French Street (M 5 485), in 1844. It was the only place he and Abigail lived from that date forward. From time to time, the Hares took in borders, some of whom were potters that William employed. Then in 1846, William acquired "a stone pottery and other buildings" (R 5 278) that he had been leasing for several years prior. This placed the Hare home and pottery in the same block between Second and Third streets. Spring Alley, probably used to access some stables within the block, cut through from French Street to Walnut Street. The home was above while the pottery was below the alley. By 1855, Hare owned three more parcels in the same block. Two were adjoining the sides of his pottery and the third was at the northeast corner of French and Second streets. In all, these four lots provided him with 128 feet of continuous frontage beginning at the corner of Second Street and running northeast toward Spring Alley and Third Street. The combined purchase price of the five plots totaled $5,315.

Willian Hare's French Street Properties

Date of Indenture	Purchase Price	Use	Apparent Address	Reference
March 21, 1844	$495	Home	230 French	M 5 485
April 18, 1846	2200	Pottery Mfg	206 French	R 5 278
December 1, 1848	570	Unknown	204 French	A 6 203
March 24, 1853	900	Pottery Mfg	212 French	M 6 429
April 26, 1855	1150	Unknown	200 French	T 6 207
TOTAL	$5315			

No photographs of any of these properties during Hare's ownership have been found. However, William sold the property at 200 French Street to McLear & Kendall, a carriage manufacturer, in May of 1865 for $1,500. This corner building does not appear to have been conducive to manufacturing or displaying carriages so it is likely that they rented the building to other merchants or used it as an office. In fact, a photograph (Hagley Museum & Library, S81-3) taken about seven years after Hare's disposition of the property shows the building occupied by cigar and tobacco merchants, Hayes & Rice. A photograph during their occupancy is the closest portrayal we have of the architecture and life on French Street in the third quarter of the nineteenth century.

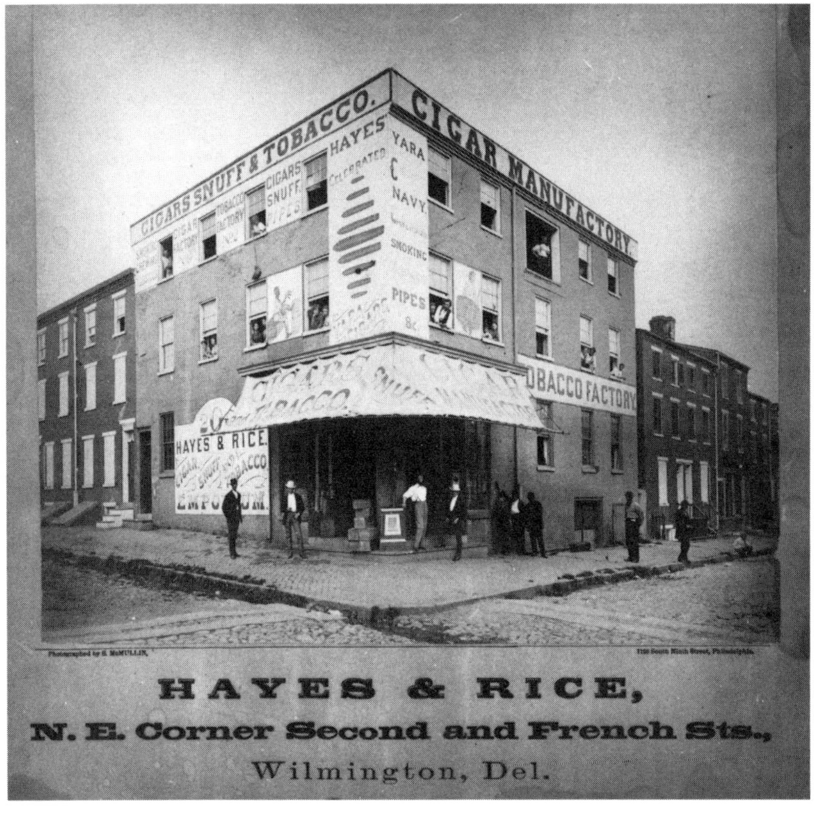

This property at the corner of French and Second streets, shown circa 1872, was a few doors down from William Hare's pottery. Hare owned this building from 1855 until 1865. *Photograph S81-3.Courtesy of Hagley Museum and Library*

His Pottery

Earlier it was shown that William Hare was in business on French Street in 1840, and in Chapter IV it was suggested that he took over this pottery from Hayhurst in 1839. The circa 1839 date matches well with a capsule found in an 1880 publication edited by Richard Edwards entitled *Industries of Delaware*. There it was written: "Wm Hare, potter, ...whose establishment has had a history of 42 years of continuous existence." So by the time of his death, this potter from Pennsylvania had operated his business on French Street without interruption for some 46 years. As a business owner, there is no evidence that Hare ever entered into a partnership with another potter or financial backer, although others held mortgages on the properties.

Hare's business address prior to the 1860s was French Street above Second Street or French Street between Second and Third streets. The city then instituted a block numbering system and for some time the address was usually given as 206, though in the 1870s and into the '80s, the number 212 was more often used. At some point, probably before 1866, Hare enlarged the size and manufacturing capability of his pottery after he acquired the adjoining lot to the north in 1853. The potters who preceded him had street frontage of 40 feet whereas William enjoyed 89 feet excluding the corner property at Second Street. The change of address may have had something to do with his expansion since sketches along French Street in the *Wilmington Atlas* of 1876 show the building at 212 labeled "POTTERY." The sketch of these properties in the *Hexamer's Atlas* of 1866 depicts essentially the same layout but without any labeling of buildings. However, based on boundaries cited in land indentures, the original pottery acquired from Hilles and Smyth was on the property matching 206 French Street. As for the location of his kiln house, the 1884 *Sanborn Map* is the first to label it and places it at the rear of the original site.

Earlier, an argument was made that William Hare apprenticed in Wilmington for Andrew Maxwell under a formal indenture. Hare also played the role of the master. On April 6, 1844, he contracted to bind **William Rogers** and teach him the art, trade and business of a potter. The eventual fate of this apprentice is unknown.

In the 1850 Census of Manufactures, William claimed his pottery's capital was $1,000 and valued his year's production of "earthen and stone wares of all kinds" at $3,600. He used 100 tons of clay and 100 cords of wood and employed, on average, four individuals.

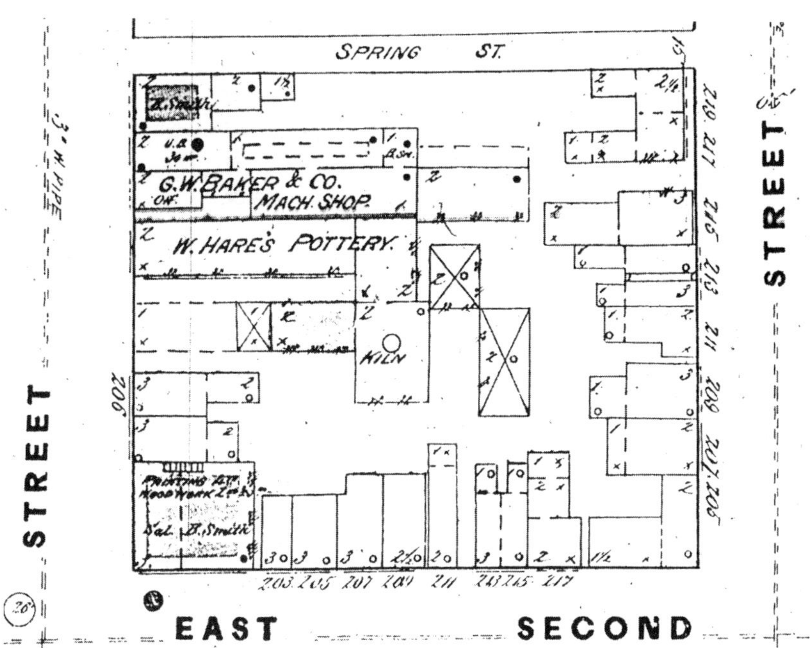

William Hare's pottery was depicted on the *Sanborn Map Wilmington, Delaware, 1884.*

Three potters - **Henry Bell, William Desney** and **Benjamin McShone** - boarded at the Hare residence and most probably worked for him during this period.

By the 1860 census, William Hare claimed that the value of his real estate had grown to $10,000 plus an additional $3,000 in his personal estate. That year, with $6,000 of capital, he produced $5,400 worth of earthen and stoneware. Compared with the previous decennial census, Hare had invested another $5,000 of capital in his pottery. That was a sizeable outlay then, but it is unclear to what extent he improved and added to his facilities. A new or enlarged kiln is one possibility. Though doubtful, if his working capital was now included, that would help explain the rise. Employing an average of seven workers, the French Street pottery consumed 300 tons of clay and 120 cords of wood in 45 loadings and firings of its kiln, the largest ever reported. Potters and others who probably worked for Hare during this period were **Levi Adams, Samuel Bradford, Charles Decker** and **Randolph Weir**. Most certainly **Jacob Schiller** was also at the pottery about this time since his signature was on a receipt provided to Samuel F. Du Pont in 1863 to document the purchase of several dozen flower pots. Another potter, Englebert Neumayer, boarded with the Hares per the 1860 census, though as we saw in Chapter III, he was about ready to enter into partnership with George Ziegler to lease a pottery near the Christina River.

By applying some math to the census data and using information that has been published regarding nineteenth century pottery making, one can gain some understanding of the number of pieces Hare probably produced in 1860. Each of his 45 kiln firings used an average of 6.7 tons of clay. The amount of clay per piece would have depended on, for one thing, the size of the "thrown pot." In *American Stonewares*, Georgeanna Greer discusses pottery making methods and writes that a four-pound ball of clay was the usual size for producing a one-gallon jug. Preserve jars were most of Hare's stoneware production and the majority was smaller than a gallon. On the assumption then that he averaged three pounds of clay for each piece, a kiln burn would have produced nearly 4,500 pots. That is exceedingly high. Others have estimated that typical kiln loadings comprised 250 to 1,000 pieces. Even if one considers that some clay was used to make bricks and kiln furniture, either Hare operated an unusually large kiln or else the 300 tons represented the weight of the clay as dug. As such, it contained a significant amount of stone and grit that was removed during washing and then discarded. Or a ton of clay by William's measure may have been less than the 2,000 pounds as we know it. In any event, William Hare must have produced well over 500,000 pieces of pottery between 1839 and 1885. Either he or Mathew Crips must hold the state record.

How does the size of Hare's operation stack up against that of some of his contemporaries? Of the several that operated in neighboring Pennsylvania in the third quarter of the nineteenth century, the Mount Jordan Pottery of the Grier family near Oxford, Pennsylvania, was the most active in Chester County. John in 1860 and Ralph in 1870 reported producing both earthenware and stoneware. Product values, not unlike the Wilmington pottery, totaled $5,400 and $7,000, respectively. The Griers reported employing eight to nine workers and using 250 and 300 tons of clay. Hare employed seven in 1860 and consumed 300 tons of clay. So Hare was on par with the largest operations in the area during this period.

According to 1870 manufacturing statistics, the activity at Hare's pottery was down somewhat from ten years earlier. Clay and wood consumption dropped by 50 tons and 20 cords, respectively. The value of "stone and clay ware" produced was $5,000, about 10 percent less than in 1860. Though his costs for materials were virtually identical, labor costs for four employees were less than half of those in 1860. William claimed capital of $10,000, once again a sizeable increase since the previous census. In the early 1870s, the pottery's address evolved to 212 French Street. Maybe there is a connection between this change and that influx of capital. Though the value of his personal estate apparently remained at $3,000, his real estate holdings doubled to $20,000. In the 1860s, Hare acquired several properties, especially in the area around Fourth and Spruce streets. Based on an 1849 county map that also shows parts of the city, these parcels were in a residential area. Presumably they were not connected to his business, but rather rental properties he used to generate additional income. Potters who may have worked for Hare about this time included Randolph Weir, **James Mahan** and Samuel Bradford. Weir's son, Samuel J., was listed as a laborer in the *Wilmington Directory* and may have also worked at a pottery.

By 1880, Hare reported his pottery produced $6,000 of "stone and earthen ware pottery." That year he consumed $2,000 worth of materials and paid out $1,500 in wages to an average of four employees. Capital was again listed at $10,000; real estate holdings were not part of this decade's census. A listing in the *Wilmington Directory* suggests that Samuel Bradford was still employed on French Street.

In each census recording Hare's manufacturing statistics, stone and earthen or clay wares were reported. Production of both salt-glazed stoneware and earthenware can pose a dilemma for the potter. Hare's stoneware was commonly salt-glazed but the surface of earthenware is typically not so treated. This glaze is formed by adding salt once the kiln is brought up to temperature. The salt then vaporizes and the sodium reacts with the surface of the ceramic to form the characteristic salt-glaze. But invariably, some salt deposits remain throughout the interior of the kiln at the end of the firing cycle only to become involved in glazing action during subsequent firings. Said another way, the kiln becomes contaminated with salt. So how does the potter produce both types of ceramics? The master could operate two kilns with one dedicated to salt-glazed products and the other for unglazed ones. But the second kiln takes extra space and capital, the latter being the larger hurdle. Or one might produce earthenware before salt taints a new or rebuilt kiln. But that approach would limit the amount of earthenware the pottery could produce to those firings following the infrequent, major overhauls of the kiln. On the other hand, some potters took advantage of the cooler operating temperatures in certain parts of the kiln and loaded these with earthenware to minimize the effect of the salt. But, based on the size of his operation, Hare most likely operated two kilns. In fact, if one looks closely at a drawing showing an 1874 panoramic view of Wilmington, the top of Hare's kiln house appears to show two stacks.

The French Street pottery ceased operation upon Hare's death near the end of 1885. Soon thereafter his executor, George Allmon, arranged for Robert Fraim and A.B. Gillespie to appraise his estate. An exhaustive inventory, consisting of 12 pages and valued at $983.15, was completed on January 7, 1886. Most of the items were wares from his pottery, though a few personal effects from his home on French Street were also listed. In the January 23, 1886, edition of *Every Evening,* Allmon advertised an executor's sale of the entire stock of the ware rooms and pottery of William Hare, deceased. The sale was held on the site of the pottery at 212 French Street. Proceeds fell short of the earlier appraisal by $287.37.

But the appraisal and sale did not include real estate. Disposition of the property that had held the pottery did not occur until October 26, 1889. The Hare estate still owed the heirs of Eli Hilles a substantial amount of money and a court order forced a sheriff's sale of two parcels. Harry Emmons was the high bidder on both. One was the original property that Branch Green and others had worked (V 14 242) and the other (V 14 244) was the location of Hare's later business center at 212 French Street. The *Every Evening* reported the sheriff's sale two days later and named Charles B. Lore, Esq. as the new owner. He and Emmons were both attorneys; their practice under both names was located at 847 Market Street.

The deeds recording Emmons' purchase of the properties contained no reference to a pottery or kiln. Soon after Hare's death, the Warren Athletic Club moved their facilities to one of the parcels. *The Warren Athlete* dated May 13, 1886, and in the collection of the Historical Society of Delaware, provides some details. The club reported that "They removed to the second story of the Third

EXECUTOR'S SALE

At 212 French street commencing on

MONDAY, January 25 th,

At 9 o'clock,

And to continue until sold, the entire stock of the ware rooms and pottery of William Hare, deceased.

GEORGE ALLMON,
Executor

Every Evening, January, 23, 1886

Street Market House on Dec. 11th, 1885, from which they removed on March 25th to their present location, Hare's Building, No. 212 French street, where they have fitted up the gymnasium on the first floor, the room being about 25′ X 115′. They also use the second floor for dressing rooms, &c." The dimensions of this lot as described in the deed were 30 X 114 feet so that the structure the club refurbished covered nearly the entire lot. The size of the building corresponds to that shown on the survey of Wilmington published by Hexamer in 1866. During Hare's occupancy, his kiln house sat on the adjoining parcel to the south and was attached to part of this structure at the rear of the property.

While William Hare was able to maintain the operation of his pottery for over 45 years, he was not very well-to-do at the time of his death. The proceeds from his personal and business inventories were slightly less than $700. Once these were combined with other receivables and offset by claims, the remaining balance was $137.90. The two properties that comprised his pottery were eventually disposed of through a sheriff's sale to satisfy a debt of $2,200 to the heirs of Eli Hilles. Earlier in his life, for example in the 1860s, his financial status was much sounder. In 1866, the *Delaware Gazette* listed the incomes of Wilmington residents and based on a rough estimate, William Hare's was in the top third. Surely his net worth was growing as he turned pottery profits into rental properties. But as the 1870s and '80s came, market pressures heavily impacted the business of the local potter. Soon after, most had disappeared. More will be said about those circumstances in Chapter IX.

Hare's Wares

Surviving examples of known ceramics from the Hare pottery confirm that he manufactured both stoneware and earthenware, though almost all are stoneware. The potter identified many pieces of his salt-glazed and dipped stoneware using one of his two maker's marks. However, his branded redware is extremely rare. But that is not unusual. This type of ceramic tended to be even more utilitarian and less decorated than stoneware, and so nineteenth century potters did not take the time to sign their less artistic work.

By far, the more common of Hare's impressed marks reads: "Wm. HARE/WILMINGTON DEL." However, W. HARE/WILN DEL" has been observed on a handful of pieces, especially on the bottom of diminutive examples. Maybe this design was developed to fit in a smaller area since the second line, "WILMINGTON DEL.," in the more familiar mark is quite broad. Also, two of the vases on which the second style of mark is found are more characteristic of forms of the late nineteenth century suggesting that this mark was fashioned well into Hare's years of operation. One stone jar scripted on the bottom with Hare's signature is also known and is in the collection of the Historical Society of Delaware.

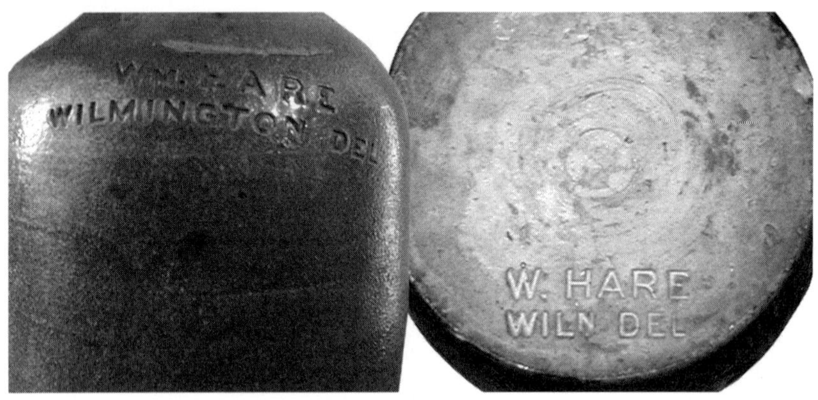

William Hare used two impressions to mark some of his pottery. Wm.HARE/WILMINGTON DEL. was by far the more common. The less frequent mark, W. HARE/WILN DEL, can be found on the bottom of a vase. *Courtesy of the Historical Society of Delaware*

For a number of other reasons, we know that Hare produced earthenware on French Street. First, he reported the production of earthenware in each decennial manufacturing census from 1850 to 1880. Second, in the June 25, 1852, issue of the *Delaware Gazette*, Hare "respectfully informs his friends and the public generally that he still manufactures Earthen and Stone Ware." Third, the inventory of his pottery upon his death lists hundreds of pieces of earthenware.

So, what forms of earthenware did Hare's pottery produce? Again, while the number of signed examples is few, a closer look at his estate inventory and newspaper advertisements help answer the question.

Twelve different pottery forms totaling over 1,200 individual pieces were described as earthenware in his estate inventory. These included crocks, jars, jugs, cake and pudding dishes, pie plates, pitchers, pans, mugs, teapots, chamber pots and spittoons. Numerous other forms were also listed. Although they were not specifically described as earthenware, some assuredly were.

STONE AND EARTHEN-WARE!

WILLIAM HARE,

RESPECTFULLY informs his friends and the public generally, that he still manufactures

Earthen and Stone Ware

at his long established pottery in French street near the corner of Second, one square from the East end of the Lower Market House, Wilmington, where he keeps on hand a large stock of ware, such as *Milk Pans; Cream Pots; Large Stone Pots* for potting butter; together with a large assortment of Stone-ware, Jars, Jugs, Pitchers, &c. Also, a general assortment *Rockingham Ware; Tea Pots and Pitchers*, of different sizes, *Spittoons* of various patterns and sizes; a large lot of *Yellow Ware*, a very superior article for standing fire for baking purposes.

He also keeps on hand a general assortment of *Fire Bricks* for cooking stoves; *Clay Cylinders and Furnaces*. It is unnecessary to enumerate all the articles kept on hand, as persons are particularly requested to call and examine his stock for themselves. They will find it to their advantage to do so, as every article can be purchased at very low rates.

☞ A large lot of defective ware for sale very cheap

Wilmington, Del., June 3.—1m*

William Hare mentioned a variety of clay products in this early newspaper advertisement found in the June 4, 1852, issue of the *Delaware Gazette.*

In 1852, Hare also advised the public that he kept on hand firebricks for cooking stoves and clay cylinders for chimney flues. This is the earliest of his advertisements that has been found. Three years later, drainpipes were also mentioned, and the City of Wilmington purchased some from Hare in 1861. According to the *Delaware Republican* on October 7, the city council approved a payment of nearly $27 to the potter for drainpipe. Though he never seemed to have abandoned the manufacture of earthenware, subsequent advertisements are almost completely focused on other products. But quite clearly, earthenware was a market segment that was important to the overall success of his business.

Flowerpots were a common nineteenth century earthenware form. Two receipts mentioned earlier and held by the Hagley Museum and Library recorded sales of several dozen each to Samuel F. Du Pont in 1863 and again in 1864. In one case, Du Pont paid $2.88 for a total of eight dozen flowerpots. Ranging in size from four to seven inches, the potter charged from two to five cents each. This document was signed in William Hare's own hand.

W. 9- 16170

Wilmington March 2/64

Mr S. Dupont.

Bought of Wm Hare

3 Doz 4 inch Flowerpots 24 " " .72
3 " 5 " do " 36 " " 1.08
1 " 6 " " " 48 " " 0.48
1 " 7 " " " 60 " " 0.60
$2.88

Recd payment Wm Hare

A receipt signed by William Hare acknowledged payment for flower pots purchased by S. Du Pont, March 2, 1864. *Courtesy of Hagley Museum and Library.*

Now what about Hare's stoneware? His French Street pottery produced stoneware in several forms but probably well over 95 percent was what the potter advertised as an air-tight preserve jar. These jars came in at least four sizes, nominally a pint, quart, half-gallon and gallon, though their volumes were not very exact. While many potters made jars in various shapes for preserving foods, the form of Hare's jar is quite distinctive. Collectors can spot them immediately. The jars are narrow-mouthed and short-necked. Most are straight-sided, though there are some known examples in an ovoid shape. Decorated jars, however, are rare; the Historical Society of Delaware owns two. One is brushed with a hint of cobalt blue and the other is decorated with a manganese glaze over a creamy yellow slip. Infrequently a jar may show a narrow raised ring around the outside of the neck. Otherwise, the jars are without enhancements. The flat bottoms show the three patterns—crossed twisted, plain cut and straight plain twisted—which Georgeanna Greer describes as resulting from the type of wire and cutting technique used to separate the finished vessel from the potter's wheel. These patterns were probably the work of different potters. Most of Hare's stoneware fruit jars were salt-glazed and are found in a range of colors from off-white to gray to rusty brown. Color variations were the result of differences in clay composition and firing conditions. But others had an Albany-slip type of brown glaze. This glaze was applied by dipping the jar. It was held upside down and immersed to within an inch or so of the jar's bottom. In fact, fingerprints showing where and how the jar was held are usually present near the bottom. Like most of his contemporaries, Hare glazed the inside of his stoneware jars with Albany-type slip. More will be said about how these jars meshed with Hare's business strategy in Chapter IX.

In looking closely at the marks on several jars, one sees the two lines of the mark are not always parallel nor equally spaced from jar to jar, indicating that the lines were applied separately. And the location of the mark on the piece of stoneware varies. Fruit jar examples are found marked near the top just below the shoulder, midway down the body and very close to the bottom. Different potters working for Hare may have placed "his signature" in their own way or, in the haste of producing large numbers of jars, paid little atten-

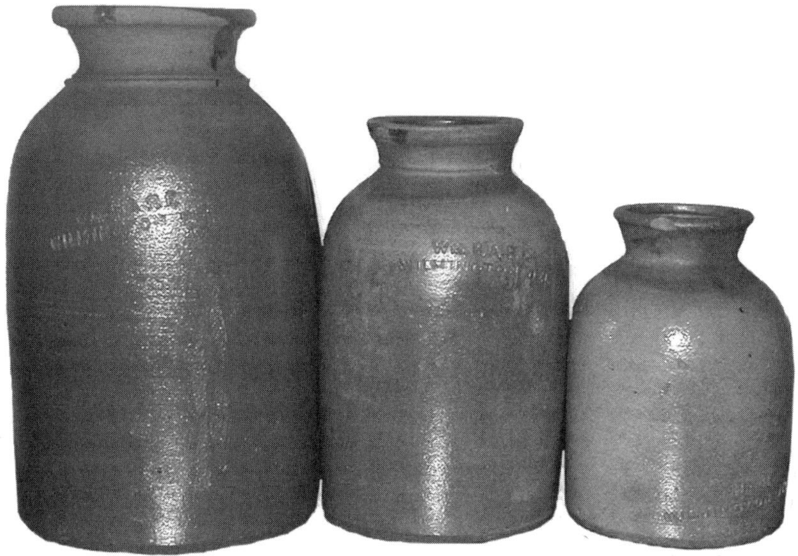

William Hare's salt-glazed, air-tight stoneware preserve jars were produced in at least four sizes ranging in height from about 5.5 to 11 inches. The tallest jar is not included in this photograph.

tion to where they impressed the marks. Also, the care taken in applying the lettering was sometimes less than stellar. One sees examples where not all of the letters are clearly impressed or some are missing, especially part or all of the "DEL." And occasionally one will see an example where one of the lines, more than likely the "WILMINGTON DEL.," double impressed. One does see great similarity from jar to jar in the style, size and spacing of letters in each line of his mark, though whether he had more than one instrument for each of the two marks is uncertain.

To varying degrees, nineteenth century potters decorated their stoneware with hand-painted designs in cobalt blue. And indeed,

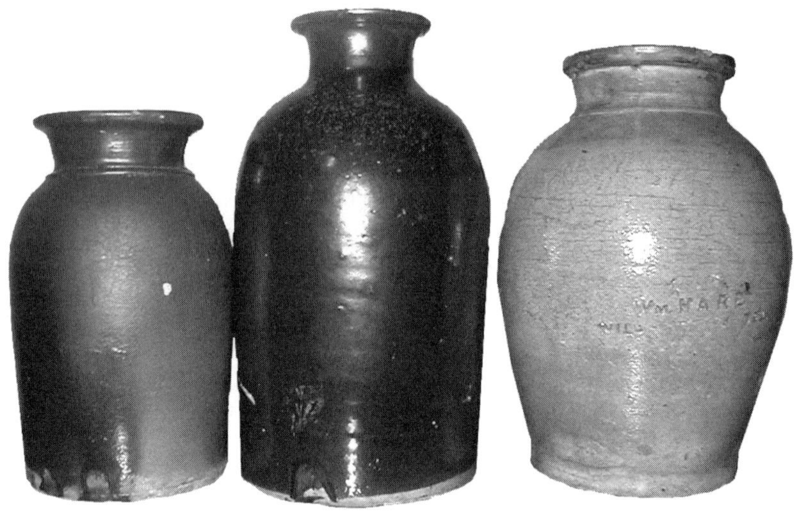

The Hare pottery produced stoneware preserve jars (left and center) which were externally glazed with an Albany-slip. The glaze was applied by inverting the jar and dipping it. The potter's fingerprints remain as a testament to the glazing technique. The salt-glazed jar (right) is ovoid rather than straight-sided suggesting it was one of Hare's earlier jars.

both decorated and undecorated salt-glazed wares other than preserve jars were made at the pottery on French Street. In his estate inventory, approximately 800 pieces of stoneware were listed, though not enough information is provided to tell how many of these pieces were artistically enhanced. Identified as stoneware were bottles, butter crocks, jars in a variety of sizes, jugs, pitchers, spittoons and water fountains. Many of the jars listed were undoubtedly the narrow-mouthed ones previously discussed. All but the last item are common forms but it is unclear what constitutes the one the appraiser called a water fountain. Photographs showing several marked examples from a private and a museum collection are included here. The undecorated pieces include a bottle, jar, jug, and syrup jug.

Compared to some contemporary potters like Richard C. Remmey of Philadelphia and Peter Herrman of Baltimore, the Hare pottery produced relatively few pieces of stoneware decorated in cobalt-blue. Presumably Hare saw much more of a market need for his preserve jars than for decorated forms of stoneware so that is where he concentrated. Decorated cake crocks and wide-mouth jars of various sizes impressed with the characteristic Hare mark have survived. Referring again to Remmey and Herrman, many pieces of decorated but unmarked stoneware have been attributed to their potteries based on the similarity of the blue decorations to those on marked wares. Comparing some known Hare pieces, the 4-gallon jardinaire and the cake crock pictured here along with another cake crock in

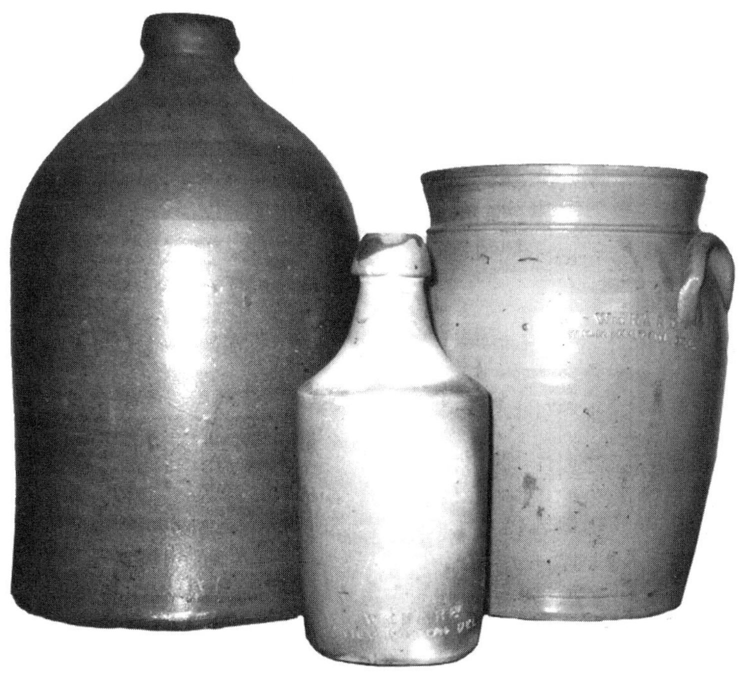

The Hare pottery produced typical forms of undecorated stoneware. *Private collection of Andy Scari, Wilmington Delaware.*

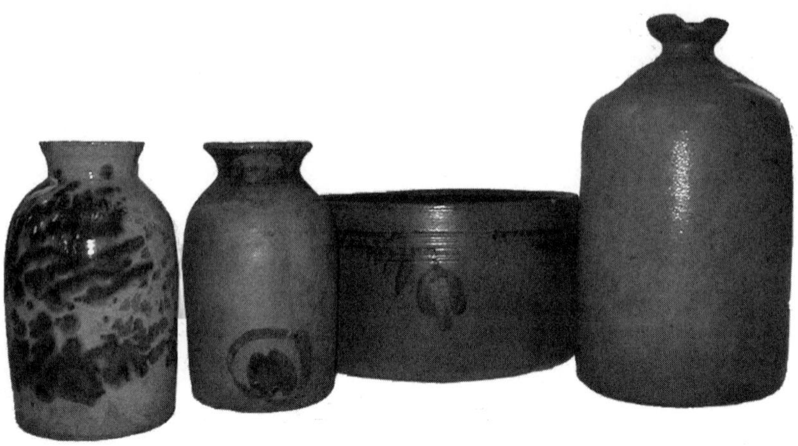

Three examples of stoneware made by William Hare are decorated; the fourth is a rare undecorated syrup jug. Manganese over a creamy yellow glaze was applied to the jar to the left. *Courtesy of the Historical Society of Delaware.*

the Historical Society of Delaware's collection have very similar decorations. A drooping flower at the end of a tendril was used to circumvent each piece. Two pieces held by the Delaware State Museums show similar brushings. But other pieces show some different decorations. A 4-gallon, wide-mouth jar whose photograph is on file at the Winterthur Museum was brush-stroked with two leaves in a fashion similar to one of Remmey's designs. There also appears to be one of those withered flowers between them, though they are not attached to a tendril. But with so few pieces to examine, it would be a substantial stretch to conclude that the presence of this drooping flower is a design feature that allows similarly decorated, but unmarked pieces, to be attributed to the Hare pottery. In fact, potters like the Chester County Griers and Remmey used similar designs. But not all of Hare's work favored this design. There is a marked 4-gallon jar of his that has both an unusual and quite striking ornamental blue design. This decoration is repeated on both the front and back and the color is very vivid compared to other Hare pieces.

No other Delaware potter created name recognition throughout the First State as did William Hare, and fittingly so. Mathew Crips was much wealthier, John Jones had his hands in more businesses and Abner Marshall dug clay that supplied the ceramics industry in Trenton. But William Hare left a legacy of pottery that was manufactured in Delaware and "signed" with his name. He was the only one to do so. Thus, William Hare "lives on" through his air-tight stone preserve jars which he impressed with his mark: Wm. HARE/WILMINGTON DEL.

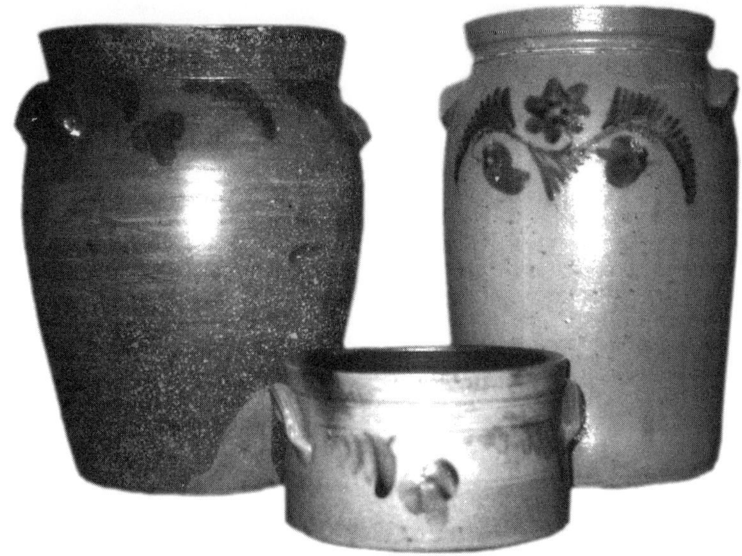

Some stoneware produced by William Hare was hand-decorated in cobalt blue. The 4-gallon jar has an unusual brushed design. *Private collection of Andy Scari, Wilmington, Delaware.*

Chapter VI

Other New Castle County Potteries

Six

In addition to the pottery sites and operators detailed in earlier chapters, ceramics were manufactured at three other locations in Wilmington and New Castle County. Two German immigrants attempted to fashion and fire fine porcelains. A member of the Marshall family helped to arouse Delaware's kaolin clay industry and he also produced pottery in his own kiln. And in 1880, an experienced potter established a new factory at a time when the doors of most others had already closed. The story of each is unique in its own way.

A Porcelain Factory in Wilmington

The first half of the nineteenth century saw a number of attempts to manufacture fine porcelains in America and the Philadelphia area was no exception. But "white china" is more difficult to produce than other types of ceramics, and competing with European imports on both a quality and cost basis proved insurmountable for most who attempted its manufacture in the United States. The major raw materials, kaolin and feldspar, were available within the Delaware Valley, but as Arthur James points out, even a large influx of capital could not keep one of the more well-known porcelain manufacturers of Philadelphia viable over a long period of time. Operated under a variety of names and supported by a variety of partners and investors, the Tucker, the Tucker and Hulme, the Tucker and Hemphill and the Hemphill porcelain works that began in 1826, were finally closed in 1838.

In a book by Edwin A. Barber, the author speaks of the American Porcelain Manufacturing Company of Gloucester, New Jersey, which was incorporated in 1854 and operated under that name until 1857. It produced soft porcelain, and marked pieces impressed with "APM Co" are known. One example is pictured in Ellen and Bert Denker's book entitled *North American Pottery and Porcelain*. They describe this white pitcher as molded in chinoiserie design with a mask under the spout. One of the principals of the firm was **William Reiss** who, according to Barber, experimented with firing porcelain in Philadelphia and Wilmington, Delaware, prior to establishing the firm in New Jersey.

William Reiss (sometimes spelled Riess) probably acquired his knowledge of ceramic production in Europe. According to the 1850 Delaware census, he was born in Prussia. At the time of that census, Reiss was 48 years old and listed his occupation as "china factory." The same census recorded that William and his wife, Joanna, had eight children. The youngest was a year-old daughter, who like all of her siblings, had been born in Prussia. So, as of 1850, Reiss and his family were very recent immigrants.

Thanks to the then editors of one of Delaware's nineteenth century newspapers, the *Blue Hen's Chicken*, some understanding of the Reiss venture can be assembled. In its weekly issues, this newspaper included a section called "Local Intelligence," in which a number of references to a porcelain manufactory and pottery were found there beginning in late 1849 and ending in early 1853.

In the issue of December 21, 1849, the newspaper mentioned that two Germans had been visiting New Castle County with the intention of manufacturing porcelain. Both kaolin and feldspar were found in Mill Creek Hundred, a section of the county to the west of Wilmington and bordering Chester County, Pennsylvania. This newspaper, noted for its heralding of Wilmington as a great place for new manufacturing enterprises, went on to say that if the venture succeeded, it would prove a valuable addition to the business of the county, as $40,000 worth (of porcelains) alone were imported annually into New York. About six weeks later, the newspaper reported that the Porcelain Manufactory was now in the process of erection.

About the middle of March of 1850, the editor visited the porcelain factory to see what progress the entrepreneurs were making. He reported that the facility, located on Seventh Street near Madison Street, was expected to begin production in about three weeks. Start-up had been delayed since all preparations were under the sole charge of Mr. W. Reiss while his partner was paying a visit to Germany. The article then went on to stretch the truth as it reported that this was the first manufactory of its kind in the United States. The next statement again reflected the newspaper's focus on Wilmington as a haven of opportunity for new businesses: if this venture succeeded, it would more than probably be followed by a number of others and would also prevent a great deal of money from being sent out of the country.

The May 17, 1850, issue of the *Blue Hen's Chicken* named the other partner in the porcelain undertaking when it reported that Mr. Reiss, of the firm of Reiss & Huttmann, had arrived in Wilmington last week following a two-month visit to Europe. The article made clear the purpose of his trip. The traveler had returned with both his wife and two children and his partner's wife and eight children. The paper apparently confused the names of the partners, however. According to the census of 1850, the Hutman family was the smaller of the two and he was the partner referred to in the March newspaper notice as visiting Germany. This census provides another important piece of information. Hutman's (census spelling) first name was William. He was a 45-year-old immigrant who along with all members of his family had been born in Prussia. With his occupation referred to as "Gent" and the value of real estate owned as $2,000, **William Huttmann** was most likely the financial arm of the partnership. But based on a search of land indentures, whatever property Huttmann held was apparently not in New Castle County.

The Reiss & Huttmann pottery had some product success. On one Saturday in October of 1850, several stands in the Wilmington market were filled with china ware manufactured locally by Mr. Reiss. The wares looked well and sold very fast. But this outcome was short-lived. Three months later, under the byline, *Factory Stopped*, the newspaper regretfully reported that the porcelain factory at the corner of Madison and Seventh streets had ceased production again, and went on to say that this was the third or fourth time. It also added that while in type, the newspaper was informed that there was talk of switching to manufacturing yellow ware and stoneware. John Ramsay, in his book entitled *American Potters and Potteries*, briefly mentions William Reiss, circa 1851, as a potter producing redware and stoneware in Wilmington. But if Reiss did alter his product line, it was not for long. Neither Reiss nor Huttmann are listed in the *Wilmington Directory* of 1853 and recall that Edwin Barber found William Reiss in New Jersey by 1854.

Like other nineteenth century attempts to produce fine ceramics in America the Wilmington enterprise failed rather quickly. But while the experiments in Delaware did not produce the desired outcome, Reiss was not deterred from trying again. Sadly, the run in Gloucester, New Jersey, was also brief. It too, was a commercial and financial failure. Barber wrote that wares would often come from the kiln melted into a conglomerated mass. Similar firing failures may have also plagued the Wilmington operation and eventually led to its demise. So Reiss & Huttmann went from identifying raw material sources to ending an attempt to manufacture fine porcelains in Wilmington in less than 15 months.

As for how long Reiss and Huttmann remained in Wilmington following the failure of their porcelain venture is unclear, but another newspaper account suggests they had departed before the middle of 1852. In the June 18 issue of that year, the *Blue Hen's Chicken* reported that Messrs. Aumer and Hallworth had taken over the old china factory and begun to manufacture enameled, Rockingham and yellow wares. They must have produced some saleable ceramics since the writer described these products as beautiful in color, remarkably strong and suitable for the table. Again, the newspaper wished the new operators well and encouraged the citizens of the city to patronize this new venture.

The new partners at Seventh and Madison streets were potters who had recently settled in Philadelphia. A **Peter Auner**, potter, is listed in the *Philadelphia Directory* beginning in 1851, and the following year, **Phillip** and **William Hallworth** are enumerated as potters along with Auner. Peter and William continue to be logged in the directory over the next few years, though entries for them are not continuous. On the other hand, Phillip is only found in 1852. It is very likely this group continued to maintain some presence in Philadelphia during their attempt to fire up the Delaware operation. That foresight presumably served them well, for the Wilmington venture only lasted about six months. On January 11, 1853, the *Blue Hen's Chicken* reported that Messrs. (Gabriel) Arnaud and (Ferdinand) Mace had purchased the building at the corner of Seventh and Madison streets, lately used as a china factory. The new owners were in the starch making business and were granted the property by Samuel Wollaston (L 6 108), a well-known Wilmington farmer and land owner. Samuel had held the lot since 1838 and must have leased it to the German porcelain makers and the Philadelphia potters. At some point during Wollaston's ownership, bricks may have been produced there since the deed of 1853 describes the property as consisting of a brick factory and lot. (Or maybe a remaining kiln was misinterpreted as one for bricks rather than ceramics.) According to this record, the property was located at the southwest corner of Seventh and Madison streets with a frontage of 160 feet along Madison Street. Arnaud and Mace were in the market for a new home for their operation since their factory had been destroyed by fire a few weeks earlier. Thus, with this change in use, the attempts of two sets of entrepreneurs to turn clay into legal tender ended on the west side of Wilmington. Today, that lot is part of a city recreational area and most, if not all of it, is a paved tennis court.

Abner Marshall at Hockessin

A first inkling that **Abner Marshall** was working with clay and firing a kiln can be found in local newspaper notices in 1853. In the *American Republican* of West Chester, Pennsylvania, it was announced that Marshall had commenced the manufacture of fire bricks in New Castle County, Delaware, on the farm of Thomas Little. Meanwhile, the *Blue Hen's Chicken* reported much the same story on July 22, though it mistakenly placed Little's acreage across the state line in Chester County. The news note also mentioned that furnaces for the manufacture of iron were creating a demand for these bricks. A few days earlier, much the same information had been published in the *Delaware Gazette*. In actuality, the property was in Mill Creek Hundred, Delaware, about a half mile below the Pennsylvania border. One of its boundaries was a new public road at the bottom of Hockessin Hill leading from the Old Wilmington Road to Garrett's Snuff Mill. Hockessin Friends Meeting was across this road from a corner of Thomas Little's property. But as we will see later, Abner did not limit his wares to specialized bricks. The 1860 census tells us he also produced at least two types of pottery.

In his book entitled *Hockessin: A Pictorial History*, Joseph R. Lake, Jr., wrote of Abner Marshall's discovery of kaolin on the farm of Amos Sharpless in 1854, though he provided no source of this information. But as referred to already, newspaper notices placed the location of Marshall's kiln on the farm of Thomas Little and mentioned a commencement date a year earlier. A decade later, it was Little's land that Abner purchased along with its clay pits.

Abner Marshall, of Kennet, has commenced the manufacture of fire brick on the farm of Thomas Little, in New Castle County, Delaware, which he has leased for several years; and his success with the first kiln has been all that was desired, producing bricks of a very superior quality.

American Republican, July 19, 1853

According to an obituary in the *Daily Local News* of West Chester, Abner, son of Robert and

Mary Hoopes Marshall, was born on August 27, 1814, probably on land which later encompassed the Marshall Paper Mill. This property was located about three miles south of Kennett Square, Pennsylvania, where John Marshall first constructed part of a family homestead in 1767. Abner died as a widower in his 91st year on January 9, 1905, at Lansdowne, Pennsylvania. Both Abner and his wife, Ann Elizabeth (Pyle), were buried at Longwood Meeting. Ann was apparently his second wife for Abner's spouse was identified as May Jane in an 1846 deed, and four years later Ann E. was named as his wife in another deed.

As one follows Marshall's career, the image of a risk-taker and entrepreneur clearly emerges. Early on, like his father, Abner was engaged in farming. While census records of 1840 do not include occupations, in Abner's case they provide a clue. As a head of household in Christiana Hundred, Delaware, Abner Marshall's entry lists five men between the ages of 20 and 39. All are identified as employed in agriculture, so besides Abner, four must have been farm hands who boarded and worked with him.

Marshall had entered into a farming partnership with William E. Garrett in late 1835 in which the major emphasis was grazing. The farm was owned by Garrett and situated in Christiana Hundred on the border with Mill Creek Hundred, where Garrett operated a snuff mill. Two years later on March 25, their arrangement was altered and Abner began leasing the farm under a four-year agreement at $350 per year, which was renewed for a like period. During the ten years of this relationship with Garrett, Abner became involved in much more than farming. One finds that he arranged for improvements at the mill, built a stone wall and hauled bricks for the construction and repairs of furnaces. Marshall even provided board for mill workers along with the owner's hired tradesmen and William Garrett himself. This account of the relationship between Abner Marshall and William E. Garrett can be found in the latter's "Mill and Farm Accounts, 1832-1845," which is held in The Winterthur Library: Joseph Downs Collection of Manuscripts and Printed Ephemera, No. 262.

But there is still more of the Abner Marshall story to relate before he opened his firebrick operation. Though he would return to briefly work for Garrett again, Abner moved to Kennett Square, Pennsylvania. There, after purchasing property (C 5 356) in 1846, he donned a merchant's hat in the village along the road to Unionville. The 1850 Pennsylvania census confirms this occupation. Abner and

Ann apparently assumed the business of Levi W. Hoopes, who, based on an invoice of his in the collection of the Chester County Historical Society, was a general merchant. Abner and his wife, Ann, retained the property until 1858 (U 6 272), five years after he started his brickworks. Whether the Marshalls continued to operate the store or leased it out to others until 1858 is uncertain. Meanwhile, according to C.A. Weslager, writing in his book on the snuff mills, the local firm of C&A (Abner) Marshall constructed Garrett's pretentious, 19-room mansion overlooking his operations in 1850.

Finally, Abner turned to kaolin! Parts of adjoining Chester and New Castle counties were previously recognized sources of kaolin and feldspar. Israel Hoopes has been credited with an early find in nearby Pennsylvania in 1820. According to Lake, he uncovered a vein of white clay just below the surface on his farm in New Garden Township while digging a hole for a fence post. His attempts to commercialize the deposit were only marginally successful so he spent most of his life farming. After his death in 1853, his son, Isaac, turned his attention to kaolin then seeking the knowledge of consultants, improving steps in the manufacturing process, and identifying new markets. Before divesting his interests a few years later, he also began his brickworks. Once in the hands of others, this property in Chester County, Pennsylvania, became a prime commercial source of kaolin clay for a number of years. A similar story can be told about New Castle County. It was already pointed out in Chapter I that feldspar mined in Delaware was used by Philadelphia porcelain makers in the 1830s, but it was Abner Marshall's discovery and fortitude that catalyzed the large-scale commercialization of the First State's deposits of kaolin in areas of Mill Creek Hundred. More details regarding this industry can be found in Lake's book on Hockessin.

Presumably Marshall found a kaolin deposit not long before Isaac Hoopes turned his full attention to clay products. What prompted Abner to dig clay and build a kiln for bricks is unclear, though he was aware of the need for firebricks for the furnaces at Garrett's Snuff Mill. At the time of his discovery, Abner was probably farming property under lease from Thomas Little.

A few years after Abner started his brickmaking operation, he expanded his product line to include pottery. In the 1860 population census for Delaware, Abner Marshall's occupation was recorded as "fire brick maker and pottery," and his 21-year-old son, **Robert Marshall**, was listed as a potter. Per the 1860 manufacturing census for Mill Creek Hundred, Marshall consumed 30 tons of anthracite coal and 100 tons of kaolin valued at $135 and $2,000, respectively. Abner's use of coal to fire his kiln was unusual for a potter and he appears to be the first in Delaware known to have used this alternate to wood. Information cited in the census includes the following statistics:

	Potting	Firebrick Making
Capital Invested	$1,000	$4,000
Value of Materials	$635	$1,500
Number Employed	2	3
Monthly Wages	$36	$54
Value of Product	$5,000	$15,000

Abner listed his potting products as 20 crates of Rockingham and yellow ware but the value he placed on them, $5,000, is unusually high. At an average of $250 per crate, each would have had to contain hundreds of pieces based on selling prices in 1860. In comparison, the New Jersey pottery of A. Hall & Sons cited by Lelyn Branin reported its 1870 output as 200 crates of the identical types of pottery, yet valued them at $4,000. In 1860, William Hare, the most active potter in Delaware, needed seven workers to produce $5,400 in stoneware and earthenware. Similarly, Marshall's census report on firebricks is puzzling. The quantity appears to be 50,000, though the units which follow this number in the record are difficult to decipher. This quantity and the $15,000 in value equate to an abnormally high 30 cents per brick. The Hall & Sons pottery produced one million firebrick valued at five and one-half cents each. One might suggest that some "decimals were slipped" in Abner's reporting, but it is inconceivable that he could have produced 200 crates of pottery, 500,000 firebricks, or both with the five employees and the cost of materials he reported.

One would expect Abner had developed the capability to fire a kiln of pottery since he had been producing firebricks for several years. But it is unclear how he and his son, Robert, acquired the ability to form the ceramics. They probably employed and relied on one or more journeymen potters or molders. (Rockingham and yellow ware were molded ceramics so the Marshalls would not have needed the skill to hand-throw clay on a potter's wheel.) However, the identities of their craftsmen remain unknown. Glazes were also an important part of creating these ceramics, and they would have had to acquire that knowledge in some way. Moreover, there is some difficulty in reconciling the types of pottery Abner reported making with his strong interest in and attachment to kaolin. Both Rockingham and yellow ware are low temperature earthenware and are not made from the purer "white clays." So Marshall would have had to procure another type of clay for his pottery, though located where he was, that would not have been difficult. But only kaolin was mentioned in the census report.

We have no specifics regarding Abner's products or customer base. In his book, William C. Ketchum, Jr., assigned the years 1859 to 1866 to the operation of Abner's pottery, and wrote of the existence of an ornate Rockingham candlestick from his kiln. However, no photograph was provided nor was its whereabouts mentioned. As for his firebricks, Abner may have found a nearby consumer in his former employer, William Garrett, whose snuff mill might have benefited from those fired at higher temperatures.

Though originally operating on land leased from Thomas Little, Abner purchased the property in early 1864 for $3,000 (U 7 461). By this time, brick and pottery making may not have been Marshall's primary interest. Within less than two months, he turned around and sold a half-interest to Philadelphia merchants William Trucks, John Trucks and Joseph E. Parker, Jr., for $10,000 (U 7 457). In the same year, he and Trucks and Parker then purchased an undeveloped acre of land along the Philadelphia & Baltimore Central Railroad tracks in Kennett Square, Pennsylvania (Z 6 60). They presumably used this parcel to access the railroad by which they shipped their mined kaolin from the Hockessin clay pits. Two years later, Abner sold his remaining half-interest in the Hockessin site to Alfred Weeks, a Philadelphia physician, for $13,500 (F 8 410). The next year, with the proceeds from the sale of the two half-interests, Marshall acquired 114 acres along the Brandywine River in Pennsbury Township, Pennsylvania (C 7 257). He paid $19,500 for this property and returned to the practice of an occupation that had long been in his blood, farming, as confirmed by the 1870 census. There both Abner and his son, Robert, are listed as farmers. Abner held this acreage some 15 years until selling it in 1882 (N 9 485), though by 1880 he was recorded in the census as a retired farmer. The former potter then purchased a much smaller parcel (R 9 100) along Wilmington Road where presumably he lived until relocating to Lansdowne, Pennsylvania, late in life.

After Abner sold the remaining half interest in his Hockessin property, it is not totally clear what happened to his kiln and pottery making on the site. No evidence has been found to suggest that Trucks and Parker continued to turn out pottery, but they may have operated the kiln to produce firebricks for a short period of time. The 1868 Atlas by D.G. Beers shows the Fire Bricks Works of Trucks & Parker at or near where Marshall fired his kiln. But clearly these individuals were interested in mining, processing and selling kaolin, and the kaolin pits of Abner Marshall became a source of aluminum silicate-based clay for the Diamond State Kaolin Company. This company was formed on February 26, 1873, when at Dover, an act of incorporation, Chapter 653, was passed by the Delaware legislature. John Trucks and Joseph E. Parker, Jr., are identified in the act as two of the principals of the company.

Abner Marshall's involvement with kaolin clay in the area around Hockessin, Delaware, led to the development of a mining industry there that prospered for a number of years. During that time, hundreds of thousands of tons were shipped to various potteries, including those in Trenton, New Jersey.

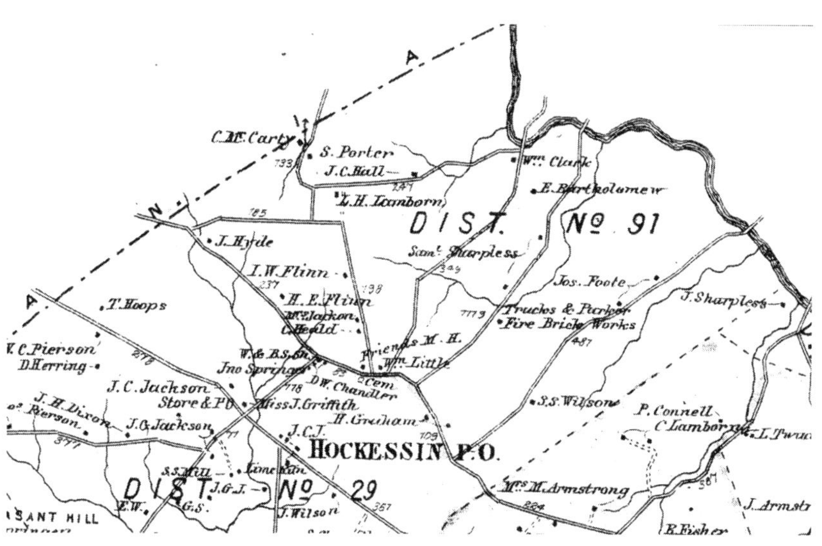

A section of a map of Mill Creek Hundred shows the Trucks and Parker Fire Bricks Works, the likely location where Abner Marshall had operated his kiln in prior years. *Atlas of the State of Delaware, D.G. Beers, 1868.*

Neumayer on Eleventh Street

Albert Neumayer can be found in the 1857 issue of the *Wilmington Directory* where he is listed as a potter boarding at 60 French Street. This location suggests he initially worked for William Hare since that address was Hare's family residence. Newmayer and Neumeier were other spellings of his surname. Born Englebert (Engelbert), he frequently used Albert after immigrating to America, though he reverted to Englebert later in life. That may have been to distinguish himself from his only son named Albert. According to the 1860 census, Englebert, the potter, was 30 years old, unmarried and, like Stüber and Ziegler, a member of the Baden, Germany, connection. The next census suggests he was married in the very early 1860s since he was listed there along with Albert, Jr., his seven-year-old son. His wife, also foreign born, died just prior to Albert's seventh birthday.

The Neumayers

Englebert Neumayer	Franziska Schmidt
b. Noverber 14, 1829	b. September 25, 1830
b.p. Germany	b.p. Germany
d. March 9, 1916	d. April 10, 1870

Married in Wilmington, ca. 1862
Albert Neumayer, Jr., son
b. May 22, 1863
b.p. Wilmington
d. June 27, 1952
Atlantic City, NJ

Information Courtesy of E.D. Bryan, MD.

As mentioned in Chapter III, Neumayer was in partnership with George Ziegler for a time. After it broke up in about 1864, he resided on Orange Street and probably worked for Ziegler until about 1870. From that point on, Albert is in and out of the *Wilmington Directory*. He is unlisted from 1871 until 1874. "Neumeier" then reappears for a time with a house address at 704 E. Fifth Street before again disappearing until 1881-82. This time Englebert is not only shown with a new residence, but 516 E. Eleventh Street is also the location of his

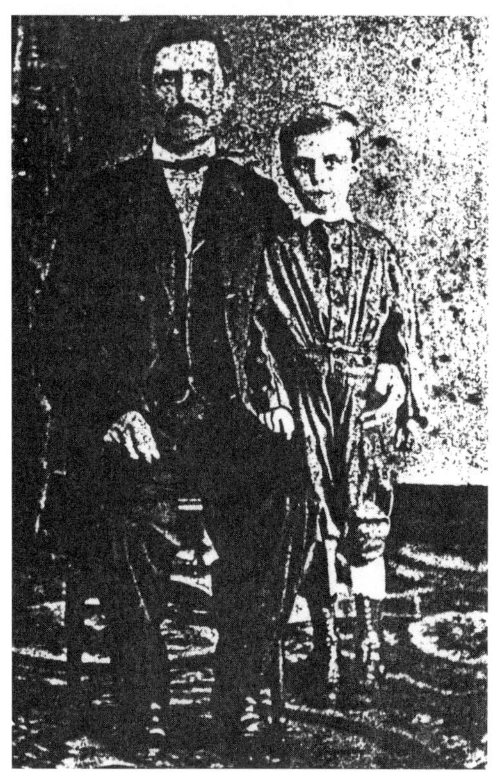

A photograph shows Englebert Neumayer and his son, Albert, circa 1870. Owned by a family descendent. *Courtesy of E.D. Bryan, MD.*

new pottery. From this point until the end of the decade, Neumayer is listed in the city and state directories under the heading of "Pottery." Though the published address of his business varied throughout this period from 510 to 516 E. Eleventh Street, it was most often shown as 510.

Neumayer purchased property on the south side of Eleventh Street between Lombard and Pine streets in April of 1880 for $375 (Q 11 344). The lot was 30 X 75 feet with the shorter side facing Eleventh Street. The site appears to have been undeveloped at the time since no buildings are referred to in the indenture nor does the *Wilmington Atlas* of 1876 show any structures there. But in 1884, the *Sanborn Map* details a two-story brick building with a slate roof labeled "Pottery," and an adjoining kiln. It seems somewhat unusual that at age 51, one would take on the task of building a pottery from the ground up. But if Neumayer still had the itch to produce his own earthenware, it may have been his only Wilmington option. The Orange Street pottery was undergoing a change in use and William Hare was still active on French Street. It's possible that Englebert tried unsuccessfully to acquire either of these locations, though the required monies would have been substantially more than what he paid for the lot on Eleventh Street. But at the new site, he needed to infuse capital. Neumayer continued in business at that location until the property was sold in January of 1890 for $1,400 (F 15 227).

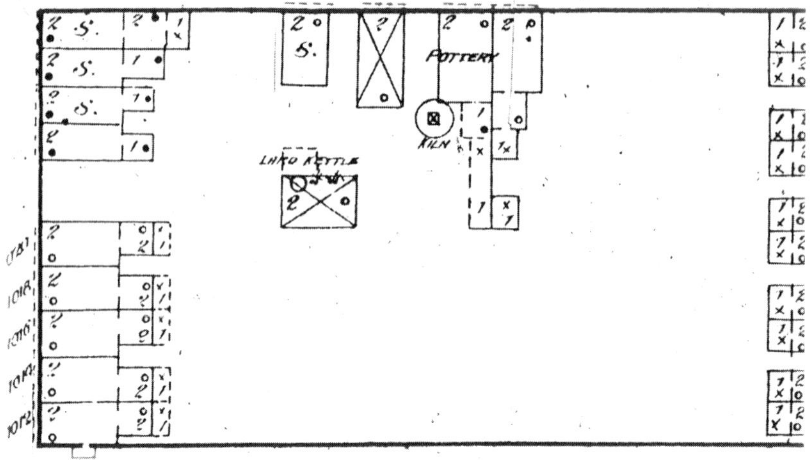

The outline of the Neumayer pottery on Eleventh Street is depicted on the *Sanborn Map Wilmington Delaware*, 1884.

It is somewhat surprising that Neumayer was already listed as the proprietor of a pottery in the Census of Manufactures in 1880, since he first purchased the undeveloped site for his new business in April of the same year. Neumayer reported that he operated for ten months and produced product valued at $1,600 using less than $300 of materials. It is quite possible that he started his new pottery before he actually owned the site. What also seems unusual is that he listed his invested capital as only $1,000 even though the potter had recently developed the site from the ground up. The potter also reported that one person was employed and annual wages paid out were $450. More than likely, he was referring to himself.

Mentioned earlier, Neumayer was not listed in the *Wilmington Directory* on a continuous basis during the 1870s. These were the years following his wife's early death as Albert, Jr., was growing from childhood to adolescence. Albert, Sr., may have been prosperous enough to concentrate on raising his son rather than working full-time. He must have been reasonably well off since he purchased three properties (W 8 367, S 10 181 and Y 10 138) in Wilmington between 1869 and 1877 and continued that trend with later acquisitions in 1888 and 1893 (K 14 300, B 16 529 and F 16 17). These likely served to provide rental income.

During the 1870s, any employment of Neumayer as a potter would probably have been with George Ziegler since their relationship continued over a long period of time. Even though he left the proprietorship of the Orange Street pottery to George in about 1865, they co-owned an unrelated piece of property until 1870 (C 9 488). Also according to E.D. Bryan, MD, probate records following the death of George's wife, Justina, assigned the power of attorney to Neumayer.

When "Neumeier" appeared in the 1880 census as a potter, his son had reached the age of 17. However, Albert did not follow his father's craft; rather, the word "confectionist" was attached to his name. Eventually Albert, Jr., changed occupations and practiced barbering for a number of years.

So with Englebert Neumayer in 1890, the era of pottery making in nineteenth century Delaware ends. For in that year, the *Delaware State & Peninsular Directory* lists, "Pottery, E. Neumayer, 510 E. 11th, Wilmington," for the last time. During the 1890s and into the first few years of the twentieth century, Englebert is shown in the *Wilmington Directory* without an occupation and residing at the address of Albert, the barber. In 1908, the name Neumayer is no longer found and the *Wilmington Street Directory* shows the son's property at 221 W. Fourth Street as being vacant. Both father and son had moved on to Atlantic City, New Jersey, and Delaware had moved on, too, without a master potter practicing the centuries-old craft of turning clay into useful ceramics.

Chapter VII

Potteries in Kent County

Seven

Pottery making in Kent County spanned a hundred years during which time ceramics were produced at four sites. Begun around 1780 in Smyrna, it concluded with the closure of a long-surviving Milford pottery in the early 1880s. Nestled between were two other operations in the Smyrna area. Shards recovered from the earliest site reveal the types of redware fired there, and two earthenware examples attributed to the pottery at Milford are on display at the Parson Thorne Mansion.

The Green Family at Smyrna

Two generations of the Green family manufactured pottery at sites on either side of Main Street in Smyrna during a span of about 50 years. Information on the three potters, a father and two sons, compiled by E.D. Bryan, MD, of Dover, has been included in this chapter. It was already mentioned in Chapter I that in-ground investigations were held at the site on the east side of North Main Street in the 1990s. In addition, a plaque was erected on this property by the State of Delaware in December of 2004, dedicating the earlier of the two pottery locations as a historic landmark. The site of this first pottery of the Greens is presently owned by Colonel and Mrs. Kenneth P. Brown.

The story begins with **Charles Green, Jr.**, of Duck Creek Hundred, who was probably a contemporary of Wilmington's John Jones. Much of what is known about Charles, the potter, comes from land deeds and Friends', tax and Orphan's Court records. He was the son of Charles the elder, and grandson of Thomas. According to a "Deed of Gift" (Q 1 255), Charles acquired a parcel of about a quarter of an acre from his grandfather for five shillings in 1764. In 1783, a triangular piece of this property consisting of 18 square perches was carved out and sold by Charles and his wife, Hannah, to Abraham Hayne, a tailor. In this land record, Charles was referred to as a potter.

The earliest tax record that provides meaningful information about his pottery is for the year 1797. At that time, Charles was assessed for a "lot of 1/8 acre whereon is erected a frame tenement, pot house, and stables, in good repair, in tenure of S. Sullivan" and himself. S. Sullivan was probably the **Samuel Sullivan** who is shown in the local tax list in 1797 as paying only a personal tax. He is not found in the Delaware census of 1800. About that time he moved to Philadelphia. One finds a potter by that name in Susan Myers' checklist and she points out that Samuel Sullivan advertised his recently acquired "Earthen Ware Manufactory" on Market Street in 1800. In fact, Sullivan followed with an advertisement in Delaware's *Mirror of the Times & General Advertiser* on April 10, 1802. Whether he was a native of Delaware or learned his craft under an apprenticeship with Charles Green is unclear.

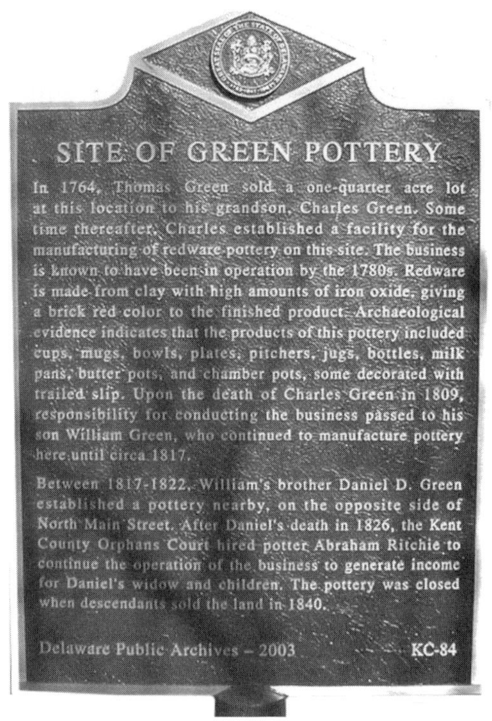

A plaque dedicating the site of the pottery operated by Charles Green, Jr., in Smyrna was erected in December of 2004. *Courtesy of Colonel and Mrs. Kenneth P. Brown.*

Tax lists for the early 1800s also refer to Charles Green's pottery. For 1803-04, the record mentions "one house and lot with a potter's shop, warehouse, stable and kitchen, in good repair in Duck Creek Crossroads," now Smyrna. By 1806, Charles and his son, **William Green,** were taxed together, suggesting the two were both working the pottery. Along with several larger tracts of land, Charles owned the site of the pottery until his death on October 3, 1809. For the next year, Charles Green's heirs were named in the tax records for his properties, including the parcel that held the house and potter's shop.

One might have expected that William learned his trade from his father. That may be but it is possible he served an apprenticeship in Philadelphia. Friends' records at Duck Creek show a certificate for removal for a "Wm Green (a minor)" in 1802. It was to the Philadelphia Monthly Meeting and requested that he be placed as an apprentice within the boundaries of that Meeting.

No intact examples of pottery from this site are known, but archaeological investigations conducted in 1991 recovered numerous earthenware shards. These show that typical redware and also higher quality, glazed ceramics were fashioned by these potters. Fragments of three manganese-glazed jugs, two of which still retain partial handles, are pictured here. Located on the book's dust cover, another photograph demonstrates the decorations used by the Greens to distinguish some wares. The shards from what appear to be plates and possibly a large charger show this shop's use of a trailing cup to apply a creamy slip before firing with a lead glaze. The rims of others, probably from bowls and pans, were decorated with a coggle wheel and fired with glazes colored with copper and

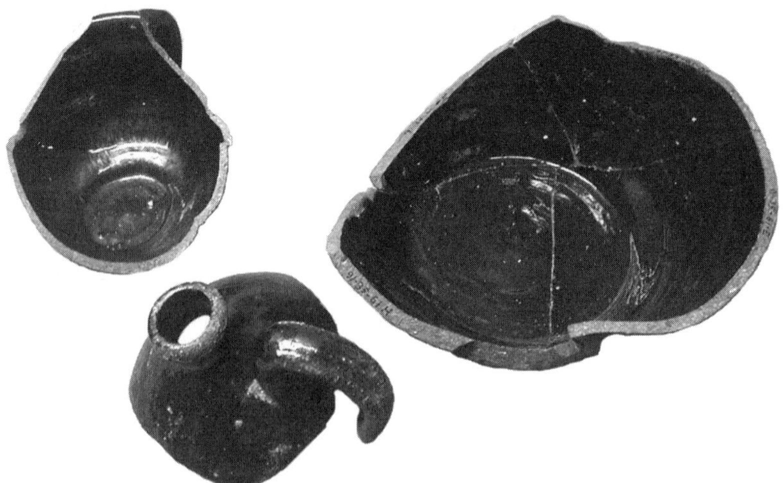

Pottery shards, recovered from the site operated by Charles and William Green on Main Street in Smyrna, show a rich black color from the use of a manganese oxide glaze. These fragments from jugs of various sizes display the ability these potters had to produce delicate forms. *Courtesy of the University of Delaware, Center for Archaeological Research.*

manganese oxides. An even wider range of colorants is exhibited on the small but rather delicate fragments.

Two account books in the collections of the Delaware State Archives provide some confirmation of the Greens' route to market and pricing structure. Jonathan Allee and Benjamin Coombe were general merchants in Smyrna in the early nineteenth century. Though purchased by the dozen, Allee paid William Green the equivalent of 3.5 pence for a bowl and 7.5 pence for a jug. But each earthenware "pott" at 18 pence was noticeably more expensive. Shards recovered from the site show a wide variation in the aesthetics of their pottery. With that in mind, it is likely that the earthenware "potts" purchased by Coombe were finer and more highly decorated than the jugs or bowls. Charles Green must have also sold some of his wares through resellers. Coombe owed the administrator of Charles' estate over £3, more than likely for earthenware he had purchased from the potter.

Pottery Sales by William Green

Jonathan Allee			
1809	1 doz	quart jugs	\$0.80
Benjamin Coombe			
1811	2 doz	jugs	£0.15.0
	6 (only)	earthenware potts	£0.09.0
	2 doz	milk pans	£0.15.0
	3 doz	bowls	£0.10.6

A review of items listed in Charles Green's estate inventory suggests two things about his livelihood at the time of his death. He was an active potter and also engaged in farming. The appraisal included saleable earthenware and potter's clay, glazing materials and wood for a kiln. In addition, 199 bushels of new corn and 32 bushels of wheat were posted at a value slightly in excess of \$151. Presumably Green's large acreage mentioned earlier served as his farmland.

The property on which the Charles Green pottery sat had a very unusual shape—a long, thin triangle. After his death, this small plot was divided into two parcels by the Orphan's Court in 1812 (Kent County Orphan's Court Case File RG 3840.006, 1811-1822). The section labeled "A" was a widow's dower ascribed to Hannah. It contained the residence and stable. The other part denoted as "B" was assigned to his son, William. It contained the pottery shop and also the parcel on which the kiln is believed to have stood. Presumably William continued to produce earthenware there until at least 1817, when he sold the property to Hannah and Robert Palmatary, his sister and her husband. Two years later, they granted this real estate to John Cummins. It is unclear if William Green leased back the pottery and continued to produce earthenware after he sold the property. He died in 1823 and his estate inventory hints that he was no longer potting by then. No burnt or unfired wares or potter's materials were included in the accounting.

Before moving on to Daniel Green and his pottery on the opposite side of Main Street, it is appropriate to digress and revisit Charles Green, Jr., and his family through several Friends' records. A certificate from the Philadelphia Monthly Meeting was produced at Duck Creek in January, 1761, recommending the acceptance of Rosamond, the wife of Charles Green. This Charles may have been Charles the elder; if so, Rosamond was the potter's mother who apparently hailed from Philadelphia.

In 1778, Charles Green, Jr., produced a certificate on his own behalf at the Duck Creek Monthly Meeting from the northern district of Philadelphia. Quite likely, this Charles is the potter and raises the question why he was in Philadelphia. Like John Jones, Charles may have been there learning his craft. Jones apprenticed under John Thompson and Charles may have done likewise. Then on returning to Smyrna, he started his own pottery, which according to the deed cited earlier, was in operation by 1783.

Continuing, in 1793, Jane Green, wife of Charles Green, requested membership with the Duck Creek Monthly Meeting and Charles asked that his three children—William, Hannah and Daniel Dawson Green—come under Friends' care. These names are identical to those children identified in Charles' estate proceedings upon his death in 1809. But the name of Charles' wife in the 1783 deed was Hannah Green. And why did Charles wait so long to seek Friends' membership for his children? Soon after returning from Philadelphia, Charles had a compliant filed against him in 1781 for his marriage that was assisted by a magistrate. He waited until 1793 to acknowledge it and then requested membership for his children. At the same time, Jane sought her own. That Jane was the potter's wife is also supported by the death record of Daniel. Duck Creek Friends scribed that Daniel, son of Charles and Jane, departed on February

11, 1826. This date matches that in the record of the Orphan's Court which acted upon the death of Daniel D., Charles' son and a potter himself. Yet the piece that doesn't fit this family picture is the reference to Hannah as Charles' wife in the early deed. And the Orphan's Court in 1809 gave his wife, Hannah, property in subdividing the potter's estate. But Jane probably predeceased Charles and he remarried. At Duck Creek in 1798, Charles Green requested a certificate to the Wilmington Monthly Meeting to marry Hannah Squib. Joined on November 15, 1798, her Meeting referred to Charles Green of Duck Creek as a son of Charles and Rosamond Green. So while these Friends records appear to mesh, it still is unclear why the deed in 1783 named the potter's wife as Hannah. Was it a mistake in the record? Hopefully the future will bring a higher degree of certainty to the life story of Charles, Jr.

Daniel Dawson Green was another son of Charles. Whether he worked with his brother during William's ownership of the pottery is uncertain, but soon after William sold out, Daniel established his own pottery on the other side of Main Street. There he continued his craft until his death, presumably manufacturing the same type and forms of low-fired earthenware that his father and brother had made. The goods on hand at the time of Daniel's death—several lots of earthenware and a large supply of wood—told of one engaged in pottery making. In addition, several articles from Daniel's estate were sold to Enoch Spruance, namely:

- 1 lot clay
- 1 keg of magnesium (manganese)
- 1 "mortar- pessel"
- 1 cart? clay

The purchase of these materials leads one to raise the question: Did Spruance carry on the potting enterprise? So far, however, no other information has been found to support his involvement in this craft. Enoch was a wealthy citizen of Smyrna and may have thought of operating the factory with hired craftsmen.

Following Daniel's death on February 11, 1826, once again the Orphan's Court entered the lives of the descendants of the Green family (Kent County Orphan's Court Case File RG 3840.06, 1832-1846). **Abraham Ritchie**, a potter who had worked in Wilmington, was hired to continue Daniel's business to provide his heirs a source of income. Ritchie carried on but in 1831 Robert Palmatary, who at one time owned the site of the earlier Green's pottery, petitioned the Orphan's Court on behalf of Daniel's children. Palmatary was their guardian. Three men were appointed to evaluate the condition of the property and they concluded that the buildings were in tolerable repair. However, unless the kiln was rebuilt, the property would be rendered quite valueless. They estimated the cost to do this at $150, using bricks from the old kiln. The court's direction must have been followed, for various records suggest that Ritchie managed the pottery until about 1838. At that point he was no longer on the tax list, and in 1840, the Federal Census counted him as a resident of Philadelphia. With Ritchie's move north, so ended the involvement of the Green family in pottery making in Smyrna. Thomas Scharf, the Delaware historian, wrote that Green's pottery closed about 1840, though the date was probably a year or two earlier.

John Denning in Milford

Two potters, John Husbands Denning and Joseph C. Gorby, were active in Milford, Delaware, largely during the third quarter of the nineteenth century. Earthenware rather than stoneware was the principal product of their hands.

Based on manufacturing census data for Delaware, **John H. Denning** was the proprietor of a Kent County pottery from 1850 until at least 1880. Thomas Scharf wrote in his *History of Delaware* that this potter started a pottery on Pearl Street (actually it was on Pear Street) about 1840. It will be argued later that John began his operation in the Milford area around 1843. This span then of about 40 years makes him one of the longest continuous pottery operators in nineteenth century Delaware.

According to family Bible records provided by Deanna Denning Wolfe, great-great granddaughter of John H., he was born on September 25, 1814, in Brandywine Hundred, New Castle County, Delaware. John married a woman by the name of Anna E. Worrall on October 5, 1837. Anna, nearly five years younger than John, hailed from Marple Township, Delaware County, Pennsylvania. That state was also the birthplace of their two oldest children, Mary and Phebe, though others were later born in Delaware. The birthplace of Anna and that of their first children suggests that Denning had a life before Milford.

Indeed, Denning's first ownership of a pottery was not in downstate Delaware, but rather in Delaware County, Pennsylvania. There he appeared as the head of household in the 1840 federal census for

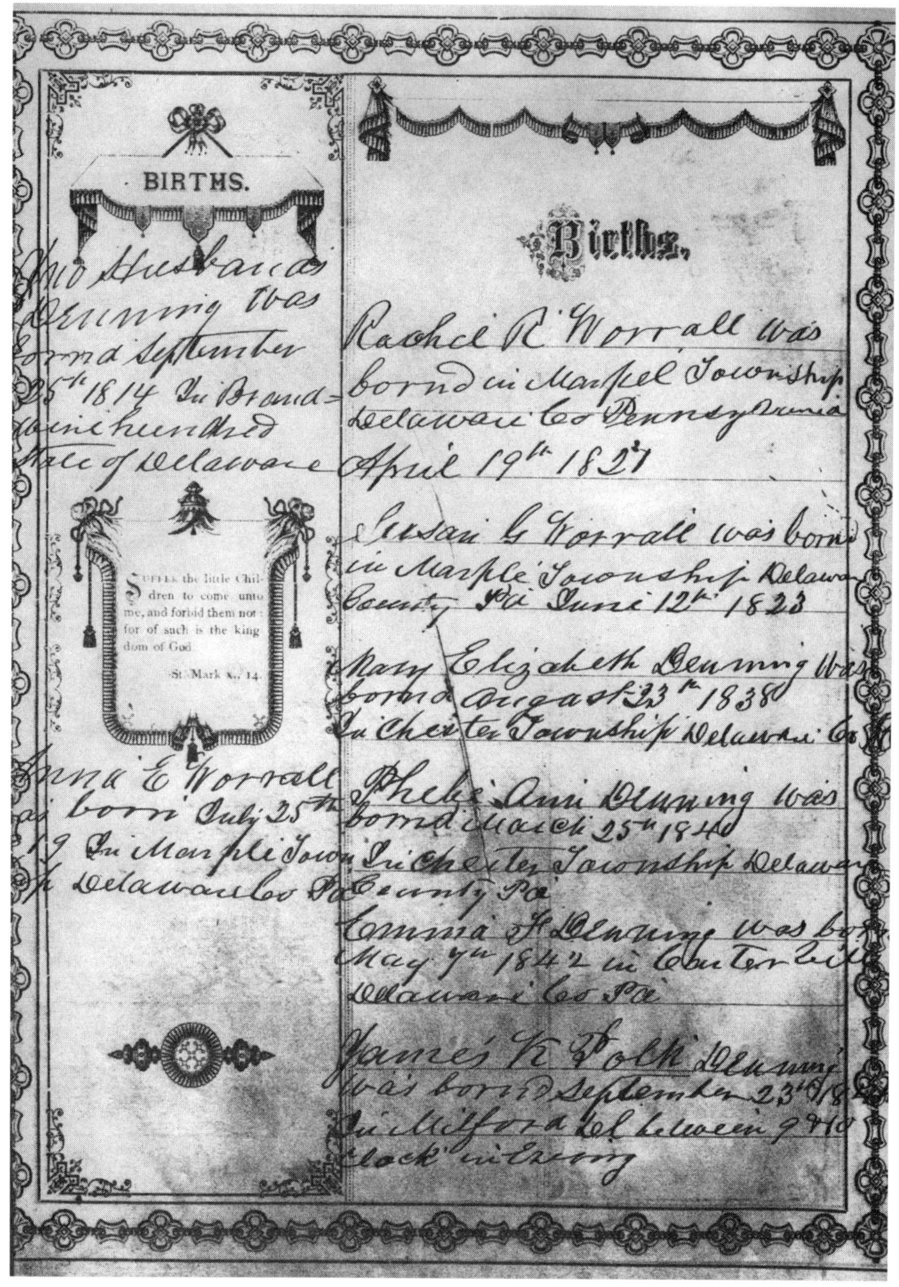

BIRTHS.

John Husbands Denning was born September 25th 1814 In Brandywine hundred State of Delaware

SUFFER the little Children to come unto me, and forbid them not: for of such is the kingdom of God.

St. Mark x., 14.

Anna E Worrall was born July 25th [illegible] In Marple Township Delaware Co Pa

Births.

Rachel R Worrall was born in Marple Township Delaware Co Pennsylvania April 19th 1827

Susan G Worrall was born in Marple Township Delaware County Pa June 12th 1823

Mary Elizabeth Denning was born August 23rd 1838 In Chester Township Delaware Co

Phebe Ann Denning was born March 25th 1840 In Chester Township Delaware County Pa

Emma H Denning was born May 7th 1842 in Centerville Delaware Co Pa

James K Polk Denning was born September 23rd 18[illegible] in Milford [illegible] between 9 & 10 o'clock in Evening

The family Bible shows "John Husbands Denning was born September 25, 1814 in Brandywine Hundred State of Delaware." *Courtesy of Deanna Denning Wolfe.*

Chester Township. In a land deed (U 218) dated March 2, 1838, John H. Denning is named as the grantee, and the record describes a piece of land, slightly in excess of an acre, which already contained a pot house. The purchase price was $600 and the property bordered Chichester Road. Four years earlier, a 73 acre farm that contained this pottery had been advertised for sale. Its description in the February 7, 1834, *Delaware County Republican* boasted a "Pot House" 26 X 22 feet and a kiln house of some 22 feet. The subscriber of the notice was Daniel Carter, the grantor of the property when Denning purchased it in 1838. Apparently the farm did not sell in its entirety when advertised in 1834, and Carter then carved out the pottery for sale to Denning.

In an 1842 newspaper advertisement, Denning thanked the public for their past favors and noted that he still manufactured earthenware near the city of Chester. At the same time, he announced that J.D. Hurtt was established as his agent with a warehouse in the borough of Chester. A similar ad was also placed in the March 29, 1842, edition of *The Upland Union, Delaware County Democrat and Peoples Advocate* where it goes on to mention chimney caps, stove pipe cylinders, bed pans, flower pots and crooked ware as products offered. Here is another probable misspelling common to earlier centuries; most likely, John meant *crockery* ware.

Where Denning learned his craft is an open question. He was 23 years old when he purchased the pottery in Chester Township, so he had had ample time to develop his potting skills by then. Since he was from Brandywine Hundred, Delaware, it is quite possible he apprenticed at a pottery in Wilmington. There were three potteries operating in the city during the early 1830s. The Orange Street manufactories, one at Water Street and the other at Third Street, produced earthenware of the type that Denning likely turned in Pennsylvania and Delaware. It

---

POTTERY – The subscriber respectfully returns thanks for past favors, and would desire to inform his friends and the public, that he still carries on the manufacturing of EARTHEN WARE, in Chester township, near Chester, where store keepers and all others can be supplied at the shortest notice. For the better accommodation of the public, J. D. HURTT has established a Ware House, in the borough of Chester, opposite the Bank, where a full assortment of ware will be kept, wholesale and retail, at the manufacturers prices.

JOHN H. DENNING

Delaware County Republican, April 1, 1842

is believed that Nathan Dalbey was then in business near the Christina River while the pottery up Orange Street was owned by William J. Hallowell. The third factory was located on French Street and under the ownership of Branch Green and followed by the management of Thomas Hayhurst. Denning could have received his training at any of these shops, though it is less likely it was at the one on French Street. There, the focus seems to have been on stoneware rather than earthenware and, while two others are known to have served apprenticeships there about this time, both were recorded under Delaware's formal indenture program. No such agreement was filed for Denning. On the other hand, one cannot rule out the possibility that he learned his art at the Pennsylvania pottery prior to his ownership of it. At this point, it is uncertain what prompted John to head for Pennsylvania, though if he had worked for Hallowell, William closed his pottery about 1838. That event could have led John to apply his skill and seek his fortune elsewhere.

How long and under what circumstances did Denning operate the pottery near Chester beyond 1842, the year of his advertisement? Apparently it was not very long. The census of 1850 provides a clue. John and Anna had several offspring. Of two daughters, Phebe was born about 1841 in Pennsylvania but Emma, two years her junior, was born in Delaware. So these data suggest John and his family left Pennsylvania for Milford, Delaware, about 1843.

On January 12, 1849, a sheriff's sale of Denning's property in Pennsylvania was announced in that day's issue of the *Delaware County Republican*. In part, the notice stated that the property of over one acre and situated along Chichester Road about a mile and a half from Chester consisted of a frame house along with a two-story, frame building, 20 by 50 feet, that had been used as a pottery. The advertisement ended by stating that the real estate had been seized and taken in execution as the property of John H. Denning.

So what was going on at the Chester Township pottery between 1843 when Denning departed for Delaware and the sheriff's sale six years later? Possibly, Denning tried to lease the property or find a buyer without success. But another theory will be offered later. Though in any case, John eventually stopped paying taxes which led to the auction.

Some later newspaper accounts related to the pottery Denning had owned bear mentioning here. On March 23, 1860, the *Delaware County Republican* reported the planned sale of four parcels of land at Carterville in Chester Township. These properties had undoubtedly been subdivided from the Carter farm advertised in 1834. According to the newspaper, Lot No. 2 was located along Chichester Road and "there is on this lot a large POTTERY, kiln, glazing house and clay mill, with all the necessary apparatus for carrying on an extensive business in the manufacture of earthenware." Eight years later in the newspaper of the same title, it was reported on February 21, that an Edward Carter planned improvements to property that had descended directly from William Penn. This article went on to note that the "old established Pot House, which enjoyed the distinction of being the only one located in the county for more than half a century, has been revived and is now in full operation." Whether Carter himself had reopened the pottery is not clear but "the ware manufactured at this establishment has a good reputation, not only in our State, but throughout New Jersey."

Before following Denning to Delaware, mention should be made of another activity of his that surfaced in Pennsylvania writings. Henry Graham Ashmead in his *History of Delaware County, Pennsylvania,* identified John H. Denning as director of Chester Township Schools in 1840. Though that seems like an unusual position for a potter, it is not known what it entailed. As will be reinforced later, Denning was one to play an active role in his community.

When Denning arrived in Milford in about 1843, he must have established his pottery on leased land since he did not purchase a site until 1850 (C 4 79). Information in the *Milford Historical Society News Letter,* published in April of 1974, placed his early business on the north side of N.W. Front Street between Walnut and North streets. Then Denning moved to the east side of Pear (now Washington) Street between Front and Water (now Park) streets. This property was about two blocks from the earlier Front Street site and bordered the lot of C.S. Watson & Company. According to the deed, the 3,400 square foot parcel contained sundry buildings used as a pottery. Though his pottery was a relatively small operation, John and Anna raised a rather large family using its proceeds. In 1874, the Dennings built a new home in Milford. According to records of Kent County Mutual Insurance, Inc., it was then valued at $1,500 and insured for $1,000. And over the years John expanded his real estate holdings. Following Anna's death in 1899, these properties were sold and the deed (E 8 108) refers to the sale of four adjacent lots on Pear Street by her estate's administrator.

Denning was in the business of manufacturing earthenware. Stoneware was not mentioned in the Census of Manufactures until

1880. As far as is known, John did not mark any of his wares. Not surprisingly, he glazed much of his earthenware as "800 lbs. glazing" is included in one census report and quantities of red lead and manganese are mentioned in another. Like his contemporaries, John made a variety of pottery forms. In the 1860 census, he reported producing the following utilitarian articles along with the values of each type:

200 dozen jugs	$300
200 dozen jars	300
200 dozen high pots	400
100 dozen crocks	75
100 dozen basins	50
sundries	75
Total	*$1,200*

That year Denning reported revenues of $1,200 compared to combined materials and labor costs of $912. However, these were not his only expenses. Besides cost of capital and maintenance, surely there was a horse to feed. In comparison, the Wilmington potter, William Hare, reported the value of his production at $5,400, four and a half times that of Denning. Meanwhile, Ziegler and Neumayer, the Wilmington partnership, produced half again as much as the Milford pottery.

Some years ago, E.D. Bryan, MD, of Dover, accidentally discovered a price list of John Denning's earthenware which is reproduced on the following page. Individual pieces ranged from about a nickel to a half dollar depending on form and size. Those prices correspond well with the census data. Based on his production in 1860 of about 10,000 pieces and a value of $1,200, his average piece of earthenware sold for 12 cents. That average suggests, to no surprise, that much of his production was of the smaller sizes that adapted well to everyday, household use.

Like most of his contemporaries Denning did not mark his wares, so examples from his pottery are almost non-existent. However, the Milford Historical Society holds two pieces of earthenware that are attributed to his Milford pottery. One is a brown-glazed pitcher and the other is an oyster pie plate, both donated by the wife of Denning's grandson, Mrs. Lee Hirsh. These examples are on display at the Parson Thorne Mansion on Front Street in Milford.

A few references identify to some degree Denning's customer base. Thomas Scharf, in his *History of Delaware*, wrote that he made

WHOLESALE PRICES CURRENT

OF

EARTHENWARE,

Manufactured and for Sale by

JOHN H. DENNING,

Milford, Delaware.

HIGH POTS.

Inches.		Per Dozen.	Single.
14—largest	size	$3 50	50
12—second	"	3 00	40
11—third	"	2 00	30
9—fourth	"	1 50	20
8—fifth	"	1 20	15
7—sixth	"	80	10
5—seventh	"	60	7

CROCKS.

16—largest	size	$3 00	40
14—second	"	2 00	30
12—third	"	1 50	20
11—fourth	"	1 20	15
9—fifth	"	80	10
7—sixth	"	60	7

BASINS.

15—largest	size	$2 00	30
14—second	"	1 50	20
12—third	"	1 20	15
10—fourth	"	80	10
8—fifth	"	60	6

FLAT PANS.

18—largest	size	$3 00	40
16—second	"	2 00	30
14—third	"	1 50	20
12—fourth	"	1 20	15
10—fifth	"	80	10
8—sixth	"	60	6

PIE DISHES.

14—largest	size	$1 75	20
12—second	"	1 50	18
11—third	"	1 20	12½
9—fourth	"	80	10
8—fifth	"	60	8
7—sixth	"	40	5
5—seventh	"	30	4

PIPE CYLINDERS.

14—largest	size	$4 00	62½
12—second	"	3 00	40
9—third	"	2 00	30
5—fourth	" short	1 00	15

FLOWER POTS WITH STAND.

Inches.		Per Dozen.	Single.
12—largest	size	$4 00	50
11—second	"	3 00	35
10—third	"	2 50	25
9—fourth	"	1 75	20
8—fifth	"	1 50	18
7—sixth	"	1 20	15
6—seventh	"	1 00	12½
5—eight	"	60	8
4—ninth	"	50	7
3—tenth	"	40	6

MILK PANS.

14 inch,	$2 00	25
12 "	1 50	18
10 "	1 00	10
3 "	60	8

Glazed Bowls & Pans.

1 gallon	$2 00	25
½ "	1 50	18
1 quart	1 00	10
1 pint	50	5
½ "	40	4

STEW PANS.

1 gallon	$2 00	33
½ "	1 50	22
1 quart	1 00	12½
1 pint	60	8

Jugs, Jars and Pitchers.

2 gallon	$3 50	50
1 "	2 00	30
½ "	1 50	20
1 quart	1 00	10
1 pint	60	6

CHAMBERS, &c.

Largest size	$2 00	30
Second "	1 50	20
Chair Pans	80	10
Bed Pans, Large size	4 00	50
Spittoons	1 50	20
Hanging Baskets	1 75	20

All articles in the above line manufactured at the shortest notice. Orders promptly attended to.

John H. Denning used this list to advertise the types of earthenware he manufactured and the wholesale price he set if purchased singularly or by the dozen. *Courtesy of E.D. Bryan, MD.*

"all kinds of earthenware supplying the country around." In *Business and Industries of Milford, 1797-1997*, edited by Harold B. Hancock, it is mentioned that the product of Denning's handicraft in clay found a ready sale to the retail dealers in all parts of Delaware. But even more telling is the account of Denning's grandson, Lee Hirsh, which was captured in *Milford Delaware and the Milford Area after 1776* by E. Dallas Hitchens and E. Mills Hurley. When springtime arrived, John would load his large rack wagon and head north as far as Pennsylvania as he dropped off his wares at numerous country stores on the way. Often, the young Lee would accompany his grandfather. As will be discussed in Chapter IX, any number of grocers, hardware dealers and merchants in china and glassware were outlets for potters like Denning. The mention of Pennsylvania probably refers to Delaware County, the locale of Denning's first operation, where he likely kept in contact with some of his previous customers.

According to the manufacturing censuses, Denning's product revenues were substantially higher in the early years of his business. John, however, controlled his material and labor expenses to keep the difference between these combined costs and revenues

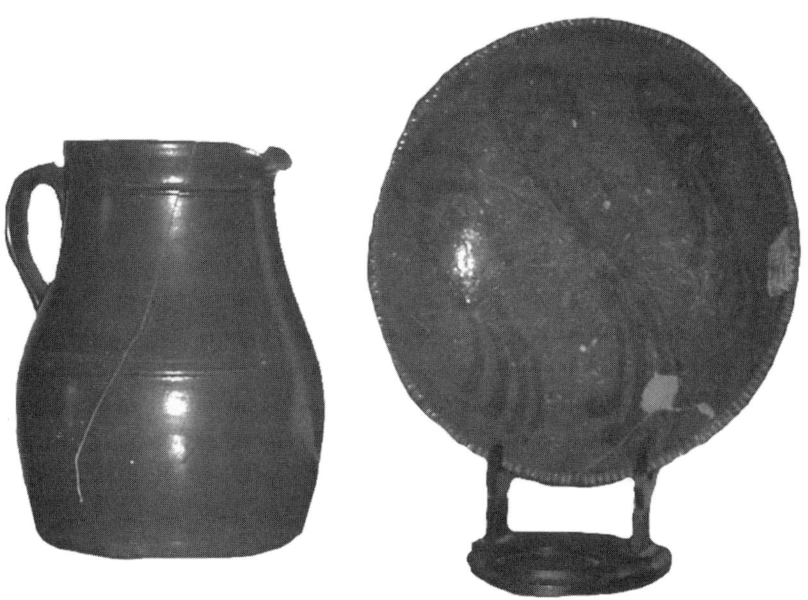

A brown-glazed pitcher and an oyster pie plate are two pieces of earthenware attributed to the Milford potter, John H. Denning. *Courtesy of the Milford Historical Society*

about equal across this 30-year period. At roughly $250 to $300 per year, he maintained a viable operation. But he may have supplemented his income in other ways. An 1859 map of Kent County in the collection of the Historical Society of Delaware lists John H. Denning as justice of the peace, a position that possibly generated some additional income. Thomas Scharf notes that he was elected a town commissioner of Milford in 1867, though this office may not have been salaried. It is quite likely that John's pottery business was aided by a low degree of intrastate competition, since he was the only long-term manufacturer below Wilmington. The only other known pottery to have operated outside of New Castle County during Denning's tenure was at Smyrna Landing, but it was only in business for a few years. The lack of other potteries may in part be due to the geology of downstate Delaware. Clay deposits were not as abundant there as they were in the northern part of the state and potters usually tried to locate near a source of that important raw material. Denning's pottery was within sight of the Mispillion Creek and its banks were possibly a source of clay.

Manufacturing Census—John H. Denning

	1850	1860	1870	1880
Loads/tons of clay	NA	50	20	NA
Cords of wood	60	40	20	NA
Cost of all materials	$345	$432	$284	$150
Number of employees	2	2	1	2
Annual wages	$600	$480	$300	$450
Values of products	$1,300	$1,200	$800	$900
Invested capital	$1,000	$400	$900	$1,000

In 1850, Denning reported he employed two men. One most assuredly was Joseph C. Gorby. He was a potter who worked for Denning for a number of years in Milford and most probably had a working relationship with him in Pennsylvania. More will be said about that later. The other may have been John himself or **Alfred Stevens**, an indentured apprentice whom Denning agreed to oversee for a period of three years and eight months. The agreement was signed on July 21, 1846. But in the 1850 population census of Milford, the occupation of Alfred, the 21-year-old son of Azel

Stevens, was recorded as "waterman." So if Alfred completed his apprenticeship under Denning's watchful eye, he chose not to pursue the life of a potter once he reached adulthood.

Besides the town positions that Denning held in Milford, he was also active in the Odd Fellows. In Scharf's *History of Delaware*, John is acknowledged as one of the charter members of the Crystal Fount Lodge No.10 which originated in Kent County on February 10, 1847. And according to the *Delaware Gazette* published on June 23, 1854, John H. Denning served as a Delaware grand officer of the I.O.O.F. A few years earlier he had played a role in state politics when, per the *Blue Hen's Chicken* of September 6, 1850, Denning was appointed a delegate to the State Democratic Convention.

It is not clear when John Denning stopped working with clay but it was some time after 1880. The listing of merchants shown on the O.H. Bailey map of Milford in 1885 does not include Denning. And the 1888 *Delaware State Directory* lists him as retired and residing in Milford. But clearly, Denning and his pottery turned out clay wares for at least 37 years and probably a few years longer. That period of time earns him the distinction of being the second longest proprietor of a pottery during the nineteenth century in Delaware.

According to the *Milford Chronicle* of January 27, 1888, John H. Denning died a week earlier at his residence on Pear Street at the age of 73 years, 4 months. Anna died in early 1899. Both are buried in the Odd Fellows Cemetery in Milford.

A Joseph C. "Garby" is listed as a 27-year-old potter in the 1850 population census for Milford, Delaware. Once again, a name has several spellings in historical records. Rather, the entry should have read **Joseph C. Gorby**. But we will also see his name spelled Gorbey. The listings for a Joseph Gorby in the 1810, '20 and '30 Delaware census records for New Castle County, Brandywine Hundred, suggest that Joseph C., born August 22, 1822, might be his son. Further review of census data, this time for Delaware in 1860, reveals that Elizabeth, the wife of Joseph C., was, like John H. Denning's spouse, born in Pennsylvania. According to the Tatnall Tombstone Collection, Elizabeth was born on September 27, 1823. Does the Gorby and Denning connection with Pennsylvania go even further? A case can be made that the answer is yes. In fact, it very likely that Joseph learned his potting craft from John and, after working for him in Pennsylvania, continued to serve Denning at his Milford pottery for some years.

Brandywine Hundred in Delaware and Chester Township in Pennsylvania are only a few miles apart. So Gorby's home and Denning's first pottery were in close proximity to each other. Joseph would have been in his early teens when Denning opened it. Since both Gorby and Denning grew up in Brandywine Hundred, it is possible their families were acquainted, which led to Gorby's apprenticeship and association with Denning. The year that he started with Denning is uncertain but Gorby was likely well versed in the business and the art by the time John left for Milford around 1843. And evidence suggests that Joseph stayed on in Pennsylvania to continue the pottery's operation or to sell off the remaining inventory before he too headed for Milford. That argument might best be made using the following chronology where years are approximate and largely gleaned from census data:

1843	John Denning leaves for Milford, Delaware
1846	Joseph Gorby marries Elizabeth in Pennsylvania.
1847	The Gorbys first daughter, Margaret, is born in Pennsylvania.
1848	The Gorbys second daughter, Josephine, is born in Pennsylvania.
1849	Denning's Chester Township property is sold by the sheriff.
1850	Joseph C. "Garby" is listed as potter in the Milford census.

Competitive forces and the severe economic depression of the late 1830s and early 1840s may have led to the demise of Denning's Chester Pottery. Both Philadelphia, less than 20 miles to the north, and Wilmington, almost equidistant to the south, had active potteries and would have provided substantial competition for Denning. But Joseph C. Gorby likely played a role in Denning's first business while it lasted, and then followed his mentor to downstate Delaware, arriving in Milford near the end of the 1840s.

There is one date that is somewhat in conflict with this scenario. Recall Denning was identified as a charter member in the Milford Odd Fellows Lodge in 1847. Thomas Scharf also lists Joseph C. Gorby as holding an identical position. That would suggest that he arrived in Milford before the birth of Josephine. But dates associated with an early census can be off by a year or so, or possibly Joseph was dividing his time between Pennsylvania and Delaware near the end of the operation of the pottery in Chester Township.

But Gorby did not remain a potter all of his life. By 1859, he was changing careers. The 1859 map of Kent County, Delaware, lists Joseph as both a potter and confectionary in Milford. And in the next year's census, he is identified as a confectioner so, while still using his hands, he had begun to shape products of the edible kind. Gorby continued so occupied during the 1860s and 1870s. Like Denning, he served the community of Milford. Thomas Scharf identifies Gorby as the tax collector there in 1869 and 1870. Joseph again changed his occupation around 1880. In 1882, the *Delaware State Directory* named J.C. Gorby as proprietor of the Union Hotel on Front Street in Milford. He apparently remained with the hotel for some years and, by 1897, had retired to his residence on Franklin Avenue. Both Joseph and Elizabeth lived long lives. He died on January 30, 1905, and she passed away on March 9, 1913. Like the Dennings, both were buried in the Odd Fellows Cemetery at Milford.

A Manufactory at Smyrna Landing

In the late 1860s, a pottery was established at Smyrna Landing on Duck Creek, a tributary of the Delaware River. Only in operation for about three years, the number of owners exceeded the number of years of its brief tenure by one. A brick and tile maker by the name of Allen and a family named Bell were involved. Start up and ownership transition dates were:

Alvan Allen & Andrew Naudain Bell	October, 1867
Alvan Allen and William M. Bell	January, 1869
Reese F. Bell	December, 1869

(Operation ceased following a fire in October 1870)

It is quite unlikely that Allen or any of the Bells were master potters, so these pottery owners must have relied heavily on the skills of those they employed. Alvan Allen, as we will see, manufactured bricks and tile, so firing a kiln was not foreign to him. Clay for this brickyard was dug on the local farm of N.T. Jerman. It was not unusual to find clay capable of producing earthenware in those types of deposits. Allen had a partner, Andrew N. Bell, who resided in New Jersey during his association with the pottery. William M. Bell then acquired Andrew's half-interest, though in less than a year, he and Allen sold out to another Bell. While Reese F. Bell may have gained some experience at the pottery before ownership, the time period was brief compared to the length of a normal learning period.

The story told here about Allen and the Bell family is largely based on the research of E.D. Bryan, MD, of Dover, Delaware. In the *Smyrna Times* published on October 23, 1867, A. Allen and A. Naudain Bell announced the beginnings of a pottery at Smyrna Landing, an area about a mile east of the town of Smyrna. Under the name of Allen & Bell, they expected to produce both stoneware and earthenware. The partners had purchased (F 5 143) and converted a large granary of some 1,400 square feet into a workshop, and also planned to add a similar sized, new building to it. A kiln was nearly complete. In addition, a shed was to be constructed over the clay mixing mill. The article went on to mention that two lathes were in operation suggesting that some of their wares were going to be turned rather than "hand thrown" on a potter's wheel. A few months later, the *Smyrna Times* briefly mentioned that they had been shown some wares manufactured by Allen and Bell at the Landing. In the February 26 issue, the editor wrote that "it is well finished and strong" and that their double-glazed ware was said to be equal to any produced in the United States. Newspapers of the time were notorious for promoting the quality of goods manufactured by local businesses.

A. Allen was **Alvan Allen** who was born on November 18, 1833. At the time of the 1860 census, Alvan was employed as a bricklayer in Smyrna, though his major occupation soon evolved to making brick and tile. With the financial backing of A.N. Bell, Alvan started this business in about 1863. Its location was on the north side of Duck Creek in sight of the eventual pottery. (Duck Creek separates Kent and New Castle counties so the brickyard was in New Castle County.) His association with the pottery was short-lived. By the early 1870s, Allen moved to Wilmington. His relocation was affirmed in his obituary published in the *Smyrna Times* on November 27, 1912, five days after his death. In Wilmington, he succeeded Jacob Lewis & Son in a brick making firm in 1872. Some ten years later, Allen began to manufacture brick in Elsmere on the outskirts of Wilmington, and served as president of Alvan Allen Brick Company. At one point in his life, while living in northern Delaware, he served as the sheriff of New Castle County. Allen was 79 years of age at the time of his death. He had married Ellen Bell in Smyrna on November 18, 1856. Ellen, born in Maryland on August 11, 1835, predeceased her husband on December 9, 1906. Both are buried in Saint Peters Cemetery in Smyrna.

A. Naudain Bell's first name was Andrew. Born on April 25, 1825, in Delaware, Bell married Mary Jane Williams in Salem, New Jersey,

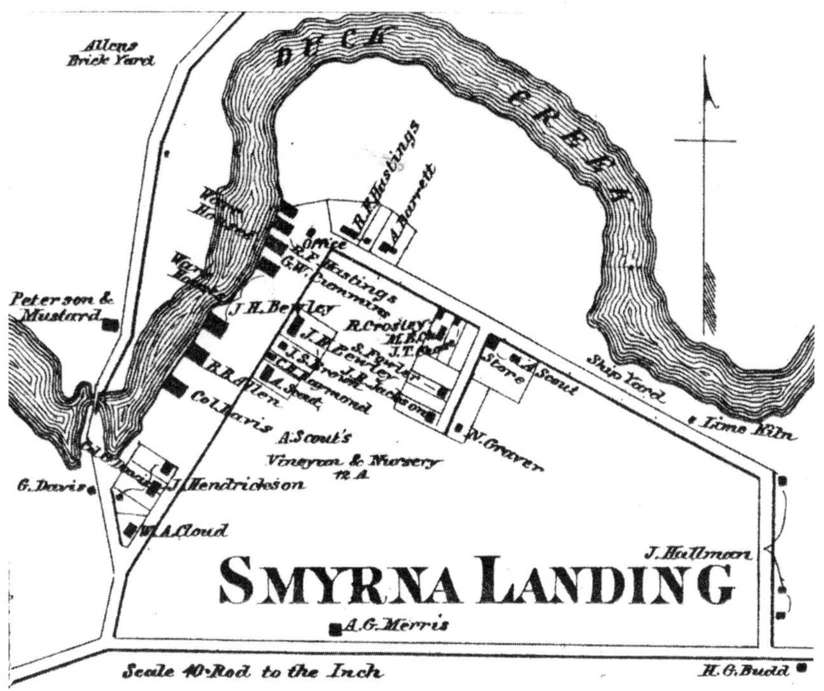

The 1868 Beer's *Atlas of the State of Delaware* shows the location of the Allen and Bell pottery in the town of Smyrna Landing, although it was labeled R. R. Allen. The brickyard was located on the west side of Duck Creek.

on July 1, 1852. Mary Jane was about six years older than her husband and outlived him by four years. She was 86 when her husband died on February 16, 1905. Both are buried in Salem. Naudain and his wife spent most if not all of their lives in Salem, where he operated a wood working mill on Griffith Street. Sashes and doors were primary products. Even in the land deed granting Allen and Bell the granary, **Andrew Naudain Bell** was identified as being of Salem, New Jersey, and when Andrew sold his interest in the property 16 months later, it was again noted that he was of that same New Jersey town. So Bell was a silent partner in this pottery venture with Alvan Allen. But what brought Alvan Allen and Andrew Naudain Bell together in this partnership? Quite likely it was family, since Andrew was the uncle of Ellen, the wife of Alvan.

Soon after Allen and Bell announced their plans for a pottery, they placed an advertisement in the *Smyrna Times* beginning February 26, 1868. In it they offered a variety of typical earthenware—

crocks, basins, flowerpots, jugs, jars and pitchers—at their Delaware Pottery. No indication was given that they had stoneware to offer. Two items that they made special mention of were hanging baskets and garden vases.

Some descriptions of the buildings at the pottery were given in the 1867 *Smyrna Times* article announcing the intended business, but more details are found elsewhere. The owners also had the

EARTHENWARE

MANUFACTURED AND FOR SALE AT THE

DELAWARE POTTERY,

SMYRNA, DELAWARE,

BY

ALLEN & BELL.

HIGH POTS,
CROCKS,
BASINS,
FLAT PANS,
PIE DISHES,
STEW POTS,
FLOWER POTS,
RED PANS.
GLAZED BOWLS & PANS,
JUGS, JARS & PITCHERS,
CHAMBERS, &c.,
SPITTOONS,
PIPE CYLINDERS.

Hanging Baskets and Garden Vases constantly on hand.

Orders promptly attended to,

TERMS CASH.

Send for Wholesale Price List. Feb. 26.

Smyrna Times, February 26, 1868.

property insured by the Kent County Mutual Insurance Company and policy #2804, dated February 21, 1868, covered the following:

Frame two-story building	56 X 24 feet
Two-story new building	24 X 24 feet
Attached mill shed	20 X 20 feet
Clay shed	11 X 24 feet

The frame two-story building was the converted granary.

But less than a year later, partial interest in both the pottery and the tile yard changed hands. Andrew Naudain Bell sold his half-interest to his brother, **William M. Bell** of Smyrna (X 7 1); the transaction occurred on January 30, 1869. The deed for the pottery mentions that the property is now used for the manufacture of earthenware. With the new ownership, the name of the firm remained Allen & Bell, though a new Bell was now "tolling" and toiling. An important piece of ephemera remains from this period of the pottery's history. A Leipsic, Delaware, general store by the name of Kirkley & Son resold earthenware that was manufactured at the Smyrna pottery. In one case, this merchant purchased nearly a hundred pieces of the typical forms of utilitarian pottery used in so many households. The transaction totaled $11.46 and the receipt, dated in April of 1869 and showing the Allen & Bell heading, has survived. Though the price for an individual piece varied from 4 to 21 cents depending on the form, the average per piece price across the entire lot was 13 cents. Much the same story had been found with John Denning, the Milford potter. His average price based on the 1860 manufacturing census was a nearly identical 12 cents.

At the end of 1869, Alvan Allen and William Bell sold the pottery at Smyrna Landing. While Allen relocated to Wilmington, William Bell continued to produce drain tile at the brickyard on the other side of Duck Creek until his retirement in 1884. Meanwhile, he was also employed by the National Bank of Smyrna as a cashier and rose to the chairmanship of that institution according to the 1880 census. Subsequent owners of the brickyard carried on that business until about 1914.

In late 1869, **Reese F. Bell**, also of Smyrna, was the new owner of the pottery near Duck Creek. In the 1870 census, he was identified as a "Manufacturer of Earthenware." Reese had purchased the lot and the buildings on it from Allen and Bell on December 30, 1869 (K 5 462). Reese's father was a brother of Andrew Naudain Bell, one of

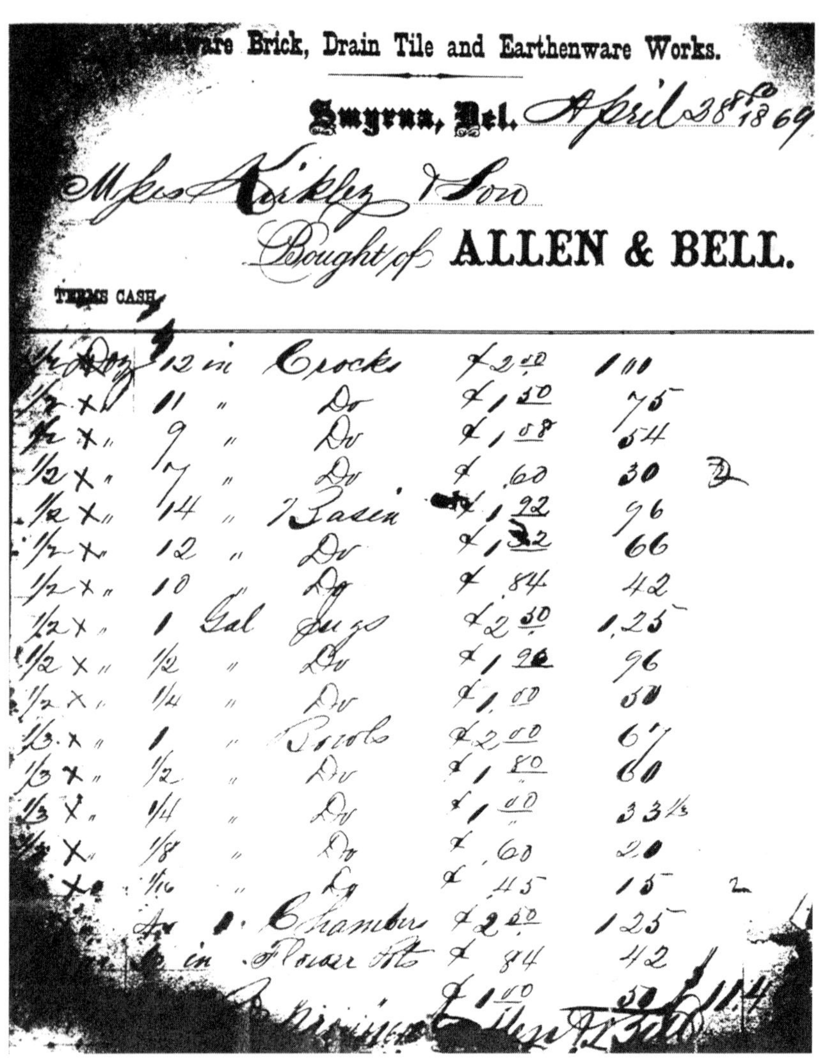

...ware Brick, Drain Tile and Earthenware Works.

Smyrna, Del. April 28th 1869

Messrs Kirkley & Son

Bought of ALLEN & BELL.

TERMS CASH.

1/2 Doz	12 in	Crocks	@ 2.00	1.00
1/2 "	11 "	Do	@ 1.50	75
1/2 "	9 "	Do	@ 1.08	54
1/2 "	7 "	Do	@ .60	30
1/2 "	14 "	Basin	@ 1.92	96
1/2 "	12 "	Do	@ 1.32	66
1/2 "	10 "	Do	@ .84	42
1/2 "	1 Gal	Jugs	@ 2.50	1.25
1/2 "	1/2 "	Do	@ 1.92	96
1/2 "	1/4 "	Do	@ 1.00	50
1/3 "	1 "	Bowls	@ 2.00	67
1/3 "	1/2 "	Do	@ 1.80	60
1/3 "	1/4 "	Do	@ 1.00	33 1/3
1/3 "	1/8 "	Do	@ .60	20
1/3 "	1/16 "	Do	@ .45	15
		Chamber	@ 2.50	1.25
	in	Flower Pots	@ .84	42

Allen and Bell sold a variety of pottery to Kirkley and Son, a general merchant in Leipsic, Delaware, on April 28, 1869. *Courtesy of E.D. Bryan, MD.*

the partners who had established the pottery. In the 1870 population census, Reese is shown as 24 years old and apparently unmarried since he was living in the household of Susan Bell, the widow of another one of his uncles.

The Census of Manufactures for 1870 reported that Reese Bell produced $4,000 of "all kinds of stone and earthenware." It's quite unlikely, however, that this statistic and the others reported with it refer to the operation solely under Reese's ownership. Having purchased the pottery at the end of 1869 and coupled with the norm that this census measured manufacturing activity for the previous 12 months, a portion of the production must have been based on Alvan Allen's and William M. Bell's stewardship during 1869. Regardless, the reported revenues and the consumption of 200 tons of clay and 80 cords of fire wood placed the Smyrna Landing pottery about 80 percent as active as William Hare in Wilmington and several times the size of John Denning at Milford during the same period of time. Reese reported that three males on average were employed at his pottery and one finds Enoch M. Donophan and members of the Trapnell family listed in the 1870 census for Smyrna Landing with the notation "Works in pottery." Donophan is believed to be **Enoch W. Donovan** since a 36 year old farmer by this name is found in the 1880 census and living in Georgetown Hundred, Delaware. So, it is likely Enoch never advanced to a journeyman potter but rather worked as a laborer during the pottery's short existence. As for the Trapnells, more will be said about them later.

The year 1870 was not a good one for Reese and, like his predecessors, his proprietorship of the pottery at Smyrna Landing was quite brief. First, the *Smyrna Times* reported in June 29, 1870, that Reese F. Bell's back was badly hurt when he was thrown from his wagon. Though brought home in an insensible condition, the article went on to say that he was recovering. Bell was hauling a load of maple wood for firing his kiln when the wagon suddenly jolted in a rut. The pottery owner was thrown from the wagon and some of its load fell on him. The accident occurred on the Kenton Road about nine miles from Smyrna. If that wasn't enough, the same newspaper reported in late October that a fire had occurred at Bell's pottery at the landing. On that night, "the pottery building" was completely consumed before any help arrived. The account suggested that the fire may have been set. The buildings, stock and fixtures were valued at about $6,000; insurance coverage was $3,600. These events within four months of each other must have led to the demise of the pottery since no evidence has been found to suggest that Bell or anyone else rebuilt the factory and resumed the firing of clay wares. However, Reese and his wife did retain ownership of the lot until 1888 (B 7 257), though what use was made of the property during those years is unknown. As it turns out, this was not the first fire which caused heavy damage to a Smyrna Landing business engaged in operating a kiln. On March 24, 1866, the *Delaware Gazette* reported that the tile yard of Alvan Allen

FIRE – On Friday night last, about half past 11, the pottery building at the Landing, owned by Mr. Reese F. Bell, was discovered to be on fire, and was entirely consumed before assistance could be rendered. The little engine "Smyrna" was pulled down by three or four thoughtful citizens, by which with the aid of buckets, the large granary and coal pile of Mr. J. H. Bewley were saved. The pottery was fired, it is generallybelieved, as there had been no fire about the building for a number of days, but whether accidentally or intentionally, of course is not known. The property was valued before the fire at from $4,000 to $5,000. It was insured for $2,400 and the stock and fixtures for $1,200, making a total of $3,600. The stock Mr. Bell valued at $1,600. Much sympathy is express(ed) for the young man, he having recently started in business. On Saturday night his smoke house was entered and robbed of meat, lard, butter, &c., to the value of eight or ten dollars.

Smyrna Times, October 26, 1870

was destroyed by a fire of unknown origin early Saturday morning. Loss was estimated at $1,200 to $1,600.

That this pottery produced stoneware was mentioned in an early advertisement and again in the 1870 manufacturing statistics. A survey of the site by E.D. Bryan, MD, and others in 1991 confirmed this likelihood since numerous fragments of this type of pottery were found.

Three members of the Trapnell family spent part of their potting years working at Smyrna Landing, Delaware, and, as we will see, none was adverse to relocation. George W. and his son, George F., appear together in the 1870 census for Delaware, where the occupations of both were noted as "Works in pottery." Shown with the same occupation was another son, John, who resided with a farmer by the name of Aaron Morris. Undoubtedly, they were employed by Alvan Allen and the Bells—Andrew, William and Reese. The Trapnells probably arrived at Smyrna about the time Allen and Bell started their pottery in October of 1867, though they may have been employed at the brick and tile yard there for a short time previously. Both Trapnell sons were Maryland volunteers during the Civil War, which places them in that state earlier in the 1860s.

Born in Maryland around 1808, **George W. Trapnell**, potter, is found in the *Baltimore Directory* in 1837 living at 82 Conway Street and again in 1840, though his address had changed. In the same year, he is also listed as a head of household in the census for Baltimore. Though absent from the directory until its publication for 1849-50, George was in the city for at least part of the intervening years. John Pearce's research of the Perine Pottery in early Baltimore found that Trapnell was employed there in 1846 when the family business was operated by Maulden Perine. In the listing of George Trapnell in the *Baltimore Directory* for 1850 and 1851, Mary Ann, his wife, was also named and identified as a confectioner. She may have operated a business out of their home. After 1855-56, one no longer finds the name of a Trapnell in the directory.

In 1860 George W. appears in the census of Cecil County, Maryland, as a head of household in the Sixth Election District. His age was then given as 53. Living at home was his 26-year-old son, **George Trapnell**, potter, and a 13-year-old son, **John Trapnell**. The Trapnells probably worked for John K. Morrison, one of two potters listed in the Census of Manufactures for Cecil County in 1860. Of the two, Morrison was the only one located in the same election district as the Trapnells. He reported producing $3,000 in stone and earthenware with the aid of three employees. A few years earlier, tax records placed the Trapnells in North East where they may have briefly potted in J.B. Magee's shop. The Trapnells remained in Maryland until sometime after the Civil War. That conclusion is reached after reviewing the applications for a military pension which each of George's two sons applied for near the end of the nineteenth century. Both had served in Maryland regiments and were eventually granted disability payments. Documents of the Department of the Interior's Bureau of Pensions provide some interesting information regarding the lives and statures of these two potters:

George F. Trapnell: Claim 799.409

Service:	Company G of the 10th Maryland Volunteer Infantry from July 10, 1863 to January 29, 1864 Company K of the 7th Regiment of Maryland Volunteers from February 29, 1864 to June 21, 1865
Born:	January 5, 1835 at Baltimore, Maryland
Married:	October 30, 1872 to Rebecca P. Carter at St. Judes Church in Philadelphia
Died:	March 9, 1911
Resident:	South Chester, Pennsylvania
Occupation:	Potter
Height:	5'4.5"
Weight:	135 lbs.

John G. Trapnell: Claim 1388.258

Service:	Company A of the 11th Regiment of Maryland Volunteer Infantry from May 26, 1864 to October 1, 1864 Company G of the 13th Regiment of Maryland Infantry from March 3, 1865 to May 29, 1865

Born: February 21, 1845 at Baltimore, Maryland
Married: June 29, 1884 to Martha Rachel Calhoun at Upper Chichester Township, Pennsylvania by Justice of the Peace
Died: September 12, 1914
Resident: Chester, Pennsylvania
Occupation: Potter
Height: 5′5″
Weight: 126 lbs.

The fire and demise of the pottery at Smyrna Landing was probably the force that caused the Trapnells to relocate once again, though for a time they may have found work with Alvan Allen, who continued to manufacture bricks and drain tiles at the nearby brickyard. In any event, before 1880, George F. Trapnell, the son, had taken on a pottery of his own in the borough of South Chester, Delaware County, Pennsylvania. Listed in the 1880 census there as a "Poterer," the younger George had purchased a lot with a two-story frame building and two brick kilns at the corner of Hayes and Front streets for $800 from Canby S. Smith on April 4, 1877 (K 4 497). But George soon ran into financial difficulties. On January 23, 1880, the property was acquired by Walker J. Hoopes for $980 at a sale held by John J. Rowland, sheriff. Trapnell had defaulted and the sheriff was commanded to take this action to satisfy a debt of $1,130.48. It's somewhat surprising. Based on the number of hands he employed, one would think that George had a reasonably active business. Working in the pottery along with the Trapnells were two boarders, James Esbin and Thomas Hawley, whom the census designated as "Works in pottery." Also recall that George F. Ziegler most likely worked for Trapnell for a short time. He was the son of George Ziegler, the Wilmington potter, who worked the manufactory at Orange and Water streets for a number of years.

George Trapnell's potting days, however, did not end with the loss of the deed. He was still listed in the *Chester City Directory* in 1885-86 as proprietor of the Chester Pottery located at Hayes and Front streets. Presumably, he was then leasing the property. Five years earlier, three Trapnells—G. F. Trapnell, John G. Trapnell and George Trapnell—are found in that publication. All were identified as potters and each was residing at a different address. By the mid-1880s, however, the senior George was no longer listed.

Though George F. ran into financial difficulties in 1880 and applied for a disability pension in 1890, he was most assuredly still operating his pottery at the time of his death. Appraisers filed an inventory of his estate in Delaware County, Pennsylvania, on March 22, 1911. This listing of goods and chattels included not only a clay mill, scales and three lathes, but over 2,500 flower pots of various sizes and about 1,000 stove pipes four to twelve inches in diameter. Above all, some flower pots and 23 dozen pigeon nests were still found "in kiln" suggesting that George had recently completed a burn. Though not identified as such, presumably these ceramics were earthenware. Not surprising, only a few chamber pots, pipkins and pans were in the inventory. By late in the nineteenth century, the market had essentially disappeared for kitchen and dining earthenware produced by the local potter.

Chapter VIII

More About Delaware Potters

Eight

Several potters, whose mention in earlier chapters was brief, deserve wider coverage. Most were the masters and journeymen who worked their trade while employed by factory owners and proprietors. In some cases though, these craftsmen went on to operate their own establishments beyond the borders of Delaware, and one finds special connections with the state of New Jersey. The first part of this chapter treats several potters in alphabetical order while the second part concentrates on those with ties to the Garden State.

John Bannard, identified as a potter in a 1799 deed, acquired real estate on Front Street near West Street for £25. A width of 20 feet was typical of residential properties so this location must have been his home rather than his workplace. In 1813, he and his wife, Jane, sold it for $400. Meanwhile in 1811, John purchased a similar property facing Second Street for $850 (S 3 561). Apparently the family moved there since the 1814 *Wilmington Directory* lists John Bannard, potter, residing at 12 E. Second Street. Throughout this period, he more than likely worked for John Jones, owner of the Water Street pottery. At least he knew the potter since John Bannard paid $23 in cash to Jones' estate, though no reason for the payment was logged. Bannard's will (NCC-S-1-87) was executed in 1824, the year before he died. In it he named Jane as his executrix. John was buried in Old Swedes Cemetery in Wilmington and, according to records there, was born in 1766. *The Delaware Gazette* of January 7, 1842, contained Jane's obituary. She died on January 1, at age 71 after a short illness.

Samuel Bradford first shows up as a potter in the *Wilmington Directory* of 1862-63. His name appears in several subsequent issues until the very early 1880s. In the 1870 census, his age was given as 54. Married to Lusanna, the Bradfords reported five sons ranging in ages from 14 to 23. The first, third and fourth, like their father, were born in Pennsylvania; the second, like his mother, in Maryland; and the fifth in Delaware. Analysis of these ages suggests the family came to Delaware in about 1855. In his book, Arthur James includes a Samuel Bradford in his checklist of potters in Chester County, Pennsylvania. There the potter worked in East Nottingham Township at the Mount Jordan pottery operated by John P. M. Grier. James lists Bradford as employed there in 1850-52, though he points out that these dates are not all rigorously inclusive. Based on the ages of his sons in the Delaware census data, one can argue that Bradford toiled in Chester County from the mid-1840s even though his wife and one son were born in Maryland. Pennsylvania's East Nottingham Township borders Maryland and the Mount Jordan pottery was no more than three miles from the state line. Less certain is where Samuel Bradford worked when he came to Wilmington, though there is a rationale that supports William Hare as his employer. The Grier pottery produced both earthenware and stoneware during Samuel's time there, and some quite unusual stoneware at that. The mid-1850s was the time when Hare started ramping up his production of stoneware preserve jars. So, experience in the use of stoneware clays and the firing of wares at higher temperatures may have been Bradford's ticket to a lengthy career on French Street.

Moses Bryan(t) of Wilmington is identified as a potter in a 1782 land record found in the collection of the Historical Society of Delaware. That year, he and his wife, Mary, granted a parcel twenty feet in width to William P. Wright, a "perukemaker" (wig maker), for £75.0.0. The property was located on the west side of King Street between Third and High (Fourth) streets. Presumably it had been the family residence. Nothing suggests that Moses operated his own ceramic manufactory. The potter appears in the reconstructed census for 1782 but is not listed in 1790.

Information found in records at the Friends Historical Library of Swarthmore College sheds more light on the life of Moses, the potter. He was born in 1751 in Chester County, Pennsylvania, the son of Thomas and Mary Shaw Bryant. Based on a certificate received for him from the New Garden Monthly Meeting, he moved to Wilmington some time in 1769. Moses married Mary Ogden in Philadelphia on May 11, 1775. Mary and he resided in Wilmington until soon after they sold their King Street property. In September of 1784, they and their four children were granted a certificate to the Philadelphia Monthly Meeting, southern district. Moses died in June of 1788 and Mary passed away in the same month, five years later. Both were buried in Philadelphia.

Moses was 18 years old when he left Pennsylvania for Wilmington. According to a genealogy of the Thomas Bryant family compiled by Miriam L. Luke, he learned the pottery trade in this Delaware city. A year earlier, a brother had preceded him to Wilmington to learn tanning. The brothers were probably drawn to Wilmington since it was closer to home than Philadelphia. New Garden Township borders Delaware. Also, if becoming a potter was on his mind, Arthur James lists no active potteries in this or surrounding townships in Pennsylvania in the late 1760s. In Wilmington, the young man must have apprenticed under Mathew Crips or John Andrews. Crips may seem like the more logical choice since his pottery was a highly active one, but Andrews was a Quaker, and that may have influenced Moses. In either case, he stayed on in the city as a journeyman potter for several years. It is likely his move to Philadelphia about 1784 was prompted by family considerations. His widowed mother and some of his siblings had already come together there.

Charles F. Decker (Dacker, Deiker) came to Wilmington from Philadelphia where he had worked as a potter after immigrating to America from Germany. Eventually Decker became well-known in Tennessee. There he operated his own stoneware manufactory for a number of years. The Tennessee State Museum holds a collection of his wares. The story of Decker's life before and after his stay in Wilmington has been assembled by Carole C. Wahler, and a summary of it can be viewed on her web site at www.cwahlerantiques.com. Thus, the discussion here will be limited to an attempt to understand the segment of Charles' life that was spent in Delaware.

Born in Baden, Germany, Charles came to this county probably about 1848 through the port of Philadelphia. After working as a potter in that city, substantial evidence points to Decker's relocation to Wilmington by 1859. He is listed in the *Wilmington Directory* for 1859-60 as a potter. And the death register (1847-1879) of the Bureau of Vital Statistics, City of Wilmington, shows that Charles' first wife succumbed to tuberculosis in October of 1859. In addition, the 1860 census lists a one-year-old son, William Decker, with Delaware as his birthplace. But as we will see, Decker's stay was brief and he was back in Philadelphia by 1862 with his second wife, Sophia Hinck Decker. It was not until near the end of the decade that he finally planted firm roots in Tennessee, though the move there was interrupted by a short stop in southern Virginia.

Sophia Hinck (Hink, Hinch) and her first husband, Henry, were also German immigrants. In the 1850 census the family lived in the North Mulberry section of Philadelphia. Henry Hink was listed as a German-born confectioner. By 1857, the Hincks were in Wilmington where Henry purchased a property on Second Street between French and Walnut streets (Z 6 205). Henry's death at age 45 was reported in the *Delaware Gazette* on September 30, 1859, six days after a liver disease ended his life. The newspaper also added that his life had been insured for $1,000, a sum that would provide a great advantage to his family. Henry's death preceded Catherine's, Charles' first wife, by less than a month.

In October of 1860, the Hinck property on Second Street was auctioned off at the direction of the Orphan's Court in order to settle Henry's estate. Interestingly, Charles Decker was the successful bidder (N 7 46) and he settled on the property on February 18, 1861. The lot held a 3-story brick building. Most likely, Charles and Sophia married soon after this real estate transaction. A Wilmington birth record shows they had a son on June 27, 1862. They must have named him Frederick since a teen by that name is later listed in the Tennessee census for 1880 under the Decker family. There he was shown as 17 years old; the young man's birthplace was recorded as Delaware. Comparison of dates suggests that his birth was just before the Deckers moved to Philadelphia. A land indenture (Q 7 214), dated September 25, 1862, named Charles and Sophia as grantors of the Second Street property in which they were identified as already residing in Philadelphia.

Two potteries were operating in Wilmington during Decker's four-year stay. William Hare was well established and busily turning out stoneware and earthenware on French Street. Meanwhile, German immigrants—John Stüber followed by George Ziegler and Albert Neumayer—were producing earthenware on a smaller scale at the corner of Orange and Water streets. While a case can be made for either pottery, it is more likely Decker was employed by Hare. William was not adverse to German potters; in fact, Neumayer had worked for him before going into partnership with Ziegler. And Hare was employing twice the number of workers and turning out numerous kilns of stoneware. Decker's primary interest was in this more highly fired, vitrified ceramic as the products of his Tennessee pottery attest. That Charles knew of Hare's pottery is surely the case. The Hinck's property on Second Street was just around the corner from it.

So with a segment of his life molded in Delaware, the questions remain—why did he come to Wilmington in the first place and then why, after seemingly putting down roots with the purchase of the property on Second Street, did he and Sophia sell it within a year and a half to return again to Philadelphia? In response to the first one, according to family tradition, Decker started his own pottery in Philadelphia a year or two before his move to Delaware. Quite possibly financial problems beset him during the widespread recession of 1857. That downturn was brought on by reduced economic activity and decreased product demand. Wilmington may have stood out to Decker as a reasonably nearby alternative to Philadelphia that included a community of German immigrants, some of whom may have even been close friends. Needing employment, Charles knew that the Hare pottery was surviving during the soft economy turning out stoneware preserve jars by the thousands. The second is no easier to answer with certainty. However, maybe Charles and Sophia needed a change from an era that had not been kind to them. Not only did each mourn a spouse but Sophia's two-year-old daughter, Elizabeth, died two months before Henry. One also has to believe that Charles' dream was to own his own pottery and he may not have seen any opportunity for that to occur in Wilmington. The market was already well supplied by existing factories in the city and several others in the surrounding region.

Two of Charles Decker's sons also became potters, although they did not work in Delaware. F**rederick Decker**, born in Delaware in 1862, was a son of Charles Decker and his second wife, Sophia Hinck Decker. Though listed in the 1880 Tennessee census as a farmer, he later worked at his father's pottery in eastern Tennessee according to the writings of Samuel D. Smith and Stephen T. Rogers in *Survey of Historic Pottery Making in Tennessee*. **William Decker** was a son of Charles Decker and his first wife, Catherine Decker. According to the census records of 1880 for Tennessee, the Delaware-born William was 21 years old by then and working in a pottery, most assuredly his father's.

Information regarding **Andrew Kime** is very limited. He is identified in the 1785 tax assessment for Christiana Hundred (Wilmington) as a potter. Andrew is also found in the 1782 census for

Delaware as over the age of 18, along with one woman in the same age category, presumably his wife. No children were recorded at the time. Kime was not found in any other census, including the reconstructed one for Delaware in 1790. His most likely employer would have been Mathew Crips.

The name **John Justis** (Justice) appears on many occasions in eighteenth century local records and writings, but recall that Mathew Crips had commercial transactions with a potter, John Justice, of Philadelphia. Is there any connection? The 1782 and 1785 tax rolls for New Castle County include a John Justis who, based on his assessment, was quite wealthy. He was referred to as a yeoman in several deeds which described large tracts of land. In the late 1780s, Crips recorded sales of earthenware to John Justice, yeoman. Thomas Scharf noted that John Justice died in 1805 at age 55 and his wife, Elizabeth, preceded him in 1795 at age 45. Jack Stidham wrote that John Justice, born in 1750, married Elizabeth Stedham who was born in 1756. (Coincidently, she had the same name as Mathew Crips' wife and they were probably cousins.) So it is quite apparent that this long time New Castle County resident was a yeoman-farmer. However, the same 1782 record shows a second John Justice; he was assessed for his father's estate. Three years later, the county taxed "John Justis, Pot. Est." These assessments were much less than for the yeoman and coincidentally, quite similar to those of John Jones, the young Wilmington potter. And though found in the tax lists, Justice is not listed in the census as residing in Delaware. So it is quite plausible that this John Justice, the potter, was raised in Delaware, trained under Crips and moved to Philadelphia. Then after opening his own establishment in Philadelphia, John and Mathew continued their relationship through the business dealings recorded in Crips' ledger and discussed in Chapter II.

Andrew Maxfield is an enigma. As pointed out in Chapter V, a hand-transcribed copy of an 1832 indenture clearly named him as the master who agreed to apprentice William "Hair." Assuredly, this apprentice was the William Hare of French Street who became the prolific nineteenth century Delaware potter, so it is important to understand what role Maxfield had in Delaware pottery making. However, after searching numerous records, including census data, land deeds, newspapers, birth and death notices and tax assessments, his name has only surfaced one time—in the copied apprentice indenture. The lack of other findings support the conclusion offered in

Chapter V: Andrew Maxfield was really Andrew Maxwell and he was only created through a clerical error made in preparing a handwritten copy of the Maxwell—"Hair" apprenticeship indenture. The original document was signed by Andrew Maxwell.

Andrew Maxwell was named as a head of household in the 1830 population census. Married with a son under five years of age, Andrew is listed as 20-29 years old then. But he was not included in either the prior or next decennial census. His life was short. Andrew died by 1835, as evidenced by an administrative memo upon his estate (T-1-198) filed that year in New Castle County. And on December 29, 1835, the estate's administrator published a notice in the *Delaware State Journal* seeking to settle claims against him. That Maxwell was a potter is borne out by the fact that he agreed to serve as a master potter in 1833 for William Henry Logan, an apprentice under Delaware's indenture program. Also recall it has been argued that Maxwell served as William Hare's master under an apprentice agreement executed in 1832. Andrew likely worked at John Jones' pottery earlier in life based on the fact that he owed $16.66 in rent to Jones' estate. Some time after the death of Jones, Maxwell probably moved on to the recently established pottery on French Street where he would have been working for Branch Green and Thomas Hayhurst when he agreed to apprentice Hare and Logan.

NOTICE.

ALL persons indebted to the Estate of Andrew Maxwell, late of the city of Wilmington decd. are requested to make payment to the subscriber, and all those having claims against said estate will present them legally attested for settlement.

FRED'K LEONARD, Adm'r.

Delaware State Journal, December 29, 1835

Identified as a potter in the 1850 census, **Benjamin McShone** was shown as boarding at the William Hare residence in Wilmington at the time. More than likely, he worked for Hare. In the mid-1840s, annual tax assessments for the city of Wilmington were published in the *Delaware Gazette* and, in some cases, the individual's occupation was provided. A potter, B.B. Mershon, was cited for tax due for 1846. Recognizing the significant number of misspellings one encounters in the nineteenth century, it is quite possible that Benjamin McShone and B. B. Mershon are representations of the same person.

Samuel Preston Moore is another individual who, according to early writings, operated a pottery near the Christina River in Wilmington. Elizabeth Montgomery in her book of 1851 penned the following:

> *Near the wharf was a shipyard of note for years. In later times, Enoch Moore built vessels there. In this neighborhood was an old pottery carried for a time by Samuel Preston Moore but for many years by John Jones, a very worthy member of Friends Society.*

The pottery was the one located on Water Street at its intersection with Orange Street. Pondering Montgomery's writings and coupling them with information regarding Jones and the riverfront shipyard of the Moore family, Samuel's connection with the pottery most likely occurred very soon after Jones' death in early 1825. The 1814 *Wilmington Directory* lists an Enoch Moore, shipwright, at Orange Street below Front Street. While he died in 1822 prior to Jones' death, another Enoch Moore, born in 1803, was also engaged in shipbuilding. So Montgomery may have been referring to this second Enoch. But does searching out Samuel Moore help understand Montgomery's reference? One finds numerous Wilmington references to a Samuel P. Moore, Samuel Preston Moore and S. P. Moore in the period covering 1787 to 1826. Presumably, they are one and the same person. One of these names appears in each of the 1787 and 1816-17 tax assessments for Christiana Hundred and Wilmington, respectively. Samuel P. is found in the 1790 reconstructed census for Delaware. A few years later, Samuel P. touted himself as a candidate for sheriff in an advertisement placed in the *Delaware & Eastern Shore Advertiser* on June 28, 1794, a position to which he was eventually elected. According to Thomas Scharf's *History of Delaware*, Samuel P. Moore was a commissioner of the Christiana Ferry from 1800 to 1805. Samuel Preston Moore, farmer, and his wife, Susannah, are named in an 1802 land indenture. Some years later, the *Delaware Gazette* reported the death of Samuel Moore in its issue for July 18, 1826. If all of these references are of the same person, then what plausible scenario explains Montgomery's connection of Samuel Preston Moore to John Jones' pottery? Sometime in early 1825, Moore, though not a potter himself, may have leased the pottery from the Jones' heirs and operated it for a year or so until his own death.

But Susan Myers mentions a potter by the name of Samuel Moore who worked in Philadelphia circa 1825 to 1836. However, she did not attach a middle name or initial to him. He seems to be an unlikely candidate. Around 1836 and beyond, the old pottery of Johns Jones was under lease to others. Furthermore, Jones died in 1825 and had been operating his establishment until then. Unless the years Susan connected Moore with Philadelphia were not quite accurate, it is unlikely this Samuel Moore "carried on at the old pottery." Future research, however, may provide a different account.

Abraham Ritchie was a potter on the move, as several references regarding him attest. An A. Ritchie was first noted as a recipient of monies during the settlement of John Jones' estate in 1826. Three payments totaled $40; a fourth was listed but the amount of the disbursement is impossible to decipher with certainty. Ritchie may have helped operate the pottery on Water Street in Wilmington for the Jones' family after John's death. Or he may have been a master potter working for Samuel Preston Moore, if Moore was a tenant of the site after Jones died. But by 1830, Ritchie was listed in the population census for Smyrna, Kent County, Delaware. E.D. Bryan, MD, of Dover, who researched the Green family potteries at Smyrna, found that Ritchie managed the later of the two factories on Main Street beginning soon after the death of Daniel Green in 1826. Abraham continued in that capacity until the very late 1830s. Ritchie's relocation to Smyrna may have been prompted through a family connection since Sarah Jones, John's wife, was a first cousin of Daniel Green's father. By the time of the 1840 census, Ritchie had moved to the Cedar Ward of Philadelphia where he was counted as 40 to 49 years old. In that census, one family member was designated as employed in manufacturing. Presumably that was the potter formerly of Smyrna and then exercising his craft in Philadelphia since Abraham Ritchie can be found in that city's directory in 1843 to 1846. In each case, he was identified as a potter. Part of this time he resided on Atherton Street within a few blocks of the Journeymen's Pottery, his probable place of employment. Ritchie's fate by 1850 is unknown since he is not listed in the census records of Pennsylvania, Delaware or New Jersey.

In the discussion of the French Street pottery, it was mentioned that **Samuel Stretch**, the 19-year-old son of William, was identified as a potter in the 1850 Pennsylvania census. Presumably he learned his craft at the Philadelphia County pottery where his father worked during the 1840s. Though Samuel probably never turned a pot in Delaware, the state was his birthplace and he definitely worked nearby. Some time during the 1850s, he moved from Philadelphia to Maryland where he appears in the 1860 census for the town of North East in Cecil County. This county borders both New Castle County, Delaware, and Chester County, Pennsylvania. Though entered in the census as S. C. Streeh, it is undoubtedly Samuel Stretch since the age of 29 is consistent with an earlier census and the place of birth was recorded as Delaware. It is also noteworthy that his occupation was given as "stone potter," hinting that he specialized in stoneware. Recall it was suggested in Chapter IV that Branch Green brought stoneware manufacturing to Delaware, and he did so in partnership with Samuel's father on French Street in Wilmington. In Maryland, Samuel probably worked for J.B. Magee who, according to the Census of Manufactures for 1860, was located in North East. The entry lists Magee's business as a "stone pottery" and its product as "stoneware," leading one to connect Stretch with this factory. But potteries close and potters move on and that is apparently what happened to Samuel within a decade. John Magee abandoned his operation in 1867 surely prompting Stretch to seek other employment. Arthur James enumerated Samuel C. Stretch on his list of potters and connected him with Ralph J. Grier, the operator of the Mount Jordan Pottery, from about 1871-1873. Actually, the potter probably arrived in the late 1860s and remained there until 1875 since, in that year, Samuel C. "Strech" purchased a building and lot on East Linden Street in Kennett Square, Pennsylvania (E 11 157). Per this deed, Samuel was residing in Oxford at the time, a town within a few miles of the Mount Jordan Pottery. Arthur James points to Samuel Stretch in Kennett Square in 1880. James must have drawn on the 1880 census for placing the 50-year-old Samuel there at that point in time. Stretch apparently remained in Kennett Square since the 1896 death record of his wife, Elizabeth, notes that she died in that borough. There Edwin Brosius owned a pottery at which, according to Arthur James, Samuel made the stoneware, a ceramic that was with him throughout his life.

Spencer Williams is listed as a potter in the 1845 *Wilmington Directory* in the section titled "Colored Inhabitants." He is the only

African American who was identified with a connection to early pottery making in Delaware. His address was given as Sixth Street between West and Pasture streets. He practiced occupations other than potter. By 1853, and in the subsequent directory in 1857, Spencer is found on Orange Street near Eleventh Street, and employed as a waiter. A few years later, the former potter was working as a coachman. These addresses are believed to be his residences since no other information about him or any suggesting he operated his own kiln has been found. In the mid-1840s to early 1850s, William Hare or the proprietors of the pottery at Water and Orange streets were probable employers.

The New Jersey Connection

Some previous chapters provided a historical perspective of two of the main potteries that operated in Wilmington in the nineteenth century. Much about the lives of their owners and operators was incorporated there since it was largely through them that the succession of proprietors was pieced together. But other information came to light in researching this subject that widens the breadth of this story and develops the relationships between some potters. Lest we forget, potters, like many artisans of the 1800s, had sons who adopted their fathers' craft. And some potters were quite transient. The book on New Jersey potters by M. Lelyn Branin serves as a key aid in connecting Delaware potters with segments of their lives that occurred on the other side of the Delaware River. Besides the discussion that follows, a road map has been included to show these associations in a more diagrammatical fashion.

Nathan Dalbey was active at Water and Orange streets in Wilmington and had a son about 14 years old in 1840. Branin mentions a **Barton Dalbey** (Dolby) pointing out that he was born in Wilmington, Delaware, and worked as a potter around 1850 in Bordentown, New Jersey. He died there at the age of 24 in 1852. Surely Barton learned to work clay at his father's pottery and probably left for South Amboy Township as the failure of his father's business was announced in 1848.

As mentioned earlier, **Henry Lambdin (Lambden)** was an apprentice under Nathan Dalbey beginning in 1847 and is shown boarding with Richard Lowe per the 1850 census. About that time, he turned 21 years of age. Lowe was the potter who took over Nathan's operation in conjunction with John Stüber in 1848, so it is quite likely that the young Henry finished out his apprenticeship under Lowe.

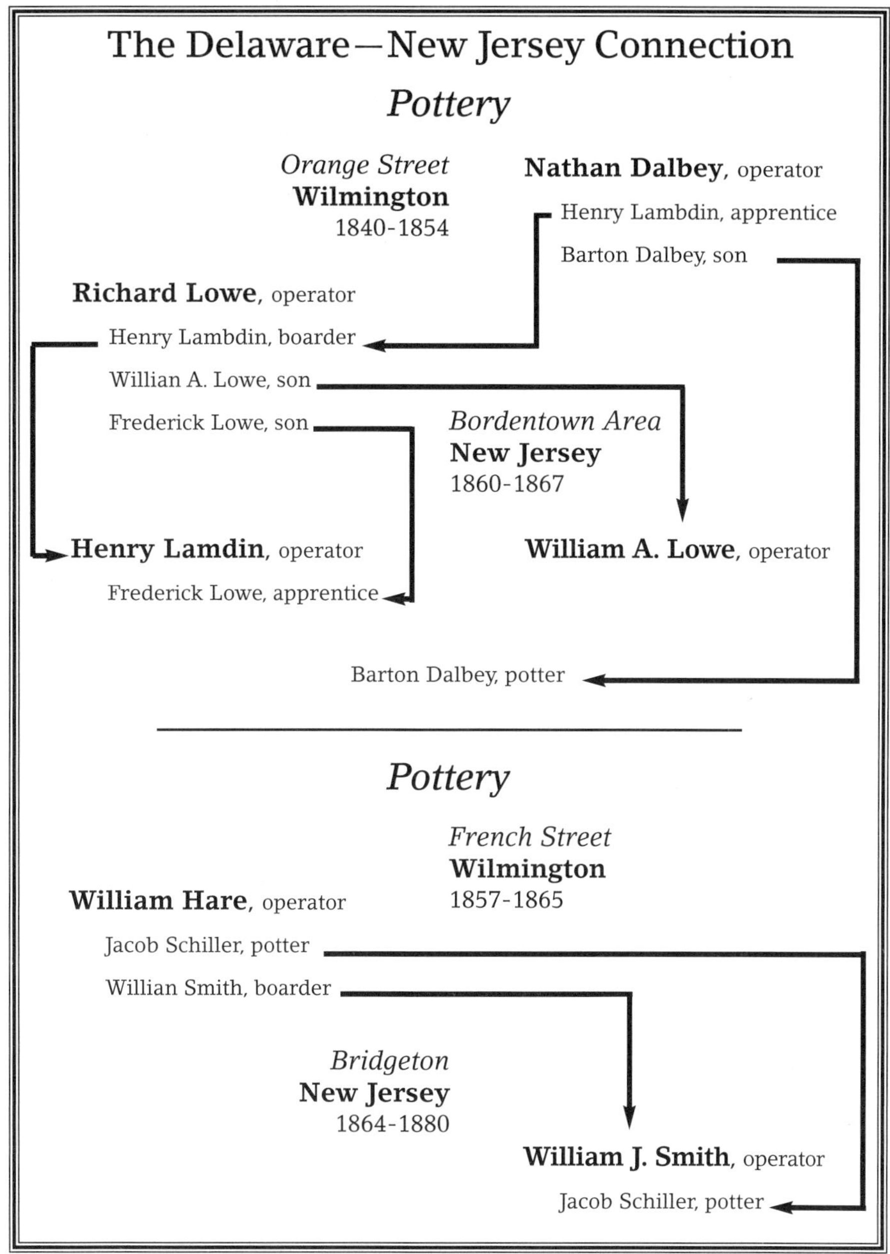

A number of potters, who were either born or practiced their craft in Delaware, also owned or worked potteries in New Jersey. All were associated in some way with one of two locations in Wilmington—French Street or the corner of Water and Orange streets.

Lambdin was born in Delaware on Christmas Day in 1829. Henry was a minor at the time of his indenture and was bound to Dalbey by his father, John S. Lambdin. According to Thomas Scharf, John Lambdin was at one time the postmaster in Smyrna.

Lelyn Branin mentions a Henry Lambdin in his book. Though some facts—born in Maryland in 1830 or 1831—do not line up perfectly, it is very likely they are the same person. In 1863, Henry purchased a pottery in Bordentown Township, New Jersey, and worked it until 1867 when he realized a 50 percent profit from its sale. Branin refers to this site as the new Thorn pottery on the north side of the Bordentown—Chesterfield Road. In fact, Lambdin arrived in New Jersey before 1860 when he is listed as head of a Bordentown household in the census. At the time, Henry and his wife, Mary Elizabeth, had a daughter; she was recorded as two years old and born in New Jersey.

But there is more to say about the connections of the Lowes with New Jersey. Branin writes that a Frederick Lew (or Low) served an apprenticeship under Henry Lambdin in 1860. Indeed, that year's decennial census shows Frederick Low boarding with Lambdin and learning potting. Richard Lowe had a son, Frederick, who at the time of the 1850 census was about 10 years old. So, **Frederick Lowe** apparently left Delaware some time after his father's death in 1854 and learned much or all of his potting skills under Lambdin, a potter who, during his own apprenticeship, had lived under the same roof with Frederick in Wilmington.

It appears that another son of Richard Lowe became active in New Jersey following the death of his father. Branin suggests that a **William A. Lowe**, who acquired the old Thorn pottery on the south side of the Bordentown—Chesterfield Road in the 1860s, may have been Richard's son. The author mentions that William was born around 1836 in New Jersey. The Delaware census of 1850 provides evidence to support Branin's suggested relationship of the two Lowes. Indeed, Richard listed a 14-year-old son, William, and cited his birthplace as New Jersey. So William Lowe, like his brother Frederick, grew up knowing his father's boarder, Henry Lambdin. And their paths crossed again since William Lowe and Lambdin were likely competitors for a few years operating the Thorn potteries on opposite sides of the Bordentown—Chesterfield Road.

The name **Jacob Schiller** was first uncovered in the 1857 *Wilmington Directory* as a potter who boarded at William Hare's address. Three years later in the decennial census, the 23-year-old Jacob, there spelled Schuler, was still listed under Hare's household. He was definitely employed by the potter since Jacob A. Schiller signed one of Hare's receipts in 1864 for several dozen flowerpots sold to Samuel F. Du Pont. For the period of 1866-68, Schiller was identified as a painter living at 230 King Street in Wilmington. However, the street named in this entry may have been an error. Wilmington had changed the system for property addresses, and Hare's home now had a number of 230, though on French Street. In any event, Jacob is no longer found listed by the time the *Wilmington Directory* was published for 1868-69. Like other potters, he had moved on. But Branin found the same Schiller in the 1880 census working for William J. Smith, the proprietor of a pottery in Bridgeton, New Jersey. That town is across the Delaware River about 30 miles southeast of Wilmington.

So how did Schiller end up in New Jersey? The likely connection was **William J. Smith**, the owner of an operation that became known as the Bridgeton Pottery. Branin goes to some length to detail Smith's life and his pottery on Cohansey Street, and tags his business with a founding date of about 1865. But Schiller was not the only potter shown in the 1857 *Wilmington Directory* as a boarder with William Hare. So was a William Smith. However, his existence in Wilmington was short-lived and by the early 1860s, Smith's name is no longer found in Wilmington. Presumably he had relocated to New Jersey. So Schiller and Smith must have met while boarding and working together on French Street and surely learned much from Hare. When reading Branin's description of Smith's business, one sees similarities with that of his former employer. Both made earthenware and stoneware. Both marked some of their wares. Both not only sold these two types of pottery but also offered products like glassware and other types of ceramics. For these, they were probably acting as resellers.

Chapter IX

In the Business of Making Pottery

Nine

During the period from 1760 to 1890, the population of Wilmington and the entire state increased several fold. In the late eighteenth century, the largest city in Delaware numbered under 3,000 people. Wilmington's residents grew to 10,000 by the mid-nineteenth century and the city's inhabitants exceeded 60,000 as the next century approached. As for the whole state, the population was over 100,000 in 1860. One might then expect the pottery industry to track this expansion in its customer base. But there were a number of other aspects—embargoes, economic downturns, business strategies, the competitive environment and consumer habits—that influenced the longevity and viability of Delaware's potteries. Hopefully a look at these will help to understand their impact during these years and why in the end, this industry went the way of the buggy whip.

Influences of Shipping Lanes and Economic Depressions

Evidence has shown that Mathew Crips, the circa 1760-1798 potter, became quite wealthy. Undoubtedly the Revolutionary War contributed much to his financial success. With the colonies blockaded, imports from Europe became sparse and local craftsmen like Crips filled the void. Once the war ended, the situation began to change, but by that time, Mathew was well-established. Shipping lanes reopened and English manufacturers, among others, returned to supplying America with their output. With the renewed competition from imports in the 1780s, Crips relied on expanding his network of resellers and one can also see from his ledger that he began to broaden his offerings beyond his manufactured earthenware. The potter sold barrels of shad and a variety of fabrics including linen and muslin by the yard and the bolt. Probably he also increased the output of firebricks from his kiln to serve local industry. One might say his business took on some semblance of a general merchant with an emphasis on the manufacture of pottery.

Following the Revolutionary War, Wilmington may have been able to support no more than two potteries. Besides Crips, a second pottery was operating in the city prior to and during the Revolution. But John Andrews died in 1778 and, while the property on which it stood was sold to Isaac Starr a few years later, it is unclear to what extent Starr leased or worked the pot house. In fact, it was not until about 1790 that Starr, the miller, was referred to in a land deed as a potter. That Starr's pottery was not very active may be suggested by the advent of a new pottery on Water Street circa 1783. There John Jones had purchased land at the Christina River and constructed a pot house and kiln. By the turn of the century, Jones may have been the only active pottery operator since Crips had retired to his stately mansion and gardens and Isaac Starr had run into financial difficulties and lost the property.

By about 1808, market forces must have again been favorable for the advent of a new pottery maker in Wilmington. With only John Jones active at Water and Orange streets, Jonathan Beeson announced that he had commenced the potting business. But while the location placed his manufactory at the former site established by John Andrews and then owned by William Robinson, Beeson did not say he was taking over the operation from someone else. That suggests the pottery was idle and that Beeson reenergized it. So what prompted Beeson to enter into competition with Jones? The War of 1812 was only a few years off and Thomas Jefferson curtailed shipping by imposing an embargo on imported goods in 1808. This period then was reminiscent of the 1770s and early '80s when demand for crafted wares had to be supplied locally. Thus, it is likely that Beeson saw an opportunity and capitalized on it during the Embargo, though not for very long since apparently he died in 1813.

But economic and market factors change and by the end of the second decade of the nineteenth century, the world was experiencing an economic crisis. During the Panic of 1819, a money-tightening policy by the country's bank helped fuel a downturn. In addition, potters, for one, were complaining about the flood of imported products which had returned from across the ocean following the end of the war. The Baltimore Census of Manufactures for 1820 tells the story. Responses from ten of the city's potteries were aggregated to produce annual statistics. Though quite wordy, the "General Remarks" under question 14 captured the potters' pleas for relief from "immense quantities" of imported Queensware. In addition, these potters sought protection by the U. S. Congress from state laws which they claimed discouraged manufacture. The plea is shown here in its entirety:

> "Our Manufactures at present are in a languishing condition and the Earthenware in a peculiar manner, for it is substituted by Queensware (of which there has been immense quantities forced into our country) more than stoneware as in the stoneware they neither make dishes or any flat shaped ware, bowls or porringers – and in addition to the injury we the manufacturers of earthenware sustain owing to the vast influx of Queensware. An ordinance of the Corporation of the City passed in 1812 prohibiting the erection of a kiln in the city after that passed under heavy penalty has had a very injurious effect on some of us who have ground located many years before this law was passed for the expressed purpose of erecting an additional kiln, and as we believe it is very unwise to throw anything in the way to discourage Manufacturers, we can but regret that such a policy has been pursued in this instance by our Mayor & City Council. And we may state in a relation to our former state by no restrictions of the corporation when we had less influx of Queensware and that by regular traders of which there are many still remaining in this city, we could make the ware and get a price to afford a profit and brisk sale which with a great deal of labour and strictest attention we could make out to get a support for our families but really the prospect appears very unfavourable at present unless you the Honorable Congress of the United States, the guardians of the public (will) should in your wisdom devise some means to protect our humble yet useful manufacture from decay it may not be presuming too much to say that we are of the opinion that if the general government were to recommend to all subordinate governments to reconsider all laws past calculated to discourage manufacture and if

> they deem it best to repeal them so as to leave no obstacle which ought to be removed out of the way of manufacturers remain looking up to our native country's council for protection we conclude respectfully."

But the situation for Wilmington's potters may not have been as severe as that experienced in other port cities like Baltimore. By 1820, two potteries were located within a few blocks of each other and still operating. John Jones had long been situated on Water Street at the corner of Orange Street and William Hallowell had taken over the earthenware manufactory at the corner of Orange and Third streets. For one thing, the population of Delaware's largest city had nearly doubled since 1794 from about 2,900 to over 5,200. But Jones' pottery may not have been as active by this time since, as was mentioned in Chapter III, he was also operating a brewery. In fact, he had been engaged in the brewing business since before the War of 1812 and may have used this source of income to help cope with the return of clay-based imports from across the Atlantic once shipping lanes reopened. By 1822, economic recovery was underway and, in fact, it was a year later that Hallowell purchased the property at Orange and Third streets which included the pottery he had been leasing.

Quite possibly some of the hardest times felt by Delaware potters occurred in the late 1830s and early 1840s. Soon after the presidency of Andrew Jackson, the county fell into a deep economic recession often referred to as the Panic of 1837. Governmental policies and a change in money supply played a major role in creating this economic downswing. Historians, however, are mixed on the primary cause or causes of the event. By mid-1830, at least two, and most likely three potteries were operating in Wilmington. Hayhurst was on French Street and Hallowell was at Orange and Third streets. Nathan Dalbey had probably taken over Jones' site on Water Street a few years earlier. As we saw in Chapter IV, Thomas Hayhurst met financial disaster about this time. The pottery he was leasing was put up for sale in January of 1839, and fourteen months later all of his goods, chattels and rights were assigned in trust for the benefit of his creditors. A year or so prior to the first hint of Hayhurst's dilemma, William Hallowell closed his Orange Street pottery and no evidence has been found that anyone took up the turning and firing of clay at this location. By this time, Hallowell was in his middle fifties and he retired to Philadelphia to reside with his daughter and son-in-law, a physician. His decision was probably heavily influenced by the hard times that were descending on the country. Meanwhile, John H. Denning, an eventual Milford potter, was in business in neighboring Pennsylvania, but by 1843, he left the Chester area to start over in Delaware. A few years later, his Pennsylvania pottery was auctioned at a sheriff's sale. It appears he tried to ride out these hard economic times for a while but eventually could no longer make ends meet just north of the Delaware-Pennsylvania border.

But there was one potter who took a chance and started his own manufactory during these trying times around 1840. William Hare established his business at Thomas Hayhurst's old location sometime during 1839. This timeline, based on the Census of Manufactures and Wilmington Fire Insurance Company records, were discussed in Chapter I. So how could Hare survive when others had failed? Several factors likely played a role. He had probably worked at the Hayhurst pottery for some years before then and knew the facilities, products and customers. Unlike Hayhurst, Hare was himself a potter and he also stressed earthenware along with his stoneware. And as one looks more closely at Hare in later years, one finds a hard-working man with excellent marketing and business sense—an entrepreneur. He was also aided by the fact that Hallowell had closed so there was one less pottery operating in Wilmington. Generally speaking, business in the United States started to improve after 1842 and William Hare purchased his first property, the family residence, in 1844. Two years later, he acquired the pottery on French Street.

The remainder of the nineteenth century in America was not without economic downturns, including a crisis in 1857 and the Panic of 1873. But the three venerable Delaware potteries continued to survive. Both Wilmington's economy and population saw substantial growth during the second half of the nineteenth century that was spurred on by carriage and railroad car manufacture, shipbuilding, foundries and a tanning industry. William Hare and John Denning continued their long, uninterrupted runs in the cities of Wilmington and Milford, respectively. And at the corner of Water and Orange streets in Wilmington, while John Stüber moved on to become a merchant grocer in 1859, George Ziegler leased the location from heirs of the Jones' family and produced earthenware there until 1880, first in partnership with Albert Neumayer and then on his own. But keep in mind that no new pottery of any consequence came on the scene during this period, but more about that later.

Marketing and Business Strategies

Delaware potters used a variety of methods to market and deliver their ceramics. While some of these were touched on during the discussions of individual potters, treating this subject as a whole helps to place a better perspective on how this group of craftsmen merchandised their wares. This discussion will also include much about William Hare's business and marketing strategy.

One obvious route to market was to sell to local inhabitants from within the walls of one's manufactory. Mathew Crips' ledger recorded a large number of sales to residents of Wilmington and neighboring New Castle County. Records of Joseph Bringhurst, proprietor of a Market Street drug store, show that he purchased pottery from William Hallowell and Branch Green. Surely word of mouth helped potters reach this market segment.

Potters were known to traverse the countryside offering their wares from their horse-drawn wagons. John Denning of Milford even had his wagon outfitted with racks so that he could carry a large stock and was known to travel as far as Pennsylvania, probably Delaware County, during his springtime runs. Others used wagons filled with straw in which their earthenware or stoneware was packed to protect it from breakage during long and bumpy sales excursions.

Reselling through general merchants was a key route to market for many potters. None appears to have built a broader network than Mathew Crips. This proprietor sold much of his production through resellers as far north as New York and as far south as North Carolina. When Jonathan Beeson announced the opening of his earthenware manufactory, he specifically targeted "country storekeepers" in his newspaper advertisement. Early deliveries to these store owners were by wagon or ship, though later railroads surely provided a means of moving large quantities of product to others.

Some potters sold their wares to other potters either for cash or in exchange for other materials. Mathew Crips' ledger recorded transactions with John Justice, a Philadelphia pottery operator, in which Mathew's tea pots were an article of commerce. Years later, Richard Lowe's estate inventory suggests he may have been reselling some stoneware made by William Hare.

Always interested in a sale, these craftsmen took advantage of any situation that would put their product in front of the consumer. Porcelain from the factory of Reiss and Huttmann was sold on one October Saturday in 1850 at stands located in Wilmington's market. Nine years later, William Hare displayed some handsome stoneware, preserve jars and earthen pipe at the fall agricultural exhibition of the New Castle County Agricultural Society. His participation was first mentioned in the October 14, 1859, issue of the *Delaware Gazette*. A week later, the same newspaper's list of prize winners included Hare, who had received a diploma for the clay products he exhibited. In September of 1868, according to the *Smyrna Times*, Allen and Bell from Smyrna Landing exhibited "beautiful earthen hanging baskets" at the annual fair sponsored by the same society. The editor added that "the baskets were especially admired by the ladies, as well as their other pottery." In the same year, the *Delaware Gazette* reported that these partners were awarded a diploma at the Agricultural Exhibition for their display of earthenware and drain tiles. A few years later, George Ziegler was named in the October 30, 1874, issue of the *Delaware Gazette* as an exhibitor at a show sponsored by the Delaware Institute of Mechanical Arts. There he displayed five earthenware vases, five hanging baskets and four flower pots.

Many of Delaware's potters advertised their businesses through various newspapers. Some of these notices announced the opening of a pottery as did Jonathan Beeson, Branch Green and Allen and Bell in 1808, 1831 and 1867, respectively. Others notified the public of a change in ownership—John Stüber in 1855—or the formation of a partnership—Richard Lowe and John Stüber in 1848. In another case, George Ziegler and Englebert Neumayer used the print media in 1862 to remind the readership that they were still manufacturing earthenware and Rockingham at the same location. But in addition, these subscribers usually took the opportunity to tout the variety of their products and the capability to deliver large quantities, while thanking the public for past business and asking for continuing favor. But no potter advertised more or used this tool better to position a product and target a market niche than William Hare. This potter was a strong marketer and a very astute businessman.

Though William Hare established his business in 1839, the earliest advertisement of his that was found was dated in mid-1852. Placed in the *Delaware Gazette*, Hare headed the notice "STONE and EARTHEN-WARE" while reminding his friends and the public of his long established pottery in French Street. Compared to ads he ran in later years, several of the features in this early one stand out:

- Besides stoneware and earthenware, he offered a full assortment of *Rockingham Ware* and a large lot of *Yellow Ware*.

- Hare not only offered the typical pottery forms used for food storage and consumption, but mentioned *Fire Bricks* and *Clay Cylinders* and *Furnaces*.
- While stoneware jars were noted, no reference was made to the product that would become his "bread and butter"—the air-tight preserve jar.
- The potter had a large lot of defective ware for sale, surely the result of mishaps during kiln firings.

In its style and content this advertisement was typical of general notices placed by potters of this era. However, Hare's mention of Rockingham Ware is somewhat puzzling. The timeframe seems early and this ceramic was typically molded. Some of Hare's stoneware jars were glazed with a deep brown color and maybe these fit his definition of Rockingham.

But three years later, William began to advertise his "AIR-TIGHT PRESERVING JARS." In the August 31, 1855, issue of the *Delaware State Journal*, the potter introduced readers to "jars with small tops to fit corks expressly for Preserving Tomatoes and other fruits which require them to be air-tight." The ad went on to say that "these jars had been tried and found to give perfect satisfaction." No doubt Hare was in the development stages with his new stone jar. And it's fairly safe to say that he had turned out prototypes over the previous couple of years and also had first-hand experience in storing fruits in them over an entire winter. As we will see, William continued to develop his jar. And while phrases like "product positioning" and "targeting a niche market" may not have been in the vocabulary of this nineteenth century potter, Hare applied these concepts extremely well, and necessarily so. Glass containers in large quantities were about to hit the market. The patent on the Mason® jar issued in November of 1858.

Hare produced stoneware fruit jars with two contrasting designs to their top closures. Both have a thin ring on the inside of the neck an inch or so below the lip. But one type also has a recessed ledge on the top for holding a round lid or disc to close the jar, although a cork could be used. The question arises whether one of these designs was used in the manufacturing of jars much before the other. If so, which variation is earlier? An answer to the first question is: possibly. To the second question, there may be some clues in both Hare's advertisements and in a signed example of his jar dated 1856. Recall in 1855, Hare described his jars as possessing small tops to fit corks. But it's rather doubtful that he would have stressed the use of corks for those with the recessed rim. And then in his advertisement in 1856, the potter stated, "They have been improved upon which simplifies the sealing process...." But quite frankly, he could have been referring to either design in that statement. However, some observations suggest that the newer, "improved jar of 1856" was the one with the recessed top. Though not always a foolproof argument, jars more ovoid in shape suggest an earlier period. Preserve jars by Hare with this shape have not been seen with the recessed rim. But equally important, the Historical Society of Delaware holds a jar signed and dated by William Hare. The date is "1856." And the rim is recessed! Could it be that he signed his first jar that incorporated this top? One wonders then if by looking at the top of a Hare fruit jar, its date of manufacture might be placed after 1855? Though quite a simplistic view, the signed and dated jar may eventually be an important clue to better understand the evolution and timing of his sealing designs.

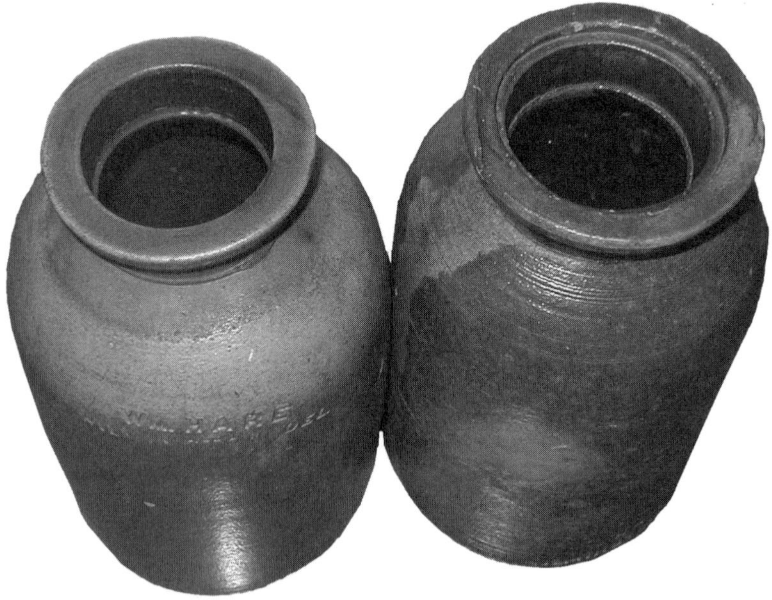

William Hare's air-tight stone preserve jars were produced with two different closure designs. The top of one rim was flat and the neck was made to fit a cork. The rim of the other had a recessed ledge that was made to hold a round lid or disc, though it too could have been sealed with a cork.

Stone Air -Tight preserving Jars.

THE SUBSCRIBER WOULD RESPECTFULLY CALL the attention of his friends and the public generally to his large assortment of **AIR TIGHT JARS**. These Jars have been tried by a number of people, and have given general satisfaction. They have been improved upon which simplifies the sealing process so that any person, by exercising a little judgment can see at once that when properly **SEALED** up they must be **AIR-TIGHT**. One important consideration in regard to these Jars is that while tin is of such a nature that acids and salt will easily corrode or rust it and can be used but a very few times, Stoneware, as every one knows, can be **USED FOR ANY LENGTH OF TIME** without undergoing any change. The great **SUPERIORITY OF STONEWARE** over any other substance for this purpose is so well known that any comments upon it are entirely unnecessary, and the proprietor feels confident that any one after having once seen these Jars will never be induced to use any other.

WILLIAM HARE
French Street near Second

Delaware Gazette, September, 12, 1856

Hare's 1856 advertisement also demonstrates his recognition of the benefits of stoneware over tin for storing preserved fruits. As time goes on, we will see this potter continuing to position his product against not-in-kind competition. This is also a good place to point out other characteristics of Hare's business and marketing strategies. His preserve jar was aimed at a common chore of the nineteenth century housewife, "putting up fruit," and Delaware was one of the largest fruit growing areas in the country. With the widespread availability of fruit and the extra interest that the large local growing area created, Hare was targeting a need of virtually every household, and as the only stoneware manufacturer in Delaware at the time, he had carved a niche. Furthermore, one finds the majority of Hare's advertisements in the August and September issues of Delaware newspapers, the months leading up to the home "canning" season.

Over the next dozen years or so, William Hare continued to advertise his stoneware preserve jars. In the *Delaware Republican* on August 30, 1858, the French Street potter, after long experience, offered "a receipt for preserving fruit in his Air Tight Jars." In the *Delaware State Journal and Statesman*, the word "recipe" was used instead of "receipt." He then closed the advertisement with the statement: "Prepared Cement can be furnished with the Jars." These are two more examples of Hare applying his marketing savvy to enhance his product offering. The next year the potter placed at least three different ads in two newspapers. Now he had latched onto a health benefit; in part the ad read, "Fruit Regulates the System And prevents disease." He went on to add that his jars could be purchased for 100 to 200 percent cheaper than any others, a reaction to the growing availability of a number of patented glass jars.

In a subsequent advertisement in the *Delaware Republican* on September 8, 1864, Hare still offered cement and preserving direc-

Important to Housekeepers

If you want to preserve your health, eat plenty of fruit as it is an admitted fact that

Fruit Regulates the System

And prevents disease

Now while fruit is plenty, provide plenty for the winter by preserving it in

Hare's Air-Tight Preserving Jars

The jars can be had for 100 to 200 percent cheaper than many other Jars that are offered to the public, and they will keep fruit equally as well as the highest priced Jar in the Market and are easier managed.

If it were necessary, hundreds of names could be given to testify to the above statement.

RECEIPTS AND CEMENTS CAN BE HAD together with the Jars at the pottery in French street, No. 206, above Second, WILMINGTON, DELAWARE

WILLIAM HARE.

Delaware State Journal & Statesman, September 9, 1859

tions to customers but now included a reminder that "Fruit can be preserved without Sugar which is very important in these times." Surely this was a reference to the sweetener's short supply and high price during the Civil War. And this salesman of stone jars pointed out their advantages over other products. According to the potter, "Glass is of such a fragile nature it is difficult to put in hot water without crackling." This newspaper notice also helps to confirm the timing of the original introduction of Hare's stone preserve jar. He opened the ad with "THESE JARS have been in use for TEN YEARS..." suggesting their market entry in about 1854. From information presented in an earlier paragraph, it was implied that his jar debuted about 1853.

In 1867, Hare still gave space to his fruit jars but over half of his advertisement stressed a large and general assortment of articles IMPORTANT TO HOUSEKEEPERS! He had recognized the competitive pressures his stoneware jars were facing and he was moving his emphasis to other offerings. A decade later, not only had the market essentially eroded for his fruit jars, but other utilitarian stoneware and redware were falling out of favor. So in 1878 and 1880, Wm. Hare's ads in the *Daily Republican* featured "Queensware," and a bowl labeled CHINA GLASS and QUEENSWARE was pictured. The potter, reacting to market forces, had evolved to more of a general merchant of household items. Though he still fired his kiln, a significant segment of his business resulted from reselling the products of others. As part of Hare's final estate in early 1886, large amounts of glassware and tin ware were inventoried. The accounting also contained numerous forms and pieces of yellow pottery. These could have been made on French Street or were more of the items Hare resold.

Earlier, it was pointed out that William Hare provided cement to customers who purchased his stone jars. This product would have been used to seal the jars once they were filled with fruit. Hare called it cement though in actuality it was a sealing wax. Dave Hinson in his writings about fruit jars of the 1850s and later makes the point that sealing wax was commonly referred to as cement. The lid, either tin or stoneware, was placed in the grooved top of the jar and the wax was poured over it. The corks capping earlier jars were also sealed with wax. Hare could have purchased the sealant or concocted it himself.

Recognizing then that the air-tight, stone preserve jar played a major role in the longevity of William Hare's pottery, what might have led him to develop this product? Though we'll never know for sure, the *Delaware Gazette* on June 28, 1853, allows us to stretch for an answer. In an article entitled "Preserved Peaches," the editor praised the experiment of Charles P. Matlack, a Wilmington confectioner. Charles took whole peaches fresh from the tree and sealed them in air-tight, tin jars. Stored over the winter, the fruit was as fresh and flavorful when opened as when the jars were filled. The editor added that it was hoped that others would be led to try the experiment Matlack had so successfully conducted. The year was 1853, two years before William Hare's first advertisement for his preserve jars, and Matlacks's business was located at 9 East Second Street, around the corner from the French Street pottery. Possibly the experience of his neighbor influenced Hare in the development of his fruit jar.

Five years later on September 9, the *Delaware Republican* ran a testimonial under the title, "Preserving Fruit." This time the benefactor was William Hare and his stone jars. The editor noted that these jars were the very best for this use since "They are cheaper and far more durable than glass, and are in every respect superior to tin." Peaches put up in one of Hare's jars, when opened twelve months later, were apparently as fresh as if just plucked from the tree. The article went on to warn its readership that the jars were in great demand and they should purchase them at once since the potter had just opened a fresh kiln of them.

Competitive Forces

The operators of Delaware's potteries were not immune to a variety of competitive pressures, though some of them threatened their livelihood more than others. These included the existence of other local and regional potters, imported ceramics and not-in-kind products made from tin and glass. Competition from tin and glass became more pronounced later in the period and eventually was a major contributor to the demise of the local potter.

The competition felt by Delaware's potters from their fellow craftsmen "up the street" was probably less intrusive than other forces in the late eighteenth century. Wilmington had two and sometimes three factories operating simultaneously. But we know that Mathew Crips sold much of his earthenware through resellers beyond state borders. This strong focus may have left enough of a local market for others like John Jones to serve, although we know nothing specific about Jones' customer base. Yet located within a 100 feet of the Christina River wharves, it is likely he also reached some customers by ship. Outside of Wilmington, Charles Green appears to have been the only Delaware potter of the period. His pot house and kiln were in Smyrna. While Chester County in Pennsylvania eventually became an area with numerous potteries, the early ones were few in number and largely located in the northern part of the county. It is likely then that direct purchases from these potteries by the Delaware public were infrequent. Rather it was local merchants selling European imports, especially when shipping blockades were not in place, that caused the early artisans the most grief. As an example, John Moore, a general merchant at the corner of Market and Queen streets, advertised a long list of items in the 1787 *Delaware Courant and Wilmington Advertiser* that included London superfine broadcloths and earthenware.

Several potteries were operating in Philadelphia before 1800 and surely they provided a source of domestic pottery to Wilmington and Delaware merchants along the river. Ships frequently made the short voyage up the Delaware River to Philadelphia's wharves. The publication of Delaware newspapers began in the mid-1780s but no advertisement placed by a Philadelphia potter directly targeting the general public was found until 1802. Then Samuel Sullivan publicized his recently acquired earthenware pottery. He knew the Delaware market and its potteries to a considerable extent. Sullivan had worked for Charles Green at Smyrna a few years earlier.

Chester County was alluded to earlier. The pottery operated by Thomas Vickers in Caln Township reached the early nineteenth century Delaware market. In 1808, his daybook recorded a sale to James Bringhurst of Wilmington. Though the reason for the purchase is unclear, the sale included over 50 dozen items, far more than needed by a single household. Quite possibly there was a void in the supply of pottery then because of the looming embargo or it was a low point in the number of active Wilmington potteries. Recall, Jonathan Beeson opened his pottery on Orange Street in the same year possibly sensing a market opportunity.

The situation in the first quarter of the nineteenth century mirrored the prior 40 years in terms of the types and extent of competition apparently faced by Delaware manufacturers. Wilmington still had two factories. Jones had replaced Crips as the major producer of earthenware, while now north on Orange Street, Beeson and then Hallowell were offering customers a second option. Meanwhile, the Green family enjoyed their isolation in Smyrna. And now, John Mullowny, proprietor of the Washington Pottery in Philadelphia, set out in 1813 to capture some of the northern Delaware market through resellers. In the March 17 issue of the *American Watchman & Delaware Republican*, the Market Street potter sought "MERCHANTS, residing in Wilmington and the neighboring country" for delivery of over 30 different forms of his wares. The advertisement featured "Coffee pots, red, black and yellow." But the presence of imports, except during the temporary embargo and the War of 1812, was continuing to grow. In the writings of Baltimore potters reproduced earlier in this chapter, they pleaded for relief from "immense quantities forced into our country." Merchants not averse to selling these goods occupied Market Street in Wilmington. David Smyth at No. 33 was one of the most advertised dealers of imported ceramics and glass. His notices, like one in the *American Watchman* on April 30, 1817, featured "Queen's-ware," the very product that caused the Baltimore potters to complain. While he was in this business for many years, it was a David Smyth who partnered with Eli Hilles to eventually purchase the Wilmington pottery on French Street in 1832.

Philadelphia Earthen-Ware.

THE Earthen-Ware Manufactory, for many years carried on by Mr. Wm. Standley at his Yard and Pot-House in Market between 4th and 5th streets, Philadelphia, is now in the hands of the subscribers, where a very large and general assortment of good ware may be had, and Mr. Standley's Customers and others, may be regularly supplied at the shortest notice, and at 15 per cent lower than elsewhere in the city, for Cash or the usual credit.

Orders for the West Indies, or Country, Executed with dispatch by

SAMUEL SULLIVAN, & Co.

Mirror of the Times & General Advertiser, April 10, 1802

During the next 25 years, the population of Delaware continued to grow and a new pottery came on the scene in Wilmington. Branch

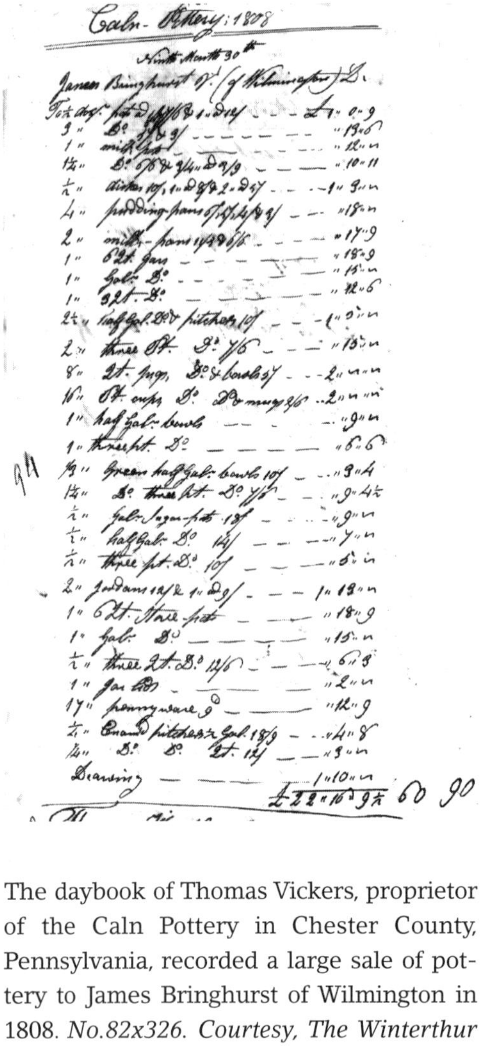

Green left Philadelphia and opened a business on French Street while the two earthenware factories a few blocks apart along Orange Street contnued to function under various operators. While Green advertised the typical clay products that had been produced by the city's potters for decades, he also introduced the manufacture of stoneware to Wilmington and Delaware. And though only in business for a few years, this type of pottery became a mainstay of the French Street operation for the next 50 years. When Thomas Hayhurst ran into financial difficulties and before William Hare had established a solid foothold on French Street, a Baltimore pottery, sensing a void, entered the market. In September of 1839, merchants Charles and William Warner announced receipt of a large supply of stoneware from Baltimore. Their source became clear early the next year when they advertised as an agent for David Parr, a Baltimore stoneware manufacturer. Over the next two years, this merchant family continued to feature stoneware from the Maryland city located some 65 miles to the southwest. And in 1842, a second Wilmington merchant, B.A. Janvier at Fifth and Market streets, notified the public that he had stoneware of Baltimore manufacture to sell, though he did not name his supplier. Meanwhile, William Hare

The daybook of Thomas Vickers, proprietor of the Caln Pottery in Chester County, Pennsylvania, recorded a large sale of pottery to James Bringhurst of Wilmington in 1808. *No.82x326. Courtesy, The Winterthur Library: Joseph Downs Collection of Manuscripts and Printed Ephemera.*

had taken over Hayhurst's pottery apparently undaunted by the clay products of others. He built a business that survived until his death in 1885. Hare also had to pit his pottery against tin ware, in part, manufactured by John L. Hadden & Co. of Wilmington. In 1840, the company advertised pudding dishes and wash bowls made of this metal. Meanwhile there was no let up in the availability of imported Queensware, crockery and earthenware as grocery and china stores continued to offer these alternatives. So while the potters of northern Delaware saw population and market growth, new products and suppliers offered stern competition for share. As for Kent County, a single pottery remained the source of locally produced earthenware. Though the Smyrna factory started by Daniel Green had closed by 1840, three years later John Denning established his business in Milford.

> **STONE WARE** – The subscribers, having been appointed by David Parr, (Stone Ware Manufacturer, of Baltimore) Agent for the sale of his Ware, are now prepared to supply any orders in that line, at Thomas Hayhurst's old prices, which in some articles are below Baltimore prices.
>
> Orders received at the Grocery Store of Wm. & Chas. Warner.
>
> CHARLES WARNER & Co.
>
> *Delaware Gazette, January 7, 1840*

The business environment the local potter faced became much more hard-hitting after 1850. Glass products and an improved understanding of food preservation started eating more and more into his market. In a book by Julian Toulouse entitled *Fruit Jars*, the author writes that he identified over 200 patents related to home canning jars and sealing techniques. After a few issuances in the 1850s, these patents proliferated in the 1860s. One of the early and most influential claims was granted to Robert Arthur in 1855 for his groove-ring seal. Though illustrated for tin and pottery containers, numerous glass companies adopted the concept and it sparked an industry that is still with us to some degree. Within a few years, the battle for the market was on, and glass jars with names like Mason®, The Gem®, The Hero® and All Right® soon followed. William Hare's stone, air-tight preserve jars were well established by this time, but he surely saw sales diminish as the decade of the '60s came to an end. Wilmington merchants like Clement B. Smyth, then at 82 Market Street, began by advertising Arthur's self-sealing tin cans and glass jars along with stone and glass fruit jars with corks. An early notice can be found in the September 9, 1858, issue of the *Delaware Republican*. The following year this proprietor announced an inventory of "Willoughby's Patent Air-Tight STOPPER for Fruit Preserved Fresh WITHOUT CEMENT." Pickels and Flinn & Jackson were other vendors selling a variety of jars. On August 18, 1869, the latter merchant's advertisement in the *Wilmington Daily Commercial* pictured three trademarked, glass jars. This issue also contained an article on fruit jars in which glass was branded "the best" and three reasons were provided to "constitute their superiority." It was ironic. Recall that the *Delaware Republican* had published a very similar testimonial in 1858 entitled "Preserving Fruit." It had embraced William Hare's stone jars. Also, one cannot discount the close proximity of the glass industry in southern New Jersey as influencing the Delaware housewife to adopt the glass jar. So, a segment of the pottery market was being captured by not-in-kind competition, and potters like Hare turned to reselling Queensware and glassware in order to remain viable.

One advertisement in the *Delaware Republican* of July 8, 1857, sheds some light on both the availability of fruit jars and their cost to the homemaker. Clement B. Smyth announced an inventory of 200 Dozen Jars for keeping fruit fresh for the winter. Pints were offered at 75¢ per dozen; a like number of quarts sold for $1.00. Though this merchant did not mention the composition of these jars, they were most likely glass as he referred to his business on Market Street as the China and Glass Warehouse. While Hare may have been able to price his more durable stone jars somewhat higher, Smyth's price point in the marketplace was one the potter surely had to take into account.

As mentioned earlier, Baltimore potters sold their stoneware through Wilmington merchants around 1840. Some years later, Kent and Sussex counties became outlets for a specialized, hand-thrown pottery from this Maryland city. Today's collectors hold a number of wide-mouth jars produced in Baltimore as advertising pieces for Delaware merchants and manufacturers. Impressed with the name, product line and Delaware town, these salt-glazed examples were probably made in the third quarter of the nineteenth century, most likely in the 1860s. Jars include those marked for H.C. Collison of Dover, Thomas Abbott of Angola and Huxford & Co. of Frankford. One large jar marked "W. M. Prouse & Co" of Magnolia, Delaware, is clearly of Baltimore origin. Not only does this piece exhibit a blue decoration characteristic of that city, but this gray stoneware jar displays a second mark, that of the Baltimore potter Peter Herrman. The attribution of other examples to this city is based on their decorative motif, characteristic hand-brushed flowers in cobalt blue.

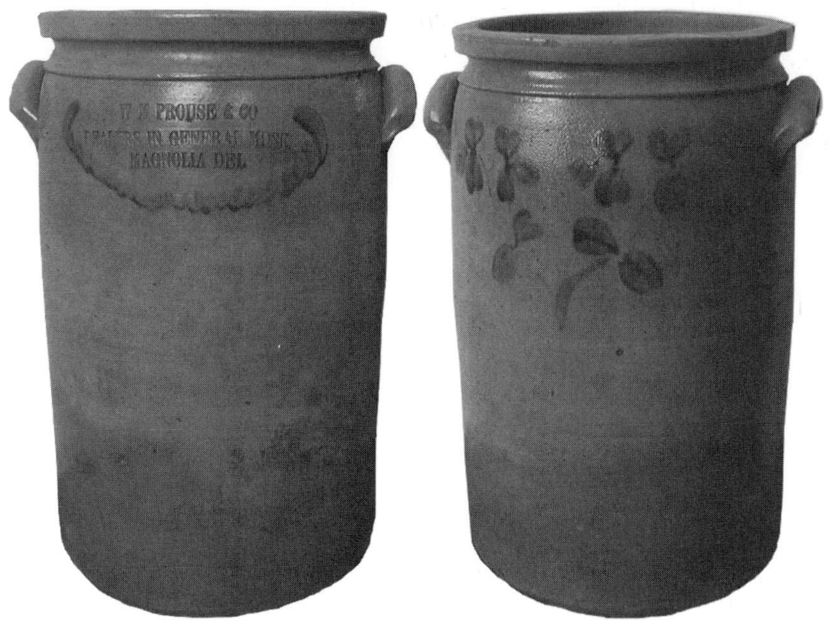

The front of this decorated stoneware jar is impressed: W. M. PROUSE & CO/DEALERS IN GENERAL MDSE./MAGNOLIA DEL. A second mark identifies the maker as P. Herrman, a Baltimore potter. The back of the jar displays a floral design in brushed cobalt blue. It stands 14.5 inches high and is just over 9 inches in diameter. *Courtesy of Colonel and Mrs. Kenneth P. Brown.*

But a Philadelphia maker may also have captured some of this Delaware market. A decoration on an advertising jar marked for Nichols & Gooden is more typical of Richard C. Remmey (RCR) who is well known for advertising pieces marked from Philadelphia, the city where he and his father, Henry, worked.

In the End

It is difficult to approximate the number of pieces of ceramics that were crafted in Delaware's potteries over this 130 year period, though it must have been several million. But for all of the clay dug, pots fashioned, wood burned and pieces sold, a combination of market forces, especially during the latter third of this era, eventually led to the disappearance of these local pot houses. Their fall did not happen over night. The markets for hand-thrown earthenware and stoneware were being severely tested over a long period of time. As evidence, while there was a sizeable expansion of Delaware's population, the number of potteries, simultaneously firing kilns, typically remained at three.

Many early forms of earthenware—cups, mugs, bowls, plates, pitchers—were used in food service. Over the years, as the purchasing power and the aesthetic cravings of the population grew, finer and more decorative wares replaced them. Early on, importers supplied the alternates but as time passed, commercial potteries began to produce molded and decorated wares in large quantities. For a time, the earthenware potter survived by focusing on garden and specialty items, although those also became the products of large establishments.

Stoneware, like earthenware, had a number of different uses, but food storage was the primary one. However, the development of new technologies and less expensive substitutes stressed the stoneware market. Experimentation led to food preserving and processing techniques that prevented spoilage over long periods of time. Stoneware could not meet this need as inexpensively. As the nineteenth century wore on, the housekeeper shifted to inexpensive glass jars with simple air-tight closures to "put up" her favorites, or bowed to the new age and purchased the products of the commercial canneries. Canning was a major industry in Delaware. Cold storage methods were also improving.

These market pressures kept prices quite stable over a long period. Crips sold much of his eighteenth century earthenware for eight to ten pence each. A stoneware milk pan from Branch Green in 1832 was priced at less than 17 cents. But stoneware commanded higher prices than earthenware. In 1860, John Denning realized an average of 12 cents for each piece of earthenware he sold. Raising prices was not an option the potter could invoke to maintain profitability.

In the end, we are left with the realization that the life cycle of the hand-thrown ceramics of these early potters, like the buggy whip, had played out. Yet today, collectors hunt down a potter's surviving wares and pay prices that approach and even exceed the revenues this early craftsman enjoyed from an entire year of his efforts.

Chapter X

Shards

Ten

Several fragments of information were uncovered which relate to the overall subject of Delaware potters and potteries but do not connect directly with earlier chapters. Some speak to the clarification of previously published subject matter, others seek closure on unanswered questions and still others provide related facts. Hopefully those with question marks will some day be resolved.

Hare's Corner

Route 13 crosses Route 273 south of Wilmington at an intersection commonly called Hare's Corner. Some Delawareans, knowing the story of William Hare, the nineteenth century potter, assume that this point on the map was named after him. Not so. The location bore that name before William Hare had reached adulthood, if not before he was born. Thomas Scharf wrote that "Hare's Corners, a few miles from New Castle, was named for an early settler." He also pointed out that even after a hotel there was renamed soon after 1820, the locality was still known as Hare's Corners. And on February 12, 1822, a notice of public sale for property "situate on the corner called Hare's Corner" was advertised in the *Delaware Gazette*. But at that time, William Hare, the future potter, was not yet ten years old and was still residing in Lancaster County, Pennsylvania, his birthplace.

A Pitcher Marked New Castle, Delaware

The Henry Ford Museum in Dearborn, Michigan, owns a pitcher which is marked with the applied letters: RIVERSIDE/NEW CASTLE/DEL. John Pearce in his short paper on the first sketches of some Wilmington potters presented a photograph of this piece. He labeled it "possibly English, ca. 1830." The body is decorated with a number of small, raised figures starting at the shoulder and continuing to the bottom of the pitcher. A private communication with the museum confirmed it is still in their collection, but they have not researched it nor attached an attribution. While this pitcher could be of American manufacture, much more likely it was crafted in England for a New Castle customer.

A New Castle, Delaware Pottery

In the same paper mentioned above, John Pearce footnoted the secondhand recollection of Judge Richard S. Rodney who spoke of an umbrella stand made at a pottery in New Castle, Delaware. Others have surmised that the pitcher mentioned in the preceding paragraph was crafted at a New Castle pottery by the name of Riverside. However, no information has been found to substantiate the existence of an early pottery in this town that was Delaware's first capital.

A Puzzle Jug

In his 1971 book entitled *Early American Folk Pottery*, Harold F. Guilland included a photograph of an earthenware puzzle jug which he captioned "...made at the Hare Pottery, New Castle, Delaware, about 1800." The author also added that the jug was inscribed:

> Hear gentlemen come try your skill
> I'll hold a wager if you will
> that you don't drink this liquor all
> without you spill or let some fall

No basis for the attribution was provided by Guilland. But William Hare was not yet born in 1800 nor has the existence of a pottery in the town of New Castle been verified. Assuming that the jug was produced well into the 1800s instead of near the turn of the century, it would seem out of character for Hare to have made such a complicated ceramic for the purpose of drinking liquor. William Hare was a maker of utilitarian pottery and also active in a temperance society. Rather the jug is likely English or at least strongly influenced by such. The National Museum Liverpool in England holds a tin-glazed puzzle jug attributed to that city circa 1750. And behold, it is decorated with the identical inscription. A photograph and description of the jug can be viewed on the museum's web site: www.liverpoolmuseums.org.

Maybe There Were Others

Very limited information has surfaced suggesting that two additional nineteenth century potting sites may have existed in Delaware but no verification of either has been established. At this point, their existence is based on hearsay. Supposedly, a potter by the name of Benjamin Milson worked in or near Lewes circa 1820 to 1830. No one by that or a similar name appears in the censuses for those years, although a Benjamin Melson is listed in Sussex County in 1840. Besides four in his household who were engaged in agriculture, one was active in manufacturing. Was Melson a "bluebird potter?" And sometime during the 1800s, a pottery may have operated off of Route 113 below Dover near Magnolia, Delaware.

Carts of Earthenware and Loads of Clay

References to Samuel Bush's account book were made in Chapter III. Two other entries from it relate to the subject of potteries but have not yet resulted in closure. Dated October 13, 1789, the name of William Wilson was attached to "2 cart loads of earthenware." Who is Wilson? Though possibly an unidentified potter, more likely he was a general merchant since other entries associated with his name mention tea, candles, chocolate and brushes. And on August 15, 1791, an entry documented eight loads of clay to a person with the surname of Warner or Worner. No first name was given. Was he a brick maker or could he have been leasing or working the Orange Street pottery owned at the same time by Isaac Starr?

John Thompson, Potter

While searching land indentures in the 1830s, one registered in New Castle County documented the transfer of property commonly referred to as "Thompson's Pot House Lot." The deed (V 4 29 1835) passed this parcel from Benjamin to Reuben Webb. Reuben was a son-in-law of John Jones, the Wilmington potter. Described as "situate and lying directly back of House No. 76 on the West side of Fourth Street from Delaware between Cherry and Sassafras Streets," the initial hope was that this was a clue to an unfounded pottery in New Castle, Delaware. But such was not the case. After pursing a number of avenues, the property was found to be in Philadelphia and had been the pottery operated in the eighteenth century by John Thompson. In her book, Susan Myers dates Thompson at that location from 1785-1801, although Friends' records indicate that John Jones began an apprenticeship with him in 1776.

While Benjamin Webb was a resident of Wilmington at the time of the sale in 1835, it is unclear why the transfer of a Philadelphia property would have been recorded in New Castle County, Delaware.

Cements for Repairing Ceramics

While scanning newspapers, two old "home formulations" from the nineteenth century for preparing cements to repair earthenware and china were found and are repeated below:

A Cement for Broken Earthenware – Take 1 oz. of dry cream cheese, grated fine, and an equal quantity of quicklime mixed well together with 3 oz. of skimmed milk, to form a good cement, when the rendering of the joint visible is of no consequence. If mixed without the milk, it perhaps might be stronger.

Delaware Inquirer,
January 14, 1860

Cement for Broken China – Take a very thick solution of gumarabic dissolved in water, and stir into it plaster of Paris until the mixture becomes a viscous paste. Apply it with a brush to the fractured edges, and stick them together. In three days the article cannot be broken in the same place. The whiteness of the cement renders it doubly valuable.

Delaware State Reporter,
June 26, 1857

Chapter XI

A Checklist of Owners, Operators and Potters

Eleven

Over 80 individuals have been identified as somehow connected with Delaware and the pottery industry during the eighteenth and nineteenth centuries. An alphabetized checklist of names has been included to serve as a quick reference. For each individual, it also includes their primary location and a short synopsis of their involvement in the industry. Most of the names are in boldface, indicating that they have been treated in one or more of the preceding chapters. This coverage of each person varies widely from a single mention to a full chapter.

Adams, Levi	Wilmington	Listed in 1845 *Wilmington Directory* as a potter on French Street between Fourth and Fifth streets; then listed as a laborer until 1868; probably worked at William Hare's pottery
Allen, Alvan	Smyrna	Established a pottery in partnership with Andrew N. Bell at Smyrna Landing in 1867
Andrew(s), John	Wilmington	Identified as a potter in 1767 land indenture; established pottery on Orange Street at Third Street
Auner, Peter	Wilmington	Partnered with Hallworths in a pottery at Seventh and Madison streets in 1852
Bannard, John	Wilmington	Listed in 1814 *Wilmington Directory* as a potter residing at 12 E. French Street; probably worked for John Jones

Beeson, Jonathan Jr.	Wilmington	Advertised a pottery in 1808 at Orange and Third streets
Bell, Andrew N.	Smyrna	Established a pottery in partnership with Alvan Allen at Smyrna Landing in 1867
Bell, Henry	Wilmington	Listed as a potter residing at William Hare's residence per 1850 census
Bell, Reese F.	Smyrna	Operated a pottery at Smyrna Landing per the 1870 Census of Manufactures and produced all kinds of earthenware and stoneware
Bell, William M.	Smyrna	Purchased half-interest in pottery at Smyrna Landing from A.N. Bell per 1869 land indenture
Bradford, Samuel	Wilmington	Listed as a potter in the 1853 *Wilmington Directory* residing at 48 French Street; listed in subsequent years through 1873 at various residential addresses; most likely worked for William Hare; came to Wilmington after working at the Grier Pottery in Chester County, Pennsylvania
Brown, John	Wilmington	Apprenticed with Mathew Crips in 1762 per Wilmington Friends' Meeting before opening his own pottery in Baltimore
Bryan(t), Moses	Wilmington	Identified as a potter in a 1782 deed who likely worked for Mathew Crips or John Andrews before moving to Philadelphia
Cooke, David	Wilmington	Purchased French Street property in partnership with Branch Green in 1831 per land indenture
Cox, Bennett	Wilmington	Listed as a potter in 1849 tax list; had worked for John Vickers at Lionville, Pennsylvania, circa 1845 according to Arthur James
Crips, Cornelius	Wilmington	Worked with his father, Mathew Crips, though also farmed in Lancaster County, Pennsylvania; identified as a potter in 1796 deed

Crips, Mathew	Wilmington	Established a pottery on King Street circa 1760 and became wealthy from his trade; regarded by many as the earliest Delaware potter.
Dalbey, Barton	Wilmington	Learned the potting craft from his father, Nathan, before working as a potter in Bordentown, New Jersey, around 1850
Dalbey, Nathan	Wilmington	Operated the pottery at Orange and Water streets for several years until his business failed in 1848
Decker, Charles F.	Wilmington	Listed as a potter in the1859-60 *Wilmington Directory* residing at 310 E. Seventh Street; went on to become an important stoneware potter in Tennessee
Decker, Frederick	Wilmington	Born in Wilmington in 1862; son of Charles F.; worked at his father's pottery in Tennessee
Decker, William	Wilmington	Born in Wilmington in 1859; son of Charles F.; worked at his father's pottery in Tennessee
Denning, John H.	Milford	Established a pottery in Kent County circa 1843 and produced a variety of earthenware forms; previously owned a pottery in Chester Township, Pennsylvania
Desney, William	Wilmington	Listed in the 1850 census as a potter residing at William Hare's residence
Donovan, Enoch W.	Smyrna	Identified in the 1870 census as 24 years old and working in a pottery
German, John M. J.	Wilmington	Listed as 27 years old and a master potter in the 1860 census
Gorby, Joseph C.	Milford	Worked for John Denning in both Milford and Chester Township, Pennsylvania, in the 1840s and '50s
Green, Branch	Wilmington	Relocated from Philadelphia after manufacturing stoneware there for over twenty years; established a pottery on French Street circa 1830; entered into a partnership with a potter, William Stretch

Green, Charles, Jr.	Smyrna	Operated a pottery on the east side of Main Street beginning circa 1781 and continued into the early nineteenth century
Green, Daniel D.	Smyrna	Established a pottery on the west side of Main Street circa 1817
Green, William	Smyrna	Inherited pottery after father's death in 1809 per Orphan's Court records
Hallowell, William J.	Wilmington	Leased and then purchased pottery at the corner of Orange and Third streets in 1823
Hallworth, Phillip	Wilmington	Probable partner of Peter Auner in a pottery at Seventh and Madison streets in 1852
Hallworth, William	Wilmington	Probable partner of Peter Auner in a pottery at Seventh and Madison streets in 1852
Hare, William	Wilmington	Operated French Street pottery from 1839 to 1885; only known Delaware potter to mark his wares
Hayhurst, Thomas	Wilmington	Served as proprietor of French Street pottery in the 1830s
Hilles, Eli	Wilmington	Owned and rented out French Street pottery in partnership with David Smyth in the 1830s and early 1840s
Huttmann, William	Wilmington	Served as partner with William Reiss in porcelain factory at Seventh and Madison streets circa 1850
Jones, John	Wilmington	Established pottery circa 1783 at the corner of Orange and Water streets; family heirs leased out site until 1880
Justis, John	Wilmington	Noted as "Pot. Est" on the 1785 New Castle County tax rolls but believed to be the Philadelphia potter with whom Mathew Crips had business dealings; probably born in Delaware where he was assessed for his father's estate in 1782

Kime, Andrew	Wilmington	Identified as a potter in 1785 Christiana Hundred tax assessment
Lambdin, Henry	Wilmington	Apprenticed under Nathan Dalbey and then resided with Richard Lowe circa 1850; relocated to New Jersey and operated a pottery in Bordentown Township
Logan, William H.	Wilmington	Agreed to serve an apprenticeship under Andrew Maxwell in 1833
Lowe, Frederick	Wilmington	Learned potting from his father, Richard Lowe; relocated to New Jersey and worked for Henry Lambdin circa 1860
Lowe, Richard	Wilmington	Entered partnership with John Stüber in 1848 to operate pottery at Orange and Water streets; became sole operator after dissolution of partnership in 1850
Lowe, William	Wilmington	Learned pottery making from his father, Richard Lowe; relocated to New Jersey and operated a pottery in Bordentown in the 1860s
Mahan, James E.	Wilmington	Identified as a Maryland-born potter in the 1870 census,though probably only an apprentice since 15 years old at the time
Marshall, Abner	Hockessin	Operated a coal-fired kiln in New Castle County and produced fire brick beginning in 1853 followed by Rockingham and yellow ware
Marshall, Robert	Hockessin	Worked for his father, Abner, as a potter, circa 1860
Maxfield, Andrew	Wilmington	Associated with the apprentice indenture of William "Hair;" however, this individual is actually Andrew Maxwell
Maxwell, Andrew	Wilmington	Executed apprentice indentures in 1832 and 1833 to serve as master potter for William "Hair" (Hare) and William H. Logan

McCoy, George T.	Wilmington	Listed in 1860 census as a youth of 14 who works at a pot house
McShone, Benjamin	Wilmington	Listed in 1850 census as a potter residing at William Hare's residence
Messick, Lawrence	Wilmington	Sold interest in pottery at Orange and Water streets to John Stüber in 1855
Miller, Henry	Wilmington	Listed as a potter from Ireland in the 1850 mortality schedule for New Castle County
Moffitt, Richard	Wilmington	Identified as a potter in the 1850 census and listed in the 1848 and 1849 tax lists
Moore, Samuel Preston	Wilmington	Associated with a pottery near the Christina River (Orange and Water streets) according to Elizabeth Montgomery's book, *Reminiscences of Wilmington;* date uncertain but possibly circa 1825
Murphy, John	Wilmington	Assessed in 1844 tax list with occupation as a potter
Namely, George	Wilmington	Listed in 1850 census record but spelling of name is difficult to decipher; noted as a potter, 28 years old and born in Pennsylvania
Neumayer, Englebert	Wilmington	Boarded with William Hare in 1857 and then entered into partnership with George Ziegler to operate pottery at Orange and Water streets; later established his own pottery on Eleventh Street which was the last one to operate in nineteenth century Delaware
Reiss, William	Wilmington	Began a short-lived porcelain factory in partnership with William Huttmann about 1850; relocated to New Jersey and became associated with the American Porcelain Company

Ritchie, Abraham	Wilmington & Smyrna	Managed pottery at Smyrna in the 1830s after working for John Jones in Wilmington; later moved to Philadelphia
Robinson, William	Wilmington	Owned pottery at the corner of Orange and Third streets from 1804 until 1823, though his occupation was a tanner
Rogers, William	Wilmington	Agreed to serve an apprenticeship under William Hare in 1844
Schiller, Jacob	Wilmington	Boarded at 60 French Street and worked for William Hare before relocating to Bridgeton, New Jersey, to work for William Smith; signed a receipt from Hare's pottery in 1864
Smith, William	Wilmington	Boarded at 60 French Street and likely worked for William Hare; relocated to Bridgeton, New Jersey and started his own pottery in about 1865
Smyth, David	Wilmington	Owned and rented out French Street pottery in partnership with Eli Hilles in the 1830s and early 1840s
Starr, Elisha	Wilmington	Purchased pottery at the corner of Orange and Third streets in 1800; he was a skinner, not a potter
Starr, Isaac	Wilmington	Purchased pottery at the corner of Orange and Third streets in 1780; though identified as a miller, he was referred to as a potter in a later deed
Stevens, Alfred	Milford	Agreed in 1846 to serve an apprenticeship under John H. Denning
Stretch, Samuel	Wilmington	Born in Delaware in 1831, son of William Stretch; later worked at potteries in Cecil County, Maryland, and Chester County, Pennsylvania
Stretch, William	Wilmington	Taken into partnership by Branch Green on French Street in 1831 after an apprenticeship in Baltimore; later worked in Maryland, DC, and Philadelphia

Stüber, Herman	Wilmington	Listed with an occupation of "porcelain" in the 1850 census; this young son of John Stüber possibly worked for Reiss and Huttmann
Stüber, John	Wilmington	Commenced partnership with Richard Lowe at the Orange and Water street pottery in 1848; though terminated after a few years, he returned to the pottery after Lowe's death
Sullivan, Samuel	Smyrna	Listed in the 1797 tax record as a tenant of Charles Green,Jr., and in 1800, advertised his own earthenware manufactory in Philadelphia
Timary, Daniel	Wilmington	Immigrated from Ireland and worked in a pot house per the 1860 census; the youth's likely employer was William Hare
Trapnell, George T.	Smyrna	Worked for Allen & Bell and others at Smyrna Landing; later operated his own pottery in Chester, Pennsylvania, by 1880
Trapnell, George W.	Smyrna	Practiced potting craft in Baltimore and Cecil County, Maryland, before working at Smyrna Landing with sons, George T. and John circa 1870
Trapnell, John	Smyrna	Worked for Allen and the Bell family at Smyrna Landing circa 1870
Webb, Jacob	Wilmington	Hired by Mathew Crips in 1783 and later worked for Aaron James in Chester County, Pennsylvania
Weir, Randolph	Wilmington	Listed in the *Wilmington Directory* as a potter who resided on both Tatnall and Fifth streets between 1857 and 1868; according to the 1860 census, he was then 22 years old and was born in Delaware; a Randolph Wine, residing with Richard Lowe per the 1850 census, is probably the same person

Williams, Spencer	Wilmington	Listed in the 1845 *Wilmington Directory* as a potter and "colored inhabitant"
Ziegler, Ferdinand	Wilmington	Worked at his father's pottery in the 1870s before changing his occupation to carriage trimming
Ziegler, George	Wilmington	Operated the pottery at Orange and Water streets from 1860 to 1880, part of the time in partnership with Englebert Neumayer
Ziegler, William (F.)	Wilmington	Worked at his father's pottery in the 1870s and then was employed at the Chester Pottery in Delaware County, Pennsylvania, before returning to Wilmington to work for Englebert Neumayer

BIBLIOGRAPHY

Books

Ashmead, Henry Graham, *History of Delaware County Pennsylvania*, Philadelphia, L.H. Everts & Co., 1884.

Barber, Edwin Atlee, *Marks of American Potters*, Philadelphia, Patterson and White, 1904.

Barber, Edwin Atlee, *The Pottery and Porcelain of the United States*, New York, G.P. Putnam's Sons, 1909.

Bjork, Gordon C., *Stagnation & Growth in the American Economy, 1784-1792*, New York and London, Garland Publishing, Inc., 1985.

Booth, James C., *Geological Survey of the State of Delaware*, Dover, Printed by S. Kimmey, 1841.

Branin, M. Lelyn, *The Early Makers of Handcrafted Earthenware and Stoneware in Central and Southern New Jersey*, Cranbury, NJ, Associated University Presses, Inc., 1988.

Broderick, Warren F. and William Bouck, *Potter Works*, Cranbury, NJ, Associated University Press, Inc., 1995.

Denker, Ellen and Bert Denker, *North American Pottery and Porcelain*, Pittstown, NJ, The Main Street Press, 1985.

Edwards, Richard (Editor & Publisher), *Industries of Delaware: Historical and Descriptive Review*, Wilmington, 1880.

Ferris, Benjamin, *A History of the Original Settlements of Delaware and A History of Wilmington*, Reprint of 1846 Original, Gateway Press, Inc., Baltimore, 1987.

Greer, Georgeanna H., *American Stoneware: The Art & Craft of Utilitarian Potters*, 3rd Edition, Atglen, PA, Shiffer Publishing Ltd., 1999.

Guilland, Harold F., *Early American Folk Pottery*, Philadelphia, Chilton Book Company, 1971.

Hancock, Harold B., *Businesses and Industries of Milford 1787-1987*, edited with M. Catherine Downing, Milford, Milford Historical Society, 1987.

Hancock, Harold Bell, *The Reconstructed Delaware State Census of 1782*, Wilmington, Delaware Genealogical Society, 1983.

Hinson, Dave, *A Primer on Fruit Jars*, The Federation of Historical Bottle Collectors, Bottles & Extras, Volume 7, Number 12, 1996.

Hitchens, E. Dallas and E. Mills Hurley, *Milford Delaware and the Milford Delaware Area after 1776*, Wilmington, Delaware Genealogical Society, 1985.

James, Arthur E., *The Potters and Potteries of Chester County, Pennsylvania,* Reprint, Exton, Schiffer Publishing Ltd., 1978.

Ketchum, William C., *The Pottery and Porcelain Collector's Handbook*, New York, Funk and Wagnells, 1971.

Lake, Joseph R. Jr., *Hockessin: A Pictorial History*, Hockessin, Friends of Hockessin Library, 1997.

Leibowitz, Joan, *Yellow Ware: The Traditional Ceramic*, Exton, Schiffer Publishing Ltd., 1985.

Lewis, Fannie Land, *Descendents of Dr. Tymen Stiddam*, Pocatello, ID, n.d.

Lincoln, Anna T., *Wilmington, Delaware: Three Centuries Under Four Flags,* 1609-1937, Rutland, VT, The Tuttle Publishing Co., Inc., 1937.

Montgomery, Elizabeth, *Reminiscences of Wilmington*, Wilmington, Johnston & Bogia, 1872.

Myers, Susan H., *Handcraft to Industry – Philadelphia Ceramics in the First Half of the Nineteenth Century*, Washington, D.C., Smithsonian Institution Press, 1980.

Ramsay, John, *American Potters and Potteries*, New York, Tudor Publishing Co., 1947.

Ries, Heinrich, and Henry Leighton, *History of the Clay Working Industry in the United States*, New York, J. Wiley & Sons, 1909.

Sawin, Nancy C., *Up the Spine and Down the Creek*, Hockessin, North Light Studio, 1982.

Schaltenbrand, Phil, *Big Ware Turners: The History and Manufacture of Pennsylvania Stoneware 1720-1920*, Bentleyville, PA, Westerwald Press, 2002.

Scharf, J. Thomas, *History of Delaware, 1609-1888*, Philadelphia, L.J. Richards & Co., 1888.

Skaggs, Jimmy K., *An Interpretive History of the American Economy*, Ohio, Grid, Inc., 1975.

Smith, Elmer L., *Pottery: A Utilitarian Folk Craft*, Lebanon, PA, Applied Arts Publishers, 1975.

Smith, Samuel D. and Stephen T. Rogers, *Survey of Historic Pottery Making in Tennessee*, Tennessee Department of Conservation, 1979.

Stradling, Diana and J. Garrison Stradling, Ed., *The Art of the Potter*, New York, Main Street/Universe Books, 1977.

Stewart, Regina and Geraldine CoSentino, *Stoneware*, New York, Golden Press, 1977.

Stidham, Jack, *The Descendents of Timothy Stidham*, Vol. 1, Wynandotte, OK, The Gregath Publishing Co., 2001.

Toulouse, Julian Harrison, *Fruit Jars*, 2nd printing, Camden, NJ, Thomas Nelson, Inc., 1970.

Tunis, Edwin, *Colonial Craftsmen*, Cleveland and New York, The World Publishing Company, 1965.

Weslager, C.A., *Garrett Snuff Fortune*, Wilmington, The Knebels Press, 1965.

Dissertations

Ng, Kenneth, *Antebellum U.S. Banking*, Ph.D. dissertation, University of Rochester, 1988.

Pearce, John N., *The Early Baltimore Potters and Their Wares: 1763-1850*, M.A. thesis, University of Delaware, 1959.

Maps and Atlases

Map of New Castle County, Delaware, Smith & Wistar, Publisher, Philadelphia, 1849.

Map of Kent County, Delaware, A.D. Byles, Publisher, Philadelphia, 1859.

General Survey of Wilmington, Hexamer, 1866.

Atlas of the State of Delaware, D.G. Beers, Pomeroy & Beers, Philadelphia, 1868.

Panorama of Wilmington, Delaware, H.H. Bailey & Co., Artists, 1874.

City Atlas of Wilmington, G.M. Hopkins, Philadelphia, 1876.

Sanborn Map–Wilmington, Delaware, Sanborn Map and Publishing Co., New York, 1884.

Map of Milford, Delaware, O.H. Bailey & Co., Lithographer & Publisher, Boston, 1885.

Property Atlas of Wilmington, Delaware, G.M. Baist, Publisher, Philadelphia, 1901.

Other Publications

W. Oakley Raymond, "Remmey Family: American Potters," *Antiques*, September, 1937.

Beverly Burbage, "The Remarkable Pottery of Charles Decker & His Sons," *Tennessee Conservationist*, Vol. 37, No. 11, Nashville, 1971.

David Kent Miller, "The Pottery Patriarch," *Tennessee Conservationist*, Vol. 37, No. 11, Nashville, 1971.

John Pearce, "A First Look At Wilmington's Potters: Mathew Crips, William Hare and Others," *The Delaware Antiques Show*, Wilmington, 1966.

John B. Kebabian, comp., *Delaware Apprenticeship Indentures: 1827-1850*, held by the Historical Society of Delaware.

Terry H. Klein and Patrick H. Garrow, editors, *Final Archeological Investigations at the Wilmington Boulevard*, Deldot Archaeology Series 29, 1984.

Charles H. LeeDecker, et al., *Archaeological and Historical Investigation of Block 1184, Wilmington, New Castle County, Delaware*, Deldot Archaeology Series No.78, 1990.

Mathew Crips' Ledger, Hagley Museum and Library, Accession Number 1756.

United States Department of Treasury, *Documents Relative to the Manufactures in the United States*, A.M. Kelley, New York, 1969.

Future Publication

Espenshade, Christopher T., et al., *William Hare: Master Potter of Wilmington Delaware*, Delaware State Museums, Dover, 2005-06.

INDEX

A

B

C

D

N

P

Q

R

S

T

V

W

Y

Z